The Light Crust Doughboys Are on the Air

Celebrating Seventy Years of Texas Music

by John Mark Dempsey

Foreword by Art Greenhaw

Number Two in the Evelyn Oppenheimer Series

University of North Texas Press
Denton, Texas

Permissions:
University of North Texas Press
P.O. Box 311336
Denton, TX 76203-1336

The paper used in this book meets the minimum requirements of the American
National Standard for Permanence of Paper for Printed Library Materials,
z39.48.1984. Binding materials have been chosen for durability.

Library of Congress Cataloging-in-Publication Data

Dempsey, John Mark, 1954-
  The Light Crust Doughboys are on the air : celebrating seventy years
of Texas music / by John Mark Dempsey ; foreword by Art Greenhaw.
     p. cm. — (Evelyn Oppenheimer series ; no. 2)
Includes discographies (p.   ), bibliographical references (p.   ), and
index.
  ISBN 1-57441-151-9 (alk. paper)
  1. Light Crust Doughboys. 2. Country music groups—Texas. 3. Western
swing (Music)—Texas—History and criticism. I. Title. II. Series.
  ML421.L53 D46 2002
  781.642'092'2—dc21

                                        2002004971

All photos courtesy of the Light Crust Doughboys Museum, Mesquite, Texas,
from the collection of Marvin "Smokey" Montgomery and Art Greenhaw.
Bottom jacket photo © J. Griffis Smith, courtesy of *Texas Highways* magazine.

Design by Angela Schmitt

The Light Crust Doughboys Are on the Air: Celebrating Seventy Years of Texas Music
is Number Two in the Evelyn Oppenheimer Series

Contents

♩ ♪ ♩

Illustrations
following page 153

Foreword
by Art Greenhaw

It's been said that years after the breakup of The Beatles, George Harrison told Keith Richards of The Rolling Stones, "You don't know how lucky you are, mate. . . playing with your own band for all these years!"

Such is also the life of a Light Crust Doughboy. There have been many times in my life when my dream has been to make music side by side with marvelous instrumentalists and singers such as Smokey Montgomery and the current Light Crust Doughboys: Jerry Elliott, Bill Simmons, John Walden, Jim Baker, and Dale Cook.

Being a Light Crust Doughboy is being able to count your blessings. Smokey often said, "I'm the luckiest banjo player in the world." What a wonderful personality trait! What a tremendous philosophy of life: To delight in one's journey and not one's destination; to bloom where one is planted; to find happiness from within instead of from without. And Smokey's personal philosophy shines through, even in his absence, in the authenticity of The Light Crust Doughboys' stage shows . . . the purity of non-formula, non-commercial music, the music of the soul.

We Doughboys were further blessed when we learned that John Mark Dempsey was going to preserve the history of the group in this book. His love of the Light Crust Doughboys and his deep knowledge of the Texas broadcasting history of which the group is an important part meshed with our vision of how we wanted to be remembered, even as we continue to perform and record. Maybe we're not making Billboard Top Ten hits yet, but we are getting Grammy nominations for Top 5 in the world in our categories!

Other blessings of being a Light Crust Doughboy include being able to do the music we want to be doing; being able to run our own bandstand-type independent record label; being able to compose and arrange as we choose and according to our visions; having the freedom to pick who we want to collaborate with in a musical sense; and having the opportunity to inspire new generations of young people to be participants in the most dynamic and popular art form of all—music! And while we're at it, we also like to strike some blows along the way for individuality, self-reliance, non-conformity, and the overcoming of fragile and unworthy authority.

In 1996, a newspaper editor asked Smokey what he'd like to be doing at the end of his life. "Exactly what I'm doing now: making music," was his reply. I've always had as my goal both that Smokey philosophy and the words of the old monk who was asked as he was hoeing his garden, "Master, if you knew you had one hour left to live, what would you do?"

The master answered, "I would just keep on hoeing my garden."

To Smokey and The Light Crust Doughboys who have fought the good fight and run the race: rest high on some eagle's wings.

To The Light Crust Doughboys still doing it and doing it so well: play on, old friends, play on. . . .

Introduction

♩ ♪ ♪

This book was a race against time. We lost. But, even so, it was a triumphant experience.

When work on this history of the Light Crust Doughboys began in the summer of 2000, 87-year-old Marvin "Smokey" Montgomery was still regularly performing with the group, indeed, was the on-stage leader of the Doughboys. He had joined the group in 1935 at the height of its radio popularity, and became its undisputed leader when the Doughboys were reorganized after a hiatus during World War II. He was not wheeled out for sentiment's sake, to take a bow or perform a token tune on his beloved four-string tenor banjo; as any-one who saw the Doughboys perform in recent years will attest, he was a powerful musical force, right up to the end. But as time went by, the leukemia that had been under control for awhile began to as-sert itself once again, and his health became increasingly frail. Every-one hoped, of course, that he could somehow recover and continue to play with the Doughboys for many more years. But, if that was not to be, we hoped we could complete the book and publish it while he was still around physically. We didn't make it. Smokey Montgomery's remarkable life came to an end on June 6, 2001 at the age of 88.

But a saving grace was that Smokey, still very clear of mind, was able to read an early manuscript of this book less than two weeks before he died. He went through it page by page, and made a few small corrections. The one thing he most wanted to correct was an anecdote that portrayed the Depression-era Doughboys, at least on one particular occasion, as having a little too much to drink and getting too raucous. "Never happened," he told me. "We were not a rowdy bunch." He was not overly upright about it, but he wanted to set the story straight. Done.

Another vignette from Smokey's final days is related to this book. As I was going through the process of checking facts, I had sent a list of questions to Smokey and his wife Barbara by e-mail (Smokey was very up-to-date). He wanted to answer the questions over the phone rather than by responding to the e-mail message, but he was going into the hospital that day for a leukemia treatment and would be there overnight. Barbara called and told me they would be home the next day and Smokey would call. Of course, under the circumstances, I didn't really expect a call. The next day, Barbara called and said, "Smokey is very tired and wants to take a nap, so he won't be able to talk to you today, but he wanted me to call and tell you." Wow. I'm accustomed to people not returning phone calls and forgetting to do what they say they'll do. Happens all the time. I sometimes do it myself. But here was a man within weeks of his death, and he was still taking the trouble to be thoughtful. Exceptional.

Smokey Montgomery received a funeral service befitting his status as a Texas music legend. The Hall of State at Fair Park in Dallas was the setting. Smokey's Dixieland group, the Bearkats, performed, as did the Dallas Banjo Band, which was Smokey's brainchild. And, of course, the Light Crust Doughboys took center stage, with Smokey's stool placed before his microphone, and his beloved tenor banjo resting on its stand between keyboard player Bill Simmons and fiddler John Walden. The Doughboys performed Art Greenhaw's gospel composition, "Sending Me You," Smokey and his wife Barbara's song, "Lord, Take All of Me," and "How Great Thou Art." After the service, the Bearkats led a New Orleans-style musical procession to the hearse, and again from the hearse to the grave.

The Light Crust Doughboys will carry on, as Smokey wished. Of course, if the Doughboys had never performed again after Tojo and Hitler knocked them off the air in 1942, their story would be worthy of a book. But, under Smokey's leadership, a new Doughboys group came together after the war, and that group continues performing and recording to this day. Theirs is a record of longevity, musical excellence, and popularity that is unrivaled in country or pop music.

Chapter 1 describes a Light Crust Doughboys performance in the last year of Smokey Montgomery's life, when they were in their 66th year of performing as a band, not including the wartime years when the band was inactive. Under the leadership of the youthful Art

Greenhaw, the Doughboys are continuing to perform and record. As a member of a younger generation of Texas troubadours, Robert Earl Keene, says, "The road goes on forever and the party never ends." And so, this book presents the story of the Light Crust Doughboys—yesterday, today, and tomorrow, from their beginnings with Bob Wills, Milton Brown, and W. Lee O'Daniel to the present and whatever the future may bring.

It is not possible to thank everyone who helped me in developing this book. But special thanks to Art Greenhaw and all of the Light Crust Doughboys, Fran Vick and Karen DeVinney with the UNT Press, Cary Ginell, Kevin Coffey, Janis Stout, and, most of all, Smokey.

"The best show group I've ever had"

♩. ♪ ♪

When the tale of the Light Crust Doughboys began, Herbert Hoover was president. The majority of Texans, indeed, the majority of Americans, still lived and toiled on the farm. Car travel had begun to transform the nation, but the great interstate highway system existed only in the minds of a few visionary dreamers. Of course, there was no Internet and no television, and while the medium that would make the Doughboys stars all over the Southwest—radio—had already captured the imagination of millions of listeners, it remained only a rumor to many rural Texans. So what would have been the chances, back in 1931, that the Light Crust Doughboys would be taking the stage on a warm summer night amidst the opulent, high-tech ambience of North Dallas in the first year of a new millennium?

The 90-degree heat does not deter a crowd of Doughboys fans, standing in line, patiently waiting for the dinner theater doors to open. Many of them are gray-haired and wear bifocals, but others would not look out of place waiting in line for a Dixie Chicks show. Young or old, they're all here to enjoy an evening of Western swing (along with a gaggle of other musical styles), played by a band whose roots reach down to the very beginnings of the music.

Backstage inside the small theater, the Light Crust Doughboys filter in one by one for the show, still more than an hour away. They're dressed in starched, pale magenta and indigo Western shirts and bolo ties. The talk is easy and familiar, and only occasionally touches on music. Someone brings up Louis Armstrong, and ventures that he was a part of a vanishing breed of jazz musicians. "We're very close to a vanishing breed ourselves," another Doughboy reminds him. "These old Western swing guys—there aren't too many of 'em left."

Finally, a wiry man with steel-gray hair, a bristling mustache, and dark piercing eyes saunters in. He has the air of relaxed, confident authority. Someone anxiously asks Marvin "Smokey" Montgomery, a Doughboy since 1935, about the arrangement of a particular song on the set list for that evening's show. "We'll make it up as we go along," Smokey replies reassuringly. "I'll do like Bob Wills used to do, I'll point at you, and you play every lick you know. . . . We rehearse, but we never do 'em the same way we rehearse 'em." He may sound casual, but before the show begins, Smokey will instruct all of the Doughboys on the parts they'll play.

Time has mellowed Smokey. He notices when someone plays the wrong chord in a tune, but doesn't make an issue of it. Still, the intensity of his drive for musical perfection remains strong. "It doesn't make much difference. Nobody knows the difference but us. Maybe most of them [the Doughboys] don't know the difference except me, but I know the difference every time we play it, because it hits a bad chord right here. We played it last night. I almost got sick at the stomach, but I didn't. In the old days, I'd have chewed them out. Now, what the heck" (Montgomery oral history, 106–7).

"He identifies with young groups and is young. Marvin will always be young," pianist Knocky Parker, Smokey's old Light Crust Doughboys partner, commented admiringly (Interview, January 10, 1984).

Even after time eventually catches up with Smokey, he'll still have his say. "I've got them [his pallbearers] all picked out. I've got the music picked out. I'm going to do a tape recording of me talking, telling a lot of bad things about a lot of guys I know," he said, tongue definitely in cheek (Oral history, 107).

A long-time Doughboy, Muryel "Zeke" Campbell, gave Smokey due credit for holding the group together far past the time of their radio heyday. "They haven't been on the radio all these years, but they've been going continuously since the beginning. Marvin kind of took over," Zeke said (Oral history, 74).

In the dinner theater, the Light Crust Doughboy fans wait with anticipation. Some, like Virgil and Virginia Summerall of Dallas, have been Doughboy fans since the days of W. Lee O'Daniel, the flour salesman who built his fame as the Doughboys' master of ceremonies into a political career that led to the Texas governor's mansion and the U.S. Senate. In fact, Virgil sold Light Crust Flour himself in a grocery store in Corpus Christi. "Man, it was a big seller," he said.

Like many Texans, Virgil well remembered seeing the Light Crust Doughboys perform live on their many tours around the state. "I saw him [O'Daniel] several times, him and the band," Virgil recalled. "Every time they came on [the radio], I turned 'em on at the store." It's his first time to hear the group play in about 60 years, since before he went to serve in Southeast Asia during World War II.

Other fans, like Charlie Ostrander, are relatively new to the fold. "We started following the Doughboys at the Christmas show of '98," he said. "We've only missed one show since then." Charlie is from Massachusetts, but still knew of the Light Crust Doughboys. "I've heard about them all my life. But my wife got me interested in cultural events. She's my cultural director." Charlie's wife Marina is Russian. "So I said, you know, in America, we have culture, too. And I said, let's go see the Doughboys. That's American." Marina said she loves the Doughboys' spontaneity. "It seems to me they're playing for their own enjoyment as much as for ours, and it just feels wonderful," she said.

Sharon Dickerson, the president of the Light Crust Doughboys Fan Club, grew up in Nashville. Her father worked for the giant music publishing company, Acuff-Rose, and was a big fan of the Doughboys, so she grew up as a fan of the group. "I was in Mesquite to hear Hank Thompson [the County Music Hall of Fame member who has his own chapter in Doughboys history] one night, and I got there early and decided to go into Generation's Past [an antique store operated by Doughboy bass player and impresario Art Greenhaw] and met Art and his mother. We got together the following week and started talking about my love for the Doughboys, and he was infatuated with the fact that I had known Hank Thompson all of my life and grew up in the music business. And he said, 'We would love to have you aboard doing something.'" Soon, she was the volunteer leader of the Doughboys fan club. "I publish a newsletter every month. It runs anywhere from four to five typewritten pages. I put it on the Internet, I send out new fan-club applications. I attend 99.9 percent of the concerts."

"I like the traditional music that the Doughboys play, their versatility and their wholesomeness," Sharon said. "They're incredibly talented musicians, each of them individually as well as a group. I've always adored them."

Sharon, a country-music singer and performer in her own right, has a favorite moment in her association with the Doughboys. It happened at a concert. "Smokey kept telling me, 'Don't you leave, don't you leave.' And he called me on stage during the second half of the concert, and he said he thought it was time everybody knew who exactly I was. And he said, 'I think you all need to hear this lady sing.' So Art and I sang 'Amazing Grace,' both with the band and a cappella. Of all the memories, that's the one that got me in the heart the most" (Interview, May 2, 2001).

When the sold-out house has completed their dinners of sandwiches and salads, Smokey turns to the group and jauntily announces, "Shall we go out there and see what it looks like?"

While Smokey reckons the band of the late '40s was the best group of musicians to perform as the Light Crust Doughboys, the modern-day Doughboys have their own distinction in his astute judgment. "The best show group I've ever had is the guys I've got right now," he said (Interview, January 3, 2001).

On this night, the manager of the theater presents the Doughboys with a certificate naming them to the "Rockabilly Hall of Fame," along with Lefty Frizzell, Johnny Cash, Roy Orbison, Jerry Lee Lewis, and others. It's a reminder to the audience that the Doughboys cover a lot of musical territory, not just Western swing, a fact that will become very apparent before the evening is over. Smokey takes the plaque and holds it high, to the fond applause of the crowd.

"They are part of what made rockabilly music bigger," Bob Timmers, founder and curator of the Rockabilly Hall of Fame, said. "They were part of the tradition of rockabilly. The Doughboys' innovative Texas swing has a direct link to rock 'n' roll," he said. "Swing helped inspire rockabilly, which inspired Elvis Presley and ultimately rock 'n' roll," Timmers asserts (Barber, June 18, 2000).

By no means is it the only recent honor in the astonishing career of the Light Crust Doughboys. In early 2001, the Doughboys received a Grammy nomination for their recording *The Great Gospel Hit Parade* with legendary gospel singer James Blackwood and the Jordanaires, Elvis Presley's vocal group. (Blackwood, who died in early 2002, was closely associated over the years with Elvis Presley, Johnny Cash, the Statler Brothers, Larry Gatlin, and Tammy Wynette, and, as of 2001, had received nine Grammy awards and 29 Grammy nominations of his own.) In 1999, the Doughboys were nominated for a Grammy award in the category of "Best Southern, Country or Bluegrass Gospel Album of the Year" and for a Gospel Music Association "Dove" award. The nominations were for their collaboration with Blackwood and his quartet, *They Gave the World a Smile: The Stamps Quartet Tribute Album*. In 1998, the Doughboys were nominated for *Keep Lookin' Up: The Texas Swing Sessions*, also with Blackwood. The Light Crust Doughboys were charter inductees in the Texas Western Swing Hall of Fame in 1989, and in 1995, the Texas Legislature named the Doughboys "Texas' official music ambassadors." In recent years, they have performed in unique collaborations with the Lone Star Ballet in Amarillo and the Southern Methodist University Mustang Band, and performed in a series of concerts in Europe. In 1999, Mel Bay Publications, Inc., published two books of Doughboy compositions, most of them by Smokey Montgomery and Greenhaw.

The Light Crust Doughboys' place in Texas music history is secure. John Morthland, a contributing editor to *Texas Monthly* magazine, has been writing about music since 1969 when he began working as an associate editor at *Rolling Stone*. Morthland related a story that is often repeated about the powerful presence of the Doughboys in the 1930s and '40s. "Johnny Gimble [a former member of Wills' Texas Playboys] has said this to me, and I've read it or heard it from others too, that when they were growing up, you'd walk down the street at noon and every window was open and the Doughboys were coming out of every window. You could hear their whole radio show as you walked down the street," Morthland said (Interview, May 4, 2001).

After the Rockabilly Hall of Fame presentation, a local radio personality steps to the mike, and intones the historic words, "The Light Crust Doughboys are on the air!" Immediately, the Doughboys launch into their time-honored theme:

> Now listen everybody from near and far,
> If you want to know who we are
> We're the Light Crust Doughboys,
> From Burrus Mill.

> Like our song, think it's fine,
> Sit right down and drop a line,
> To the Light Crust Doughboys,
> From Burrus Mill.

> And I declare, (oh, yeah!) we'll get it there (ah-hah),
> And if we have the time to spare,
> Sometime when we're down your way,

We'll stop in and spend the day.
We're the Light Crust Doughboys,
From Burrus Mill.

Never do brag, never do boast,
We sing our song from coast to coast,
We're the Light Crust Doughboys,
From Burrus Mill.

Smokey cradles his celebrated tenor banjo on his lap as he sits at stage left on a stool, the only concession to his 87 years. Throughout the evening's two-hour show, he will hop from the stool to the mike to announce the tunes, josh with the other Doughboys, and charm the audience. "We'll dedicate this next song to Joe Dickinson [the theater manager] because it really fits him. It's called 'Bubbles in My Beer,'" he confidently offers. Keyboardist Bill Simmons sits in front of Smokey, and slightly to the left at the edge of the tiny stage. Fiddlers John Walden and Jim Baker stand at the back, and bassist Art Greenhaw holds down stage right, as guitarist Jerry Elliott steps forward to sing the classic Texas Playboys barroom number.

Jerry has been a Doughboy since 1960, a record of longevity that would be astounding if not for Smokey's 65 years with the band. "He was the 'Fort Worth singing sensation of 1949,' which is strange since he tells us he's 32," Greenhaw tells the room. Elliott's resume includes serving as an arranger for the late, great singer and songwriter Roger Miller. Jerry dips his head and grimaces as he reaches for the high notes, and then rares back and wails, still climbing the scale with considerable ease. He recalled that when he joined the band, the Doughboys were still playing at grand openings of grocery stores that bought a big load of Light Crust Flour, and the Cargill foods company, which had bought out the Burrus Mills and Elevator Co., was still paying the group. "But Smokey wanted to get off the road," he said, and the group has been playing shows for the simple pleasure of its fans ever since, never mind the flour.

The next song, "My Mary," was perhaps original Doughboy Milton Brown's best-known song, recorded in 1935 after he left the band to

7

launch his own group, the Musical Brownies. The Doughboys themselves recorded the song in 1934 (Ginell, *Milton Brown*, 291–92). Jerry sings the beautiful melody, which sounds as contemporary as any recent hit by George Strait.

While the Doughboys are closely identified with country music, their music actually predates what we today call "country." Smokey Montgomery: "They didn't write country tunes then. There wasn't a Nashville where they made tunes just for country. We were playing all the pop tunes, trying to play them like a big band. We listened to Benny Goodman and Tommy Dorsey and all those bands, Artie Shaw, Glenn Miller. We played a lot of tunes that they played, pop tunes. We would get a lot of songs from south of border: 'La Cucaracha,' 'El Rancho Grande,' and all those tunes. We did a lot of old breakdowns and old-time East Texas running waltzes" (Oral history, 124).

Early in the show, Smokey shows that, after more than six decades with the Doughboys, he is still very much a banjo virtuoso, as he tears up "Sweet Georgia Brown," fingers racing up and down the fretboard.

Smokey plays a four-string tenor banjo, different from the more familiar five-string variety. His favorite instrument is a 1948 model Silver Bell Symphonic banjo. He also has a gold-plated Silver Bell Bacon made in 1922, the year when he picked up the banjo for the first time (Tarrant; Montgomery interview, May 3, 2001).

Doughboys shows tend to be informal affairs, not unlike a spontaneous jam in Smokey's den. Smokey, the undisputed leader and a jovially hard taskmaster, may announce at any moment that the band will play an unrehearsed number. Or he may good-naturedly upbraid one of the Doughboys for some real or imaginary transgression. At the end of "Sweet Georgia Brown," Smokey, in mock indignation, instructs Bill, "Don't hit that last chord till I hit the last chord." The audience enjoys the feeling of "sitting in" as the Doughboys have fun with their music.

A Light Crust Doughboys performance is a guided tour through the American musical landscape of pop, country, early rock 'n' roll, gospel, and jazz, besides the group's home base of Western swing.

They launch into a countrified version of Pat Boone's "Love Letters in the Sand." Smokey relates a story about '50s teen idol Boone hitchhiking back and forth from the University of North Texas campus in Denton to WBAP-TV in Fort Worth, where he sang on a daily program. "Pat's almost a genius, but sometimes he goes over to the other side," Smokey jokes cryptically. Fiddler John Walden steps to the mike and croons the tune in a rich, smooth baritone, his prominent eyebrows and handlebar mustache bobbing, his eyes twinkling.

Backstage before the show, John tells how his father led an orchestra in Wichita Falls, and how he slyly led John into music. "'See that fiddle in this case,' he told us boys," John recalled affectionately. "'I'm going to put it under this bed, and I don't want you to touch it. You'll get a hard whipping if you mess with it.'" Of course, little John picked up the fiddle. "'Which one of you boys got the fiddle out? I'll have to whip you all if you don't own up to it,'" he told John and his brothers. So John admitted playing with the old fiddle, expecting the worst. "But he made me study four hours instead," John said. "He made me run scales."

Art is a frequent contributor of new songs to the Doughboys' repertoire. Smokey introduces Art's song, "Texas Women," saying, "This song was written by Art. He's still researching it." Art, responds, "I had a good teacher in Smokey," to which Smokey shoots back, "As much as I can remember." The song is a bouncy paean to the women of the Lone Star State, in much the same spirit as "California Girls" by Brian Wilson of the Beach Boys.

> You mix champagne with guacamole,
> Sparkling water, hot tamales,
> Got a Texas woman from head to toe.
> There's nothin' like 'em in the whole wide world,
> They're even better than a honky-tonk girl.

Besides playing the bass guitar, Art sings in a powerful bass voice. Along with Jim, he forms the younger generation of Doughboys and serves as the group's business manager.

"I have to stay spiritually, physically and mentally alert or they'll [the other Doughboys] just run circles around me," Art muses. "Music is our calling, it's not just a career" (Thibodeaux).

For "Pistol Packin' Mama," the World War II-era Bing Crosby/ Andrew Sisters hit, Jim Oliver, an honorary Doughboy, joins the group on trumpet. "Gene Autry had trumpet on some of his songs, but Bob Wills had 'em on everything," Smokey, ever the instructor, advises the crowd, which breaks into spontaneous applause after Oliver's trumpet solo. Jim Baker (our "poster boy," Smokey calls handsome Jim) joins Jerry to sing the lead vocals.

After Jerry receives a big ovation for "Faded Love," the beloved song made popular by Wills and Ray Price, it's time for Smokey to shine. "This is one of the first banjo songs I ever learned," Smokey comments. "Just for a change, Bill," he offhandedly says to Simmons, "let's play the first part in waltz time." Smokey's banjo has been very prominent all night as a rhythm instrument. But as they launch into "Bye Bye Blues," Smokey demonstrates the intricate and lightning-fast picking that has made him a legendary player on the instrument, "the man who brought Dixieland banjo to Western swing," as Art calls him. As Smokey unveils the surprising licks, the admiring crowd bursts into applause. It's easy to forget that the man "smoking" the banjo (it's how he got his nickname) has been pickin' like this since Franklin D. Roosevelt was giving Fireside Chats.

"If he is not the best musician in the history of the band, he is certainly among the best," historian Charles R. Townsend, the author of the Bob Wills biography *San Antonio Rose* wrote in a brief sketch on the Doughboys. "Bob Wills referred to Smokey as a 'genius on that banjo,' and added he would select Marvin as banjoist if he were forming an all-star western swing band" (Townsend, "About the Light Crust Doughboys").

Then it's time for the Doughboys to tip their hats to rockabilly, the raw musical genre for which they had been honored earlier in the evening. Giving credit to composer Arthur "Big Boy" Crudup in his tongue-in-cheek fashion, Art launches into a medley of "That's All Right, Mama" (Elvis' first hit) and "My Baby Left Me." Unexpectedly hearing Oliver join the arrangement, Art's eyes widen in mock alarm. "I think it's time for a trumpet solo," he announces.

For "M-I-S-S-I-S-S-I-P-P-I," Bill Simmons' own composition, which has been recorded by the likes of Ella Fitzgerald, Smokey calls to the sound technician, "We need a mike, Bill's gonna sing, and I don't have a union card." Simmons, his features dominated by a long, white beard, gets his mike, and he plays it for laughs when the mike attached to a boom starts to droop, but it is the way his dexterous fingers flit across the keyboard that stands out.

"I was working with Curly Williams when I first went to Memphis, Curly Williams and his Georgia Peach Pickers," Simmons recalled. "One day he came in and he said, 'You want to help me write a song? M-I-crooked letter-crooked letter . . . ' He hummed a little bit, and he didn't have much, he just had the idea. They said kids used to jump rope to that, you know. My wife remembered it [the jump-rope chant]. I told him I'd go home and work on it. I was sitting there at the kitchen table, with an old pencil and some manuscript paper. It was three o' clock in the morning and I woke my wife up, and said, 'How do you spell 'Mississippi?' Anyway, I finished the thing up, and I did the words and most of the music, but it was his idea. We put it together, made a demo, and sent it to Fred Rose with Acuff-Rose [publishing company] in Nashville. A couple of days later they called and told Curly, 'Boy, you've got a hit!' They were trying to get [Bing] Crosby and the Andrews Sisters to do it. But instead, Red Foley did the first one [recording]. Of course, we made one with Curly." Others who have recorded the song are Kay Starr, Ella Fitzgerald, Art Mooney, Snooky Lanson. Bill's favorite version was Ella Fitzgerald's (Interview, March 16, 2001).

Doughboys shows are characterized by a striking variety of musical genres. Could Bob Wills or Milton Brown ever have imagined that the Light Crust Doughboys would share the stage with a pair of Russian classical musicians? Two friends of the Doughboys' faithful fan Charlie Ostrander, Sergey Vaschenko on the balalaika, a triangular-shaped stringed instrument, and Vladimir Kaliazine, on the bayan, an accordion-like apparatus, step forward for a brilliant interlude. Charlie and his wife Marina regularly invite the Doughboys to their home for parties. There he introduced Sergey and Smokey. "He [Sergey] just has magic in his fingers. And then I heard Smokey, and he has magic in his fingers. And I said, these two guys have got to meet each other. So we had them over to the apartment for a party, and they had a jam session, and they've been going strong together ever since." Thanks to the Doughboys' penchant for a wide range of styles, the sprightly, intricate sounds created by the two Russians seem not at all out of place, and they are warmly received by the Doughboys fans.

The Doughboys perform "Fraulein" and "Cool Water" before Smokey introduces the rare tune that has been around longer than the band, "Listen to the Mockingbird." It's a fiddle *tour de force* for John, who, among other flourishes, reaches over the top of the fiddle's fretboard to hit the high notes. The enthusiastic audience pays him back with wild applause.

It would be hard to top John's rip-roaring performance, so the Doughboys break for intermission, after Art formally introduces the band. Finally, turning to Smokey, he announces. "He's been a Light Crust Doughboy since 1935. That's about 30 years longer than Mick Jagger's been a Rolling Stone. And he looks younger than Jagger and Richards." Smokey puts the spotlight back on Art, saying sincerely, "If it wasn't for him, we wouldn't be here today." Mauvehaired waiters and waitresses too young to remember The Eagles, let alone the early Doughboys, circulate among the crowd taking new orders, as Art jokingly admonishes the fans, "The break'll be a lot shorter if you buy everything on that table." The counter at the front of the theater, covered with new CDs and videotapes, is a testament to the Doughboys' modern-day productivity. Fans mix easily with each other and with members of the Doughboys in the relaxed atmosphere.

In the second half of the show, the Doughboys stretch out. They're joined by Bob Krenkel on clarinet and saxophone, Bud Dresser on trombone and flugabone (a rare hybrid of the flugelhorn and trombone), John Anderson on trumpet and Art's father Frank on euphonium. Smokey nonchalantly announces, "Let's get the horns out, get a little Dixieland going. . . . Scramble one muskrat, I'll be home for dinner." The Doughboys then kick off the lively New Orleans classic, "Muskrat Ramble."

"As their current recordings reveal, the band has always borrowed from all areas of American music," Townsend wrote. "Everything . . . from country to Dixieland, from western swing to big band swing, from blues to cool jazz" (Townsend, "Doughboys— Yesterday"). Besides James Blackwood and the Jordanaires, the Doughboys have also recorded in recent years with Nokie Edwards, the lead guitarist for the 1960s surf band The Ventures, and with steel guitarist Tom Brumley, best known for his work with Buck Owens and Rick Nelson.

Besides serving as banjo man and master of ceremonies, Smokey serves as the group's musical arranger. Before the next number, he offers, "I want to show you how the Doughboys learn a new song. I wrote a new arrangement this afternoon, none of these guys have seen it before. I'll show you how well these guys can sight read. If it doesn't sound right, it was the computer, it wasn't me." The song is "Marie," the beautiful Irving Berlin chestnut first popular in the big-band era, and a song that one-time Doughboy bass player and vocalist Joe Frank Ferguson helped to popularize while he was with Bob Wills and the Texas Playboys. Smokey confides to the audience that Berlin never liked Tommy Dorsey's arrangement of the song. "So I wrote a Bob Wills arrangement," he said. The Doughboys, reading Smokey's fresh arrangement note-by-note, perform a near-perfect rendition of the old favorite, twin fiddles to the fore. Satisfied, Smokey beams, "You played every note I wrote, band, just like I wrote it. That's kind of unusual."

Smokey Montgomery, it is revealed from his stage comments, has stepped into the computer age with the ease of a person 50 years younger. "Looking at my computer, I see that this next song is the most-played song by the Light Crust Doughboys. We're going to play it again tonight." It's Bob Wills' best-loved song, "San Antonio Rose," sung with consummate skill by Jerry Elliott, with harmony vocals from Art Greenhaw and John Walden. There is no dance floor in the dinner theater, but a couple is inspired to find a spot large enough to enjoy a spontaneous two-step.

On another occasion, Smokey revealed how the computer helps him maintain his amazingly busy schedule, which also includes performances with a unique group he formed called the Dallas Banjo Band, and reflected on his long-standing love of composing and arranging music. "I've got too many irons in the fire," he said. "One of them is sitting at home, playing with that computer, and writing arrangements for the Dallas Banjo Band. That's fun. . . . When I was with the Doughboys [in the group's radio heyday], I could write a new song, and I wrote a new song almost every day, and we'd put it on the air the next day, because I was making out the [radio] programs" (Oral history, 182–83).

Later, Smokey announces, "A couple of months ago, a fella came up and asked me why we didn't play this next song. I looked on my computer and saw we never have played it. I helped [Dallas Cowboys quarterback] Don Meredith make a record of this." The song is the old country and folk standard, "Wabash Cannonball." Jerry nevertheless sings it with great familiarity, and Smokey, with complete aplomb, crosses the stage to give on-the-fly directions to the four-man horn section, which they pick up easily, knowing to expect the unexpected from Smokey.

Now, Smokey stirs the pot with, "Let's pep it up a little bit. How about the 'Pinetop Boogie'? That'll get it going." The tune, which Smokey learned from old-time bluesman Clarence "Pinetop" Smith (Tarrant), is a vehicle for Bill to show off his barrelhouse piano playing. At one point, he picks up the electric keyboard and brandishes it like a 25-year-old rock and roller. On the beat, Smokey hops out the mike to shout, "Boogie!" When it's over, Smokey gives his ironic seal of approval: "Thank you, Bill. He gets better all the time . . . so they tell me."

"Bonaparte's Retreat" features a swinging, sophisticated arrangement. Smokey, perched on his stool, nods approvingly as he looks over Bill's shoulder at his artful fingers dancing across the keyboard.

Another Western standard performed by the Doughboys comes from their brief but successful movie career. In 1936, the Light Crust Doughboys traveled to Hollywood to make a movie, *Oh, Susanna*, with the singing cowboy star, Gene Autry. While in California, they made friends with the popular Western singing group, the Sons of the Pioneers, which then featured young Leonard Slye, who soon would be known as Roy Rogers. The Doughboys learned "Tumbling Tumbleweeds" from the Sons of the Pioneers, and have been performing it ever since. The three-part harmony from John, Jerry, and Art conjures visions of mesas and big-sky vistas.

"Everybody listen—this is how we're going to do it, whether it's right or not," Smokey announces. "This is my theme song, I want it played right. It's called, 'I Can't Get Started Anymore.'"

The musical styles and references fly by in kaleidoscopic fashion. Now the Doughboys are venturing into the territory of jazz and blues, with a detour into Elvis country. A bawdy "Sugar Blues" is followed by "Crying in the Chapel," with Art informing the crowd that Presley's popular gospel number was composed by one-time Doughboy Artie Glenn.

Glenn is one of the dozens of talented musicians who have been members of the Light Crust Doughboys at one time or another over the past 70-plus years. He played bass and guitar with the Doughboys for a few years in the 1950s. In 1953, as he was recovering from spinal surgery in a Fort Worth hospital, he made a promise to become closer to God. After leaving the hospital, he went to pray at the Loving Avenue Baptist Church. As he walked to the front of the church, tears coursed down his cheeks and the famous words suddenly came to him:

> You saw me crying in the chapel,
> The tears I shed were tears of joy.
> I know the meaning of contentment,
> Now I'm happy with the Lord.

The song first became a hit as sung by Glenn's son Darrell. The Orioles, Ella Fitzgerald, Rex Allen, Sr., and Eddy Arnold later recorded the song, in addition to Elvis' definitive version (Jones).

After "Crying in the Chapel," it's a sharp turn into traditional jazz with the Jimmy Van Heusen tunes "Darn That Dream" and "Here's That Rainy Day." And then, hammer down, they hit the

15

homestretch. On the old standard "You Are My Sunshine," John, all knees and elbows, nearly stops the show with a sensational fiddle solo. Then they tear into the "Orange Blossom Special," with the crowd impulsively joining in with rhythmic clapping. John pumps his right arm and leg in locomotive fashion, bends over at the waist, stomping the floor and hopping on one foot as the music reaches a crescendo. So exuberant are his contortions that his glasses fly off and he nearly topples over.

"It's a natural thing that I do. The music gets to going so fast that I can't hardly keep up with it," Walden said, almost sheepishly. "It happens every time I play it" (Interview). The crowd responds to John's solo with a howling cheer.

They send the happy audience into the summer night with the old Roy Rogers-Dale Evans theme, "Happy Trails," and, of course, a final chorus of the Doughboys theme. Art pronounces the benediction; he is part of the Light Crust Doughboys present and future, but the words are from the earliest days of the band's existence: "Remember the words of W. Lee O'Daniel, the governor of Texas and the only person to defeat Lyndon Baines Johnson in an election ('And live to tell about it,' interjects Smokey): Fellows, won't a 50-pound sack of flour make a great big biscuit?"

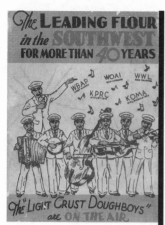

"The Light Crust Doughboys are on the air!"

♪ ♫ ♪

"Yahoo! The Light Crust Doughboys are on the air!"

It's no coincidence that the words most associated with the Light Crust Doughboys contain the phrase "on the air." In their 1930s and 1940s heyday, the Doughboys were creatures of broadcasting. "There is no way of knowing how many millions of people heard their broadcasts," wrote historian Charles R. Townsend (Townsend, Display). But while the Doughboys were certainly talented musicians and popular live performers, first and foremost they were salesmen for a household food product—Light Crust Flour. The Doughboys' impresario, W. Lee O'Daniel, was one of the first politicians to use broadcasting

17

to sell himself to voters. The Doughboys embodied the very essence of the "golden era" of radio—live performances, the dominance of programming by advertising agencies, union disputes over the broadcasting of recorded music, and, finally, the decline of network radio programming with the emergence of television. And so it is ironic that one of the giant figures in television history has a role in the Doughboys' story.

Over and over, the young University of Texas journalism student practiced the Doughboys' signature greeting, to the point that his fraternity brothers were ready to toss him out of the house. The inflection of "Yahoo!" had to be just right. This was his big chance. The hugely popular Doughboys, making one of their many tours of the state, were coming to Austin for a live broadcast from the KTUT studios, and they needed an announcer to open the show. The young broadcaster had a part-time job announcing the sports news on Austin station KTUT, but this would let him show off his announcing skill to a much larger audience on the far-flung Texas Quality Network.

"On maybe four occasions [during 1934 and 1935], the manager at KTUT called me and asked could I fill in the next morning as an announcer," remembered Walter Cronkite. "I, of course, agreed. I was anxious to do it. It meant a couple of bucks, not much, but that was better than the five dollars a week they gave me for the sports report" (Interview).

The future "most trusted man in America" was just one of millions of Texans and Southwesterners touched over the years by the Light Crust Doughboys. From 1930 to 1952, they faithfully tuned in to the Doughboys early-morning and, later, noontime radio program, and turned out in droves to hear the Doughboys play live on promotional tours for Light Crust Flour. Before Buddy Holly, before Willie Nelson, before Stevie Ray Vaughn, even before Bob Wills and the Texas Playboys, were the Light Crust Doughboys, "official music ambassadors of the Lone Star State," as declared by the state legislature in 1995. Improbably, they somehow have outlived all but Willie. Their historical importance is well established. "The original group was perhaps the major precursor to what became Western swing, and a very important proving ground for some of the most important musicians from [Bob] Wills and Milton Brown, to Leon McAuliffe, Leon Huff, and many others," wrote Western swing historian Kevin Coffey (Personal communication, July 29, 2001). Over the past five decades, the Doughboys persevered, against all odds, to emerge as a significant musical force in the 21st century.

In the early years of the 20th century, Texas was changing. The migration of rural people to the cities had begun. Texas historian T.R. Fehrenbach commented that, as late as 1940, Texas was still a predominantly rural state:

> The Texas cities, with a few exceptions such as Galveston and San Antonio, are all essentially twentieth-century creations. . . . And until well past the middle of this century, they were people primarily from the surrounding rural areas, from Old American agrarian stock. . . . City dwellers took up new occupations, but culture and world views did not immediately change. Farmers who saw themselves as middle class became white-collar employees – however, they did not, and still have not, become urbanites in cities with old, established urbane traditions. (83–84)

This trend brought not only the fans of the Light Crust Doughboys into the cities of Texas, but also the original Doughboys themselves, and most of their successors. As the years went by, the Doughboys' music became increasingly sophisticated, but especially in the beginning, it retained a rural, rootsy character.

Around the turn of the century, Texas land owners began to discover that the land, especially in the northern part of the state, was suitable for the growing of wheat. Mills began to pop up around the region. By 1914, the Southwest (mostly Texas and Oklahoma) produced more than twice as much flour as it had produced just 15 years earlier (Gray, 123–24).

One of the early entrepreneurs to enter the burgeoning Texas milling business was William C. Burrus, a former teacher and Confederate army officer. He and his son Jack Perry Burrus bought the Farmer's Alliance Mill at McKinney in 1890, and changed the name to the Collin County Mill and Elevator Company. It became the first mill in what would become the Burrus Mill and Elevator Company, the state's largest mill (Steen, 400–1, 407).

But the most important development leading to the creation of the Light Crust Doughboys was the emergence of radio. By the late 1920s, radio had become a major factor in American culture. At first fledgling radio stations, located mainly in urban areas, often broadcast light classical music and other selections that management thought suitable for a middle-class, genteel audience. But station management often overlooked the fact that the radio signals traveled beyond the city limits into the surrounding countryside. One early-radio historian observed that farmers and ranchers may have enjoyed some of the citified music, but what they really went for was the music that many of them played and sang themselves, "hillbilly" music some called it, with roots in rural-white and African-American folk traditions. "The mystery is that not only rural people, but city residents, not only southerners and westerners, but northerners and Midwesterners, sought out this music," Susan Smulyan wrote. "Listeners used the techniques pioneered by the distance [radio] fiends to find faraway stations playing country music" (23–24). Commercial hillbilly music had an "aroma of heartland respectability" in the South, and was better accepted than jazz, thanks to the long-standing tradition of folk music (G.H. Douglas, 176–77).

In North Texas, as in other parts of the country, radio stations were discovering the popularity of rural music. In the early and mid-1920s, "barn dance" programs became popular on many stations. On January 4, 1923, WBAP broadcast what is believed to be the first barn dance program, an hour-and-a-half of square-dance tunes led by old-time fiddler Captain M.J. Bonner, a Confederate war veteran (G.H. Douglas, 177).

Radio broadcasting, as we think of it today, was still a very new medium, having popped up seemingly out of nowhere, most fa-

mously in late 1920 in Pittsburgh, Pennsylvania, on KDKA, operated by Westinghouse. At first, radio stations were operated by department stores, churches, schools, any organization that sought to
promote itself or its ideas over the air. Broadcasters were very wary
of advertising, fearing that it would turn off the listeners. But, of
course, some method of paying for broadcasting had to found. A
great deal of support existed for government-imposed listener li-
cense fees, similar to the system that developed in Great Britain and
elsewhere in Europe. But the Department of Commerce regulated
the early radio stations and the Secretary of Commerce, future President Herbert Hoover, opposed any sort of government control.
Gradually, "goodwill" advertising, a very cautious step toward all-
out commercial broadcasting, began to gain acceptance. With goodwill advertising, the advertiser attached the company's name to the
program or the performers. Initially, no direct sales pitch for the product was made. Some early examples of this type of radio advertising
on WEAF in New York City were the "Happiness Boys," promoting
Happiness Candy Stores, the "Gold Dust Twins," touting Gold Dust
cleaning powder, and the "Ipana Troubadours," promoting Ipana
toothpaste. The programs were created and produced by advertising agencies (G.H. Douglas, 88–89).

All of this set the stage for the arrival of the Light Crust Doughboys.

Texas Monthly music writer Joe Nick Patoski said the Doughboys'
story is historic in several different respects:

> Their place in history is secure for four reasons: [Bob] Wills
> and [Milton] Brown in the early version of the band, the uti-
> lization of sponsorship which is now a standard element for
> any high profile musical act, Pappy O'Daniel's use of the
> Doughboys [actually, the Hillbilly Boys, who included sev-
> eral members who played at one time or another with the
> Doughboys] as a political vehicle (another first), and their
> sheer longevity. . . . As Texas's premier string band, the Light
> Crust Doughboys were an uplifting antidote to the Depres-
> sion, playing the kind of peppy, happy music that a listener
> could dance their troubles away to. (Patoski)

Patoski says no string or swing band has endured as long as the Doughboys. Other than the Baca family band in Fayette County, who have been playing together since the late 1880s, and the Polish Eagles from Houston's Heights, who have been going since 1903, the Doughboys are Texas's longest-running band.

It would be a mistake to give credit to one person for creating the Doughboys. Was it Truett Kimzey, the engineer for tiny KFJZ radio in Fort Worth and their first on-air announcer, who with furniture-store operator Will Ed Kemble brought them to the attention of station management? Was it W. Lee O'Daniel, the flour salesman and future governor of Texas, who saw the Doughboys' potential as pitchmen for Burrus Mill? Was it Bob Wills, the fiddling "king of western swing," who played with the original Doughboys and whose fame is greater today than in his heyday with the Texas Playboys in the 1940s? Was it Milton Brown, the smooth song stylist who has also received credit along with Wills as the founder of Western swing? The truth is, while the Doughboys' story begins with Kimzey, O'Daniel, Wills, and Brown, the group has been in a constant state of rebirth since that first performance in 1930 or 1931. In that sense, there are many people who can claim to have a role in "creating" the Doughboys.

One of the long-time Doughboys, Muryel "Zeke" Campbell, matter-of-factly summarized the history of the Doughboys and the music they helped create like this: "Bob Wills came out of West Texas; Milton Brown came out of Stephenville. They got together and got a guitar player [Herman Arnspiger]. They began a style that kind of caught on. Bob Wills carried it on after Milton died. It is sort of traditional. . . . It's kind of provincial, for this part of the country. People are used to listening to it, and that's what they expect to hear. Marvin [Montgomery] and them carry on. They still play a lot of Bob Wills' stuff because it is popular. I think it is a good idea to do it. He plays a lot of O'Daniel's stuff still, that O'Daniel did" (Oral history, 86–87).

One of the first sounds little James Robert Wills, born to John Tompkins Wills and Emmaline Foley Wills on March 6, 1905, near Kosse, Texas, ever heard in his cradle was frontier fiddle music, played by his father and grandfathers. The men of the Wills family and the men of the Foley family were known as some of the best fiddlers in Limestone County, Texas, if not all of the Brazos River valley, and they were very proud of it. As a child he was known as Jim Rob, and one of an aunt's earliest memories of the boy was of him dancing around the kitchen to the fiddling of his relatives. But times were bad and the young Wills family was forced to hit the road, seeking work as cotton pickers. In the cotton camps, Jim Rob's playmates were black children, and he became fascinated with the music their parents played. Many years later, Bob Wills would put this rhythmic influence to use in the music that would come to be known as Western swing (Townsend, *San Antonio Rose*, 1–5).

At around midnight on September 7 or September 8, 1903, Willie Milton Brown was born to Barty and Annie Brown, a sharecropper couple, near Stephenville, Texas. A daughter, Era, had been born in 1901. Milton's brother Roy Lee, born in 1921, told Brown's biographer, Cary Ginell: "Milton had a love for singing all his life. He and Era started singing together right from the start and they both loved to sing and entertain people. Wherever Milton was, it was said there was always a song" (Ginell, *Milton Brown*, 5). Milton and Era sang together at school assemblies and churches. After surviving an attack of appendicitis at 12 and the death of his beloved older sister when she was only 16, Milton and his family, including baby brother Derwood (12 years Milton's junior) moved to Fort Worth in 1918. Barty Brown played fiddle, and, while Milton showed little interest in the instrument, he sang with his father at dances. At Fort Worth's Arlington Heights High School, Milton became a "high school idol," known as an outstanding basketball player and for his singing. He learned stage presence in the Curtain Club, a drama group, and in a public-speaking class. His high school annual referred to him as "the

Harmony Boy," not only for his singing, but for his congenial personality. In the late 1920s, Brown formed a vocal group, the Three Yodeliers, that performed around Fort Worth. For a time, Roy Lee Brown said, Milton sang on radio in a group called the Police Quartet. The program was a public relations tool for the Fort Worth Police Department. Milton and his fellow singers were not paid, but they received badges that got them in to places where otherwise they couldn't go (Ginell, *Milton Brown*; Brown interview, December 21, 2001).

Herman Arnspiger was born in Van Alstyne, Texas, in 1905. Upon his death in 1984, the *Tulsa World* reported that Arnspiger and Wills met in Fort Worth in 1929. Wills was playing fiddle while in black face as part of a medicine show when Herman saw him, and invited Wills to play music with him in his rented room behind a drugstore. Wills soon asked Arnspiger to join the medicine show, but both had left the medicine show when Arnspiger heard that radio station KTAT was looking for a guitarist and fiddle player for a new program. Wills and Arnspiger auditioned for the job ("Last Original Member").

Milton's brother Roy Lee remembered the occasion when Milton met Bob Wills and Herman Arnspiger around Christmas 1929. He recalled that Milton and brother Derwood went to a party on the south side of Fort Worth where a fiddler and a guitarist were entertaining. The sociable Milton knew most of the people there, and ended up singing. "I don't know if somebody asked him to sing this particular time, but he got up and sang 'St. Louis Blues' with the fiddle player and the guitar player," Roy Lee recalled. "Well, the fiddler turned out to be Bob Wills and the guitar player was Herman Arnspiger" (Ginell, *Milton Brown*, 31).

Soon Bob, Herman, Milton, and Derwood were playing together at dances under a variety of names, sometimes joined by other musicians. Often they played at Eagles Hall, a ballroom in downtown Fort Worth. One of the musicians they played with was fiddler John

Dunnam. Dunnam went to the Aladdin Lamp Company, which marketed kerosene lamps, and made the arrangements for a sponsored program on WBAP in the late spring of 1930. Dunnam, Wills, Arnspiger, the Browns, and guitarist Clifton "Sleepy" Johnson became known as the Aladdin Laddies. Roy Lee Brown recalled that the Aladdin Laddies theme song was adapted from "Eagle Riding Papa." They sang "We're the Aladdin Laddies from WBAP." The tune, with revised lyrics, would soon become famous as the Light Crust Doughboys' theme. "Eagle Riding Papa" had been recorded by the Famous Hokum Boys, a black group featuring Mississippi country blues singer and guitarist Big Bill Broonzy. Milton Brown copyrighted the Light Crust Doughboys' version of the tune (Brown interview; Ginell, *Milton Brown*, 38).

The band knew that the Aladdin Lamp show was a shaky platform upon which to build a career. Bob Wills, for one, correctly anticipated that the program might end at any time. Indeed, by the end of summer 1930, the sponsorship of the Aladdin Laddies program had expired (Ginell, *Milton Brown*, 38). But the band members had been making friends all over Fort Worth. Before Wills and Arnspiger met the Brown brothers, they had made acquaintance with Will Ed Kemble, who owned the Kemble Brothers Furniture Company in downtown Fort Worth. In those days, it was common for furniture stores to carry a broad selection of the latest phonograph records, and that attracted young Wills. Bob and Herman Arnspiger liked to spin the latest discs at Kemble Brothers (Townsend, *San Antonio Rose*, 68).

"They rehearsed at Ed Kemble's furniture store. He had a mezzanine and they'd go up there," Roy Lee Brown recalled. "He carried these records, these old 78s. They'd go up there and rehearse." Truett Kimzey recalled: "When a new and appropriate tune, something they could use, would come out, they would sit in Kemble's playing it over and over until they were thoroughly familiar with both music and words" (Brown interview; Douglas and Miller, 82). Together, Bob and Herman comprised the grandly named Wills Fiddle Band. For a time, they played a radio program from Kemble Brothers on Saturdays (Townsend, *San Antonio Rose*, 68).

Kemble was most impressed with the young musicians. Later, after the Aladdin Laddies gig played out, the furniture merchant had a helpful suggestion. "Will Ed encouraged them to go down to KFJZ and audition, so they did," Roy Lee Brown recalled. "Al Stricklin [later a member of Bob Wills' band] was the assistant program manager at that time. Burrus Mill was looking for some advertising, and so they [KFJZ] recommended them to Burrus Mill" (Interview).

Another slightly different version of the story has it this way: Kemble noted that the Burrus Mill and Elevator Company of Fort Worth was doing a lot of advertising to promote its product, Light Crust Flour. He and Truett Kimzey, who had sat in on the audition at KFJZ, went to the general manager of the Burrus Milling Company in Fort Worth with the idea of Light Crust Flour sponsoring a radio show. Kemble told the manager how much the program featuring the Wills Fiddle Band had helped his store. The manager was W. Lee O'Daniel (Townsend, *San Antonio Rose*, 68; Ginell, *Milton Brown*, 44).

Wilbert Lee O'Daniel, was born in Malta, Ohio, on March 11, 1890, to plow-factory worker William O'Daniel and his wife Ann. When the boy was very young, his father was killed in a construction accident. His mother remarried, to an old school friend, Charles H. Baker, an easy-going tenant farmer and rancher whom young Lee came to know as "Dad." Ann, Lee, and his sister Ethel moved to Reno County, Kansas, near the town of Arlington, where Baker had settled. O'Daniel attended Salt City Business College in Hutchinson, Kansas, and went to work for the Kramer Milling Company in Anthony, Kansas (McKay). In 1925, he came to Fort Worth as the sales manager of the Burrus Mill and Elevator Company. O'Daniel has been described as a man who could "sell snowshoes on the equator." Within a short time, O'Daniel had increased the sales of Light Crust Flour by 250 percent, and he was promoted to president and general manager of the mill (Douglas and Miller). When Wills, Arnspiger, and the Browns came to O'Daniel's attention, he thought the idea of a radio show promoting Light Crust was at least worth a try. "One day in 1930 a group of jobless musicians came in to see me," O'Daniel recalled. "They had a suggestion for hooking up flour advertising with a musical radio program, using songs that would have a homey appeal to ordinary middle-class people, and it all sounded pretty good to me" (Townsend, *San Antonio Rose*, 80).

Thus begins the legend of the Light Crust Doughboys, a legend that combines the unlikely elements of music, politics—and flour.

The early history of the Light Crust Doughboys is scattered in several books written about their individual members. In modern times, biographers Charles R. Townsend and Cary Ginell have chronicled the careers of Bob Wills and Milton Brown, including their early years as members of the Light Crust Doughboys. Ruth Sheldon wrote an early biography of Wills when he was still a young man. C.L. Douglas and Francis Miller wrote a biography of Lee O'Daniel soon after he was elected governor, and Seth Shepard McKay wrote a later biography of O'Daniel while he was serving in the U.S. Senate. These books and others have provided the thread that weaves together the story of the Doughboys' early years.

The exact date of the Doughboys first broadcast is unknown. The most commonly given "date" is early January 1931, but the date "around January 1, 1931," was a guess that O'Daniel gave in a lawsuit he later filed against Wills. In fact, there is evidence that the Doughboys may have briefly performed on another Fort Worth station, KTAT, before arriving at KFJZ. A program featuring the "Light Crust Minstrels" appeared in the *Fort Worth Press* radio log on Wednesday, November 12, 1930. The program aired on KTAT from 7:45 to 8:15 a.m. The listing appeared three more times through December 17. Whether the "Light Crust Minstrels" were in fact the Light Crust Doughboys is not known, but the listing does establish that Light Crust began sponsoring a musical radio show in the Fall of 1930 (Ginell, *Milton Brown*, 46). It is generally accepted that by January 1931, the Light Crust Doughboys had begun singing and playing on KFJZ.

KFJZ started in the early 1920s using a 50-watt war-surplus transmitter. Engineer W.E. Branch acquired the equipment and put it in a small shed in his backyard. The broadcasting studio was in his living room. It became a commercial station in 1926. By 1929, department store owner H.C. Meacham had bought the station and moved it to Meacham's Department Store at the corner of Twelfth and Main in downtown Fort Worth. The Light Crust Doughboys began their career in the department store studios (Schroeder, 36–37).

Bob Wills would later show remarkable talent as a songwriter and lyricist with songs such as "New San Antonio Rose" and "Time Changes Everything," so it's not surprising that he would conceive of the group's clever name. One story has it that the name, partly a plug for their sponsor and partly a tip of the hat to veterans of World War I, who were called "doughboys," tumbled out of Bob Wills' mouth and went out over the air without much thought or advance consideration. As Sheldon told it, the Doughboys' first broadcast for Burrus Mill was a live transmission from a dance, which, if true, was ironic given O'Daniel's later stance on the Doughboys performing for dances. In Sheldon's account, Wills first spoke the words "Light Crust Doughboys" during that first broadcast (101). Townsend told it slightly differently, that Wills "perhaps flippantly" spoke the name during the first regular KFJZ broadcast, and that Kimzey soon picked up the name and used it in a catchy introduction that eventually became familiar in every Texas home: "The Light Crust Doughboys are on the air!" (Townsend, *San Antonio Rose*, 69).

Kimzey handled the announcing because the program was on the air so early in the morning, the professional announcers didn't want the job (Ginell, *Milton Brown*, 46). But, nevertheless, the young engineer had a role in the Doughboys' success and made a place for himself in music and broadcasting history. "He had a way of introducing the show that the listeners liked," Townsend wrote. "After a couple of licks on the fiddle or guitar, Kimzey announced in a very enthusiastic voice, 'The Light Crust Doughboys are on the air!' That was the cue for their theme song and the opening of the show." The tunes that followed were a mix of whatever music the Doughboys knew to be popular with the everyday people of North Texas—old fiddle tunes, ballads, blues, and even jazz. The Doughboys had no pretensions to playing "serious" music. One member of the Doughboys said they performed "strictly popular music. Whatever was popular, we played" (Townsend, *San Antonio Rose*, 70).

The Doughboys' first broadcast numbers were a sad penitentiary song, "Twenty-One Years" and an old fiddle tune, "Chicken Reel" (Townsend, *San Antonio Rose*, 68–69). Although KFJZ was Fort Worth's least powerful station at the time, the response from listeners was strong from the beginning (Douglas and Miller, 81).

"Twenty-one Years," one of the most popular "country" songs of the 1930s, was a perfect song for Milton Brown to sing, according to Ginell. "It enabled him to use the warm, convincing delivery he had perfected since singing with his sister Era in Stephenville fifteen years earlier," Ginell wrote (249, 47). Brown, singing with the Three Yodeliers, was quite aware that he had a vocal quality that pleased audiences, but to achieve wider success, he needed to be part of a dance band. This is why he joined Wills and Arnspiger, according to Ginell. Ironically, while the Doughboys' music may have been imminently danceable, their image-conscious boss, O'Daniel, forbade the young musicians from playing at dances, where liquor might be overconsumed. This would eventually lead to serious problems in the group.

In the beginning, O'Daniel kept his distance, probably only writing advertising copy for the show. In fact, Derwood Brown said that O'Daniel fired the Doughboys and cancelled the show two weeks after it went on the air, because the future governor "didn't like their 'hillbilly' music" (Townsend, *San Antonio Rose*, 69). Kimzey presented O'Daniel with bags of fan mail KFJZ had received for the Doughboys, but O'Daniel was still unconvinced (Ginell, *Milton Brown*, 48). The story goes that Wills, determined not to lose a steady-paying job in the depths of the Depression, demanded to see O'Daniel. He went and sat in O'Daniel's outer office for as long as three days before O'Daniel deigned to see him (Townsend, *San Antonio Rose*, 69).

Sheldon, perhaps creatively, recounted the conversation between the musician and the salesman:

O'Daniel: What did you want to talk to me about?

Wills: The main thing is, I want a job. I'll drive a truck, sweep the floor or anything. But I want a job.

O'Daniel: So you want to work? It's out of the ordinary for a musician to want to work, isn't it?

Wills: I've always worked and I sure know what hard work is.

O'Daniel: Well, that puts a different light on it if you're sure you want to work. (102–3)

Wills talked O'Daniel into sponsoring the Light Crust Doughboys program again. Each band member (not including Derwood Brown, still a school boy) would be paid $7.50 per week, but as a condition of their employment, they would have to work on a regular basis for Burrus Mill. Wills drove a truck. Arnspiger worked on the dock loading flour. Milton Brown, who had been a salesman, was given a job selling flour to retailers (Sheldon, 103). After five or six weeks, Arnspiger rebelled. "We had to get up in time for a 7 A.M. broadcast and then work all day at the mill. Our hands were so sore and stiff you couldn't note a guitar or play a fiddle," he said. Herman then told Wills, "He [O'Daniel] can put me one place or the other. I will play the broadcasts or work at the mill, but not both." O'Daniel relented, but the Doughboys were still required to stay at the mill eight hours a day and practice their music (Townsend, *San Antonio Rose*, 69).

O'Daniel built a practice room for the group at the mill, which was equipped with a phonograph and a large collection of the newest records. Brown's biographer Ginell wrote that Wills needed a lot of time to learn new material (49). Sleepy Johnson, who later replaced Arnspiger, confirmed Wills' deliberateness in learning new tunes when he said, "it took him a month to learn a new one" (Townsend, *San Antonio Rose*, 73).

Slow learner or not, Wills received much of the credit for the group's popularity from longtime Doughboy fiddler Kenneth Pitts, who would join the group in 1934. "In my opinion, this can be credited largely to the smooth, singing, continuous tone Wills achieved on the violin (fiddle)," Pitts wrote. "He was not a formally trained violinist, but he had the knack of handling the bow in a most expert manner and knack for producing the tone mentioned above, plus projecting a genuine, down-home country sound on the fiddle" ("Light Crust," 1).

While the Doughboys' popularity steadily grew, O'Daniel still maintained his distance. Wills, appreciating the relative security of the Burrus Mill gig, hoped to cement the relationship with the boss, so the Doughboys invited O'Daniel to attend a broadcast. Wills, in a masterstroke of psychology, persuaded O'Daniel to say a few words on the air in his capacity as the sponsor. "From that day on, W. Lee O'Daniel was the greatest fan the Doughboys had," Townsend commented (*San Antonio Rose*, 71).

A fateful event in the history of the Light Crust Doughboys and the history of Texas occurred in March 1931, when O'Daniel chartered a bus and took the Doughboys to Galveston for a bakers' convention. O'Daniel had Truett Kimzey wire the bus for sound, allowing the Doughboys to perform at stops along the way. They drew enormous crowds at their stops, and were the hit of the convention in Galveston. Kimzey still served as announcer. But O'Daniel went on the trip and was impressed enough to announce upon their return, "I think I'll buy a bus of our own" (Douglas and Miller, 84).

However, the "bus" was actually a seven-passenger, white Packard automobile, upon which signs were mounted: "Eat More Bread, Your Best and Cheapest Food" and, amidst the gloom of the Depression, "Patronize Texas Industry and Texas Agriculture and Prosperity Will Return." In fact, the Packard was christened the "Prosperity Special." It soon became a familiar sight around Texas (Ginell, *Milton Brown*, 49).

In late 1931, O'Daniel scheduled the Doughboys for a goodwill tour representing the Fort Worth Chamber of Commerce, of which he would become president in 1933 (Douglas and Miller). The tour led to an even more momentous change for the Light Crust Doughboys. Kimzey could not leave his engineering duties at KFJZ for the extended tour, and O'Daniel decided to replace Kimzey with himself as master of ceremonies. O'Daniel served as announcer for the first time at a stop in Weatherford. He immediately showed a genius for showmanship and promotion. On a stop in Houston at the Kirby Theatre, the management held the Doughboys over for two extra days. Soon, O'Daniel took over as the Doughboys' regular radio announcer, and listeners responded to O'Daniel's down-to-earth philosophizing with a flood of fan mail (Douglas and Miller, 84).

Following the chamber tour, the Light Crust Doughboys remained on the road, promoting Light Crust Flour and Burrus Mill, for more than 50 years.

Jimmy Thomason was a teenage fan of the Doughboys in Waco. Thomason himself later became a professional musician, playing with Doug Bine and the Dixie Ramblers, the Shelton Brothers, and others. He remembered the Doughboys driving into Waco with their sound system on top of the car. "Well, they were over in East Waco and they parked in front of our postman's house," he said. "One of the first songs I remember Milton doing was that deal, 'Crazy 'bout Nancy Jane.' I remember that very well. I also remember the smile on Milton's face. He sure seemed to be enjoying that work" (Ginell, *Milton Brown*, 52).

Bob Wills also made a powerful impression on the young Thomason. "Wills looked like a human dynamo at that particular time," he said. "He enjoyed it so much. I got to thinking, 'Man, these guys get to do this every day!' . . . And Milton was the idol of every boy in Waco" (Ginell, *Milton Brown*, 52–53).

Another Waco Doughboys fan was Red Varner. In 1931, he and a friend were invited to attend a Doughboys radio performance on WACO. "There they were, in the flesh, standing there right before us, dressed to the nines and ready to play for the listening audience as well as for those of us just outside the window who would see and hear the program," Varner remembered. "A moment for tuning, a word of introduction just after the 'on the air' light came on, and they were off and running. It was a grand program" (Ginell, *Milton Brown*, 53–54).

As noted before, another young Texan who came in contact with the Doughboys on their many tours of the state was Walter Cronkite. Although not then a fan of what he called country music, young Cronkite recognized that serving as the announcer for the Light Crust Doughboys, even on a fill-in basis, was a big opportunity. He said the broadcasts from the KTUT (now KLBJ) studios in Austin went very smoothly. "They were an affable bunch of guys. W. Lee O'Daniel was, of course, a big glad hander. It was a joy just to be part of the operation, although I had no ambitions to be a commercial announcer.

"This was my exposure to something other than the few thousand listeners at KTUT. I figured it was very advantageous, and I certainly didn't mind a little publicity. I didn't quite see anybody tearing my clothes off in admiration, but I was thrilled to do it. I always hoped they would need an announcer when I heard they were coming to town."

Cronkite said the Doughboys held a very elevated position in Texas popular culture at the time. "They were the only outfit of the kind whose name I remember, and I think that would probably be true of most of those in my generation. I had a feeling, though I wasn't real devotee of country music, that they almost were the founders of that kind of music."

The 7 A.M. airtime put a strain on the band because in the beginning they still played dances four nights a week (Sheldon, 103). Later, O'Daniel would put a stop to the playing of dances, because he thought it was not good for the image of Light Crust. In late 1931, after a successful run on KFJZ, O'Daniel gave the band members a raise to $15 a week and moved the show from KFJZ to the more-powerful WBAP at 12:30 P.M. each day, where they soon became famous all over Texas (Sheldon, 124).

The move to WBAP was decisive in making the Doughboys state-wide musical heroes. Like many infant stations in the early 1920s, WBAP was an extension of a powerful newspaper. The *Fort Worth Star-Telegram*, published by Amon G. Carter, Sr., and Carter Publications, owned WBAP.

Star-Telegram circulation manager Harold Hough convinced a skeptical Carter to put WBAP on the air. Carter grudgingly approved the expenditure of $300 to put the 10-watt station on the air on May 2, 1922. "But when that $300 is gone, we're out of the radio business," Carter admonished Hough, who became WBAP's most popular on-the-air personality in the early days, going by the moniker of "The Hired Hand." WBAP received its call letters from Secretary of Commerce Herbert Hoover. The commerce department then regulated the fledgling radio industry. The sensible Hoover said WBAP stood for "We Bring A Program."

After moving from the relatively weak KFJZ, the Doughboys' program was being carried on one of the most powerful facilities in the country, although on a frequency that was shared by two stations. For more than 40 years, WBAP shared air space with WFAA, owned by the *Dallas Morning News*. WFAA had been saddled with a frequency-sharing deal not to its liking with KRLD, owned by the *Morning News'* bitter rival, the *Dallas Times Herald*. *Dallas Morning News* publisher George B. Dealey apparently preferred to cooperate with Carter's station, across 30 miles of open prairie, rather than the station of his intracity rival. WBAP had been paired with KTHS in Hot Springs, Arkansas. The station found the "awkwardness" of sharing airtime with such a distant station untenable. So WBAP and WFAA petitioned the Federal Radio Commission to allow them to share the 800 kHz. channel (820 kHz. beginning in 1941). The FRC granted the change effective May 1, 1929. At the same time, the FRC authorized WBAP and WFAA to broadcast at 50,000 watts, an increase of a hundred fold from their previous wattage. The two stations later shared a second frequency, 570 kHz. ("A Brief History;" "'We'll Spend'").

Within six months, at O'Daniel's instigation, the Doughboys were broadcasting over WOAI in San Antonio and KPRC in Houston. Then in September 1934, WOAI and KPRC formed the Texas Quality Network with WBAP and WFAA in Dallas. The stations' general desire to share programming on a regional basis drove the decision to form the network, although the growing popularity of the Doughboys probably was the single greatest factor.

"'The Doughboys [radio program]' necessitated the formation of the Texas Quality Network, and the establishment of networks demanded the creation and development of more talent and programming so chains could justify their existence," Texas broadcasting historian Richard Schroeder noted. "'The Doughboys' may have been the most popular radio program ever originated in Texas" (110–11).

Hoxie Mundine, an engineer at WOAI in San Antonio related that he and the station's founder, G.A.C. Halff, traveled to Fort Worth to set up the network. "We're going up to the flour mills—Burrus Mill and W. Lee O'Daniel," Halff told Mundine. Mundine asked Halff why they were going to see O'Daniel, and Halff told him they were going to set up a radio network using Western Union telegraph lines. "That was unbelievable to me because Western Union had no lines dedicated for broadcasting," Mundine said.

The telegraph lines were used because they were cheaper than dedicated telephone lines. Mundine said the telegraph lines worked most of the time, but sometimes a Western Union operator made a mistake and transmission was lost. "The equalization necessary to overcome the loss [of sound quality] was unbelievable, but we managed to get through," Mundine said. "Then the telephone company lowered their rates, so they went to that."

The Doughboys' show was by no means the only regular program on TQN. Other programs included the "Chuck Wagon Gang," sponsored by Bewley Mills; "Gladiola Gloom Chasers" for Fant Milling; "Pepper-Uppers" for Dr Pepper; and "Riding with the Texas Rangers" for Kellogg (Schroeder, 99–100).

TQN later included KOMA in Oklahoma City, KVOO in Tulsa, KARK in Little Rock, Arkansas, KFPW in Fort Smith, Arkansas, KTHS in Hot Springs, Arkansas, KBTM in Jonesboro, Arkansas, WWL in New Orleans, and KWKH in Shreveport, Louisiana, in addition to the Texas stations. TQN lasted into the 1950s (Townsend, *San Antonio Rose*, 72; "Gold Star Mothers;" Bus photo; Campbell, 72; Schroeder, 102).

The 12:30 P.M. time slot contributed greatly to the Doughboys' popularity: "Business men and laborers are eating in restaurants and lunch stands where radios are blaring. Housewives have finished their morning work. School children are home for lunch. The farmer and his wife have left the chores for the noon day meal and invariably listen to the radio," noted Wills biographer Sheldon (124).

The Doughboys' move to the noon hour led a trend for fiddle bands. As the Doughboys' program moved to midday, so did many of the other groups. But the move was practical as well as strategic. O'Daniel kept the Doughboys busy with personal appearances many evenings, and the later start let the band members return to Fort Worth in time to get a decent night's sleep before going on the air (Ginell, *Milton Brown*, 252–53).

Texas music writer John Morthland said the noontime radio shows had a tremendous impact, in Texas especially. "They had shows like that all over the country, but it was never like it was in Texas," Morthland said. "In Lubbock, there were people who had that noon radio show, whom people still remember, and still think of as stars, who never even got to record, never toured. That format just seemed to mean so much more in Texas."

Leon McAuliffe, who later served two stints with the O'Daniel-era Doughboys and became a legendary steel guitar virtuoso as a member of Wills' Texas Playboys, remembered hearing the Doughboys growing up as a teenager on KPRC in Houston. "The people of Houston had never heard anything like it," he said. "There was no western music there at the time. . . . I would walk three blocks to the store and never miss a word of a song. In the summer every window was open, and every radio was tuned to the Light Crust Doughboys" (Townsend, *San Antonio Rose*, 73).

The "Doughboys-coming-from-the-window" story is part of the group's legend. It has often been repeated. "Even if your radio wasn't working, you could listen to your neighbor's because his was up high enough anyway," Doughboys fan Jimmy Thomason recalled (Ginell, *Milton Brown*, 53). The story may have been somewhat overstated, but, no doubt, there is a strong element of truth in it. The Doughboys became an inescapable part of daily life in Texas.

Morthland said the Doughboys had a terrific hold on the consciousness of Texas radio listeners. "Before there was Top 40 radio, which relies heavily on repetition, the repetition that hooked people was these shows like the Doughboys had that you could count on every single day. Just being there every day was a really big deal. I think that's where their greatest influence came from was that radio show. . . . The Doughboys were *it*. Radio was how you measured popularity. They were known everywhere. They were the biggest of the Texas radio stars."

A woman who attended a Doughboys show in the 1980s recalled wistfully, "I'm afraid I'm revealing my age, but I remember as a young girl running across the fields every day at noon. When we reached the yard we could hear the first few notes of the theme song, and we knew we were in for a treat. I just want you to know how much your program meant to us out in the country" (L. Johnson, 16).

The growing popularity of the Light Crust Doughboys was not lost on Burrus Mill, which quickly went "show biz." Light Crust built a new manufacturing plant on the south side of Fort Worth and placed a Broadway-style electric sign atop the building. O'Daniel and the Doughboys dedicated the building with a rooftop performance.

"W. Lee did the announcing and at the conclusion of the ceremony the records [artifacts] of the first two years' broadcasting were sealed in the cornerstone—letters, programs, photographs, flour sacks and mementos," O'Daniel biographers Douglas and Miller commented (84–85).

The Light Crust Doughboys were busy young men. Besides the WBAP programs, for a time they broadcast a program every Wednesday night on a station in the small Central Texas town of Dublin, and on Friday night, they broadcast a 30-minute program on a station in Waco. This was before the creation of the Texas Quality Network (McKay, 22).

Traveling the rural highways of Texas was not a glamorous life for the Doughboys. Roy Lee Brown recalled his brothers Milton and Derwood telling their parents that O'Daniel would stop at roadside fruit stands as the Doughboys traveled from town to town. "Of course, Burrus Mill bought the Doughboys' lunch," Roy Lee said. "He said, before lunchtime, O'Daniel would stop by and get a bunch of these overripe bananas and try to get the band to eat 'em so they wouldn't be so hungry at lunchtime" (Interview).

The authenticity of O'Daniel's contributions to the Doughboys' musical repertoire is debatable. His musical ability was extremely limited, but he was credited with composing a number of songs that became popular as performed by the Doughboys, including "Put Me In Your Pocket," "I Want Somebody to Cry Over Me," "Your Own Sweet Darling Wife." His best known song was "Beautiful Texas:"

> You have all read the beautiful stories
> Of countries far over the sea,
> From whence came our ancestors

To establish this land of the free.
There are some folks who still like to travel
To see what they have over there,
But when they go look, it's not like the book,
And they find there is none to compare
To Beautiful, Beautiful Texas—
The most beautiful place that I know.
To Beautiful, Beautiful Texas
Where the beautiful bluebonnets grow,
We're proud of our forefathers,
Who fought at the Alamo —
You can live on the plains or mountains,
Or down where the sea breezes blow,
And you're still in beautiful Texas,
The most beautiful place that I know. (Douglas and Miller, 87)

Townsend gave O'Daniel credit, at least, for significant lyrical talent. He had an "uncanny ability" to write timely songs, as when the legendary Jimmie Rodgers, a friend of the Doughboys, died. O'Daniel wrote "Memories of Jimmie Rodgers" for the Doughboys to perform on their program:

His voice is stilled forever,
His golden voice so true,
But his records keep on playing
To cheer folks when they're blue.
And in that unknown region,
From whence we'll ne'er depart,
We will meet our Jimmy [sic] Rodgers,
With his "Mother, the Queen of My Heart." (Townsend, *San Antonio Rose*, 74).

Because "the Singing Brakeman" was so popular in Texas, the Doughboys had performed many of Rodgers' songs, such as "Roll Along Kentucky Moon" and "My Carolina Sunshine Girl" (Ginell, *Milton Brown*, 249).

O'Daniel further demonstrated his knack for writing songs that were right for the moment when he wrote a song about a flu epidemic called "Kachoo! Kachoo! Kachoo!" He wrote a song about the stock market crash called the "Fall of '29," and a song for the occasion of Franklin D. Roosevelt's first inauguration called "On to Victory, Mr. Roosevelt" (Sheldon, 104).

O'Daniel played no musical instrument, but his children, taught by members of the Doughboys themselves, learned to play (Coffey, November 25, 2001). Pat strummed the banjo, Mike played fiddle, and daughter Molly doubled on piano and accordion. According to one account, O'Daniel would conceive of a tune and whistle it to his children or to the Doughboys themselves and they would complete the composition. For example, when famed aviator Charles Lindbergh's baby was kidnapped, a crime that gripped the nation, O'Daniel wrote a song called "Please Bring Back My Daddy to Me." "He whistled the melody until the Doughboys caught on, and put the piece on the air that same day," wrote biographers Douglas and Miller. "Next morning the postman stumbled into the Burrus office with thousands of requests for the song. A phonograph concern in New York heard about it and asked for rights" (89–90).

However, Milton Brown's brother Roy Lee was less favorable in his opinion of O'Daniel's songwriting ability. He said O'Daniel often simply took a traditional popular song and put new words to it. "'Beautiful Texas' is 'Just Because,'" Brown said. "And they recorded 'Put Me in Your Pocket.' That's 'When Irish Eyes are Smiling.' 'Your Own Sweet Darling Wife' is 'When It's Roundup Time in Texas.' He changed them [the tunes] just enough, I guess, to keep out of trouble, or nobody challenged him on it. . . . O'Daniel used some other tune for just about every song he ever wrote. He was good with poetry but he couldn't write a melody if his life depended on it" (Brown interview; Ginell, *Milton Brown*, 50–51).

But O'Daniel's contribution to the Light Crust Doughboys' popularity is undeniable. Besides the lively music of the Doughboys, the appeal of the noontime radio program had a lot to do with O'Daniel's folksy persona. O'Daniel wrote and delivered the announcements for the program, and frequently wrote and read poetry. The manager of WBAP, Harold Hough, would sometimes turn thumbs down on O'Daniel's poems. O'Daniel would then tuck the poem away, and pull it out for one of the Doughboys' live performances. More often than not, it would go over big with the audience.

Hough said the station often prevented O'Daniel from reading something he had written on the air, only to realize later that the flour salesman knew what he was doing. O'Daniel would not be deterred. In a day or two, he would be back with another homespun piece of poetry. "He was always several steps ahead of all of us," Hough said. "We couldn't see, for instance, how his telling little boys to walk on the right side of the street, and pointers like that, could possibly have anything to do with flour selling" (Douglas and Miller, 102–3).

Roy Lee Brown said O'Daniel was a natural salesman. "He could talk an Eskimo into buying a refrigerator," Roy Lee said. "He had a way [with words] on the air, and he'd have people eating out of his hand. It was his voice, and the fact that he made the impression he was on the poor people's side. When he ran for governor, he'd say 'I'm no politician,' but he was one of the biggest politicians ever" (Interview).

O'Daniel related well to everyday people struggling with life in the Depression. As his biographers put it: "He worked in a bit of cheer for the down-and-outer, a little sympathy for those in trouble, laughed with those who had enjoyed good fortune. . . . The program, reflecting Mr. O'Daniel's personality, had the common and the human touch, and month by month, year by year, it gained steadily in popularity" (Douglas and Miller, 105–6).

Because of O'Daniel's habit of discussing religious teachings during the Doughboys' program, many listeners thought he must be a minister. "Erring husbands were advised to correct their behavior, school children were given good advice on thrift and conduct, traffic safety emphasized, childless couples were advised to adopt babies, and religious and humanitarian movements and organizations were supported," O'Daniel biographer Seth McKay wrote (22–23).

Roy Lee Brown recalled that O'Daniel played to the emotions of his audience. "He'd come on there and he'd say, 'Ladies and gentlemen, boys and girls,' and then he'd have some sad story to tell 'em about some dear old mother, and then he'd say, 'We're going to play "That Silver-Haired Mother of Mine."' And, I mean, the people just ate it up, until they got to know him," Brown said (Interview).

O'Daniel appealed strongly to a Texas audience that was still very rural in the 1930s. He had grown up a poor farm boy in Ohio and Kansas, and he knew the hearts of country people. Praise for mothers was a popular theme. "He talked about how poor people . . . should listen to their mothers; while the Doughboys played—pianissimo—'Marvelous Mother of Mine,' he began one program: 'Hello there, mother, you little sweetheart. How in the world are you anyway, you little bunch of sweetness? This is your big boy, W. Lee O'Daniel,'" wrote Lyndon B. Johnson biographer Robert Caro (696).

O'Daniel was an instinctive radio communicator:

> It was not the content of these rambling, informal little homilies that made them so popular, nor the soft violins playing familiar sentimental tunes in the background. It was the voice in which they were delivered. The voice was warm and friendly and relaxed—captivatingly natural. And yet was also fatherly, soft but firm. It was a voice you could trust. . . . As one chronicler was later to put it . . . "O'Daniel learned early that he had Texas by the ear and from that day on he cooed and caroled and gurgled into it."(Caro, 696–97)

O'Daniel was fond of producing special programs with the Doughboys. One of these was the "Light Crust Doughboys Armistice Program" on November 11, 1931. A surviving script belonging to Herman Arnspiger provided the outline for the program. The Doughboys sang George M. Cohan's popular World War I anthem, "Over There." O'Daniel—ever mindful of who bought the flour— saluted, not war veterans, but their wives, praising "those noble Texas housewives, who 13 years ago—on bended knees—gave thanks to Almighty God for the greatest event of this generation—the signing of the Armistice." O'Daniel, ever the master of marketing, published the contents of the program, including its commercial announcements as well as its songs and poems, in pamphlet form, free upon request (Townsend, *San Antonio Rose*, 71–72).

If the reader detects a conflict between the Doughboys' reputation for ground-breaking music and the decidedly traditional material that to a great extent comprised the radio programs, the reader is not mistaken. Milton Brown's brother Roy Lee said, while the group chose its own tunes in the beginning when Truett Kimzey served as announcer, O'Daniel imposed his taste for homier fare when he stepped in as the undisputed boss. "He wanted these tear-jerking, don't-send-my-boy-to-prison-type songs," Roy Lee said. "Or my-old-gray-haired-mother songs. Now, I'm not knocking those, they're good, too. But that's what he wanted. Old-folk type songs." Roy Lee said Milton had the job of balancing the show, starting the program with a fast tune, followed by a slow one, and so on (Ginell, *Milton Brown*, 50–51).

On February 9, 1932, the Doughboys cut their first and only recordings with Wills and Brown in the band. They recorded Milton's composition, "Sunbonnet Sue," and The Famous Hokum Boys' "Nancy Jane" in the Jefferson Hotel for Victor Records. Townsend noted, "It was a simple fiddle-band recording, but this rare disc reveals that Wills already had his dance beat and the music had his characteristic swing." For some reason, Victor released the record as the "Fort Worth Doughboys" (*San Antonio Rose*, 72). The Doughboys probably changed the name themselves to avoid a confrontation with O'Daniel, who kept firm control of the group's on-air repertoire. It seems unlikely that O'Daniel would have countenanced the Doughboys performing the spicy "Nancy Jane," whose lyrics contained suggestive comments on the amazing abilities of the girl they sang about. Even so, as previously noted, the Doughboys' big Waco fan, Jimmy Thomason, said he remembered the Doughboys performing the song in public (Ginell, *Milton Brown*, 62).

According to Townsend, a representative of Victor Records approached the Doughboys to make the record, one of the first recordings ever made of Western music, but it was not a hit. Nevertheless, the qualities that would make Bob Wills, Milton Brown, and the Light

Crust Doughboys so popular can be heard in their embryonic stage (Townsend, *San Antonio Rose*, 72).

The trademark "hollers" that became so identified with Bob Wills when he led the Texas Playboys are present on "Nancy Jane," but Milton Brown's hollers are the most notable on the recording. Of course, Brown is the lead vocalist, joined by Wills and Derwood Brown on harmony vocals. Wills keeps closely to the melody, and Derwood and Sleepy Johnson, who had replaced Herman Arnspiger by this time, each provided rhythm on guitar. With only a single microphone available, Bob and Derwood probably stepped back from the mike as Milton leaned in to sing his lines (Ginell, *Milton Brown*, 63).

On "Nancy Jane" and "Sunbonnet Sue," Wills' trademark "hollers" are relatively subdued; not surprising, since it was not Wills' style to play and holler at the same time. Later, when he was leading the Texas Playboys, Wills had other musicians to carry the melody while he popped off with his famous "ah-has" and other jaunty interjections (Ginell, *Milton Brown*, 47–48; Ginell, letter).

Even on this first recording, Milton Brown's talent as a singer was apparent. Brown's vocal shows off a more "sophisticated, smoother sound," more cosmopolitan in character than the "dry, dusty sound" of popular Western singers of the time such as Carl T. Sprague or Jules Verne Allen, Ginell observed (*Milton Brown*, 63). Milton played no instrument, but he was a musician just the same. "He used his voice as an instrument," Roy Lee Brown said. "If you'll notice, he improvises with his voice, just like the instruments do. . . . He didn't copy anybody's style, he had a style all his own. He did some of Jimmie Rodgers' songs, but he didn't particularly care for them. He liked more of a jazz, pop thing, you know. But he'd do a country song, as well. He had a dynamic personality and charisma." Roy Lee said Milton was influenced in the way he made recitations in a song by Ted Lewis, who was famous for "Me and My Shadow." And, like most young people of the time, he liked Bing Crosby.

While the Doughboys are considered pioneers of Western swing, of which Bob Wills became the best-known exponent, most experts say the original Doughboys were not truly a Western swing group, even with Wills in the lineup. Indeed, in what might well be considered fighting words in Texas dance halls, Ginell took the position that Bob Wills' contributions to the original Light Crust Doughboys recordings prevented them from being true Western swing music:

> The reason I cannot consider this record the first western swing recording is, ironically, the presence of Bob Wills himself. Although considered by many to be the father of the genre, Bob Wills could not play jazz. On the Fort Worth Doughboys sides, Wills plays melody, without variation. Wills' fiddle on these two sides exists as the one holdover from the Texas string band tradition. Every other aspect of the recordings—jazzy vocals, syncopated rhythm, and repertoire—was entirely new. (*Milton Brown*, 63)

Ginell said the Doughboys lacked a true "take-off," or improvisational, fiddler, a trademark of Western swing. Bob Wills and his successor, Clifford Gross, stuck closely to the melody. Kenneth Pitts was the first Doughboys to play "hokum," as it was called (Ginell, *Milton Brown*, 245). "The hokum is when you play the hot chorus," Marvin Montgomery, the walking encyclopedia of popular music knowledge, said. "You're playing your own thing against the chords that are laid down by the tune. That's hokum. 'Uncle Art' [Satherley, the Doughboys' record producer] used to call it 'noodle'; he'd say 'noodle on the bridge' or something. We'd improvise on the melody and the chords, follow the chord progression. You'd lose the melody a lot of times" (Govenar and Brakefield, 144).

John Morthland agreed that the music of the Light Crust Doughboys during the Bob Wills/Milton Brown era was not as sophisticated as the music that Wills and Brown would later record. "It's true that Wills and Brown started there, but at that time, though, it was a pretty conventional fiddle band. It had kind of a light swing to it, but certainly nothing like what Wills and Brown became" (Interview). Roy Lee Brown made the point also. "That was a fiddle band," Roy Lee said. "They say that Bob Wills started Western swing. Well, they're wrong, cause that wasn't Western swing, that was country, that was hillbilly. Besides that, the High Fliers [a band featuring fiddler Clifford Gross, among others] were going before the Doughboys were" (Interview).

The replacement of Herman Arnspiger with Sleepy Johnson foreshadowed the unraveling of the original Light Crust Doughboys. While O'Daniel must have officially carried out the firing, it may be that Wills had a hand in the deed. While Sleepy said O'Daniel fired Arnspiger for "getting married," Ruth Sheldon wrote that Wills fired Arnspiger because the guitarist had become too comfortable in his new-found "prosperity" (Townsend, *San Antonio Rose*, 72; Sheldon, 105).

Roy Lee Brown said O'Daniel was characteristically penurious in making the change. "I've got a picture, and it's got them sitting at O'Daniel's house and Sleepy's sitting there on a piano bench. They had their initials on the sleeve of their sweaters, and it's got an 'H' on Sleepy's sleeve. That was Herman's. When O'Daniel fired him, they just gave Sleepy his sweater." Roy Lee said, oddly, O'Daniel later had Sleepy and his wife get married on the radio program.

O'Daniel showed his appreciation for the group by building them a studio at the mill and raising their salaries, but said they must stop playing dances on the side (Townsend, *San Antonio Rose*, 73). As Roy Lee Brown told it: "O'Daniel was adamantly against the Doughboys playing dances. Period. He complained about it all the time. He didn't want them to play those places because they were considered beer joints and they had dancing there and no respect for religion and all those other things. He may have thought that it might give Light Crust Flour a bad name if people knew the group was associated with those places"(Ginell, *Milton Brown*, 65).

Besides the good money, the dances allowed the Doughboys to stretch out and play exactly what they liked. O'Daniel limited the Doughboys to performing songs on the radio that met his standards of "high moral character." The Doughboys, well aware that they were fortunate to be employed at all in the Depression, let alone getting paid to do what they loved, apparently did not outwardly oppose O'Daniel's strictures. But at the same time, they avidly kept up with the latest pop and jazz recordings, and also knew that live audiences wanted to hear more up-to-date numbers than the old-fashioned numbers O'Daniel favored (Ginell, *Milton Brown*, 54–55).

The band members could earn $40 each in a single night playing dances at places like the Crystal Springs dance hall. Roy Lee Brown said Crystal Springs was a big barn-like building, "ramshackle" by today's standards, but set on a bluff on a lake fed by natural springs, and with a swimming pool below the bluff. It was located on White Settlement Road on what is now the west side of Fort Worth, but was then outside of town. For these dances, Roy Lee said, the band would often add extra players such as Sleepy Johnson and fiddler Ocie Stockard, and they would not play under the name of the Light Crust Doughboys. Their $25 weekly salary did not look like a lot compared to the money they earned at Crystal Springs to Milton Brown, and he rebelled. Wills, with a wife, Edna, and a daughter, Robbie Jo, in the heart of the Depression, still preferred the security of a regular job with Burrus Mill (Ginell, *Milton Brown*, 56, 69; Townsend, *San Antonio Rose*, 74).

In her biography of Wills, written just five years after Wills left the Doughboys, Sheldon wrote that Wills and Brown, although still friendly, clashed over who would be the band's musical leader (105). In Sheldon's view, that role clearly had been won by Wills. In any case, Brown left the Doughboys on September 7, 1932, and formed his own group, Milton Brown and the Musical Brownies. Surely, conflicts were not unknown between two young, talented, and ambitious musicians such as Bob Wills and Milton Brown. But if such clashes did happen, it seems unlikely they were the cause of Brown leaving the Doughboys.

Roy Lee Brown said there was little or no animosity between Milton and Bob. "I have heard a lot of things over the years about both Bob and Milton wanting to lead the Doughboys and that was why they split up," Roy Lee said. "Now it's true that they both wanted to lead a band, but that wasn't the reason they split up. Milton always considered Bob his close friend and likewise with Bob. Milton would never have done anything to hurt Bob. He liked Bob a whole lot and despite what people have said, there was never any conflict between the two of them from what I could see" (Ginell, *Milton Brown*, 68–69).

Roy Lee said Milton's departure from the Doughboys came about because of his family responsibilities. "He was more like a second father to me than he was a brother, because he was so much older," Roy Lee said. "He was almost 18 years older than I am." Despite the age difference, the brothers had a very close relationship. "Occasionally he'd take me to something he was going to, a singing or a ball game, and he'd ask me, 'Do you want to go by and get one of your friends?'"

But Milton was more than just a pal to young Roy Lee. "He gave me money," Roy Lee recalled. "This was the Depression years, you know. My dad didn't work [he was in poor health after working for the Bain Peanut Company in Fort Worth for 25 years] and Milton kept our family from going under and helped me finish high school. If it wasn't for his money coming in every week, I don't know what we would have done. ... He was the mainstay of our family. Even after he married, he contributed to our welfare."

"He was good to me and he'd take me places. Just out of the clear blue sky, he'd ask me, 'Do you want to sing a song on the [Brownies] radio program today?' I'd say, 'I don't care.' Well, he'd say, 'Come on and go with me to the radio station.' I'd get in his car and we'd drive to the radio station, and I'd sing one or two songs on his program."

Milton's younger brother Derwood had played informally with the Doughboys since the beginning. "He didn't get paid a regular salary like Bob and Herman and Milton did," Roy Lee said. "But he would get paid on these little trips around Fort Worth where they would go to the square, you know, some feed store or some grocery store where they would sell Light Crust Flour."

Ultimately, Milton Brown left the Doughboys as much for the sake of his family as himself. "Derwood was 16 and he had just gotten married, and he was still in school," Roy Lee said. "He was playing with Milton down at Crystal Springs. That's the only income that he had. He had a wife, so he needed a job. Well, if they gave up Crystal Springs, Derwood would be without a job. Milton went to W. Lee O'Daniel and told him, 'If you will raise my salary, and give Derwood a job, we'll quit Crystal Springs.'" Roy Lee said O'Daniel called back a week or so later and said he would give Milton a raise, but would not hire Derwood. "So Milton turned in his resignation, because he figured O'Daniel would do that, and he already had his band lined up and ready to go," Roy Lee said. Milton parted on good terms with O'Daniel, one of the few who did. "He always got along with him, but Milton got along with most people. He just had a knack for getting along with people." Roy Lee blamed O'Daniel's lack of musical understanding for not appreciating the value of Derwood's guitar playing and vocal harmonies. It was hard for Roy Lee to understand why O'Daniel wouldn't pay Derwood Brown's salary to keep him and Milton in the group given his actions after Milton and Darwood left. "When O'Daniel fired Bob, he got Sleepy Johnson to get him a band . . . and they got about four or five, where they only had three [originally]," Roy Lee mused (Brown interview; Ginell, *Milton Brown*, 67–68).

In no time, Milton Brown and his Musical Brownies were broadcasting over KTAT in Fort Worth (Townsend, *San Antonio Rose*, 73). Roy Lee said Milton played his last program with the Doughboys on a Saturday, and was performing with his new band on KTAT the following Monday (Interview). By September 19, 1932, the *Fort Worth Press* listed a special evening program featuring Milton Brown and his Musical Brownies on KTAT. Soon after that, a regular noontime program featuring the group began on the station (Ginell, *Milton Brown*, 68).

Milton Brown's exit from the Doughboys is the point at which historians begin to debate who is the rightful "king of Western swing," Milton or Bob Wills. For his part, Roy Lee strongly asserted that Milton, not Bob Wills, is the true originator of Western swing. "When Milton left the Doughboys in 1932, he had Jesse Ashlock on fiddle, he had Derwood on guitar, he had Wanna Coffman on bass, Ocie Stockard on banjo, and it wasn't long before they added Fred Calhoun on piano, who was a jazz pianist. And that was the first Western swing band," Roy Lee said. "Then he came along and added Cecil Brower [on fiddle, in January 1933], which was the first twin fiddles in a Western swing band. And then he added Bob Dunn on steel guitar, which was the first amplified steel in a Western swing band. So if you look at your bands today, they've added instruments to it, but that's still your basic instruments." Roy Lee said Milton added Iris Harper on saxophone for eight months in 1935 when one of the fiddle players left the Brownies.

"Milton used drums, but he used them on big jobs like over in Dallas at the [State Fair of Texas] Automobile Building," Roy Lee said. "He'd use drums and horns over there, but he didn't carry drums and horns with his regular band because it wasn't necessary. They had so many people where they played, they couldn't get 'em all in anyway."

Roy Lee further noted that Milton and his group recorded for the first time in April 1934, a full 17 months before Wills and the Play-boys went into the recording studio for the first time in September 1935, and had recorded 50 tunes before Wills ever recorded his first. James Austin, the producer of a collection of Wills' music released in 1991, did not dispute Roy Lee's point in the liner notes to the recordings: "Bob Wills may not have invented Western swing, but he was the man most responsible for popularizing this enduring style of country music" (Brown interview; Kienzle, 1, 7–8).

However, Joe Frank Ferguson, a member of the Texas Playboys and later the Light Crust Doughboys, said it is wrong to pit Wills against Brown as rival inventors of Western swing. "To me, it is silly to have that controversy to start with. Either way you go, you are right," Ferguson said. An interviewer observed that some writers credit Milton Brown with inventing Western swing. "Absolutely, and they would be right. They could also say that Bob Wills started it, but they were together [in developing Western swing]" (Oral history, 67).

As a youth listening to the radio, Muryel Campbell, who soon was to join the Doughboys, enjoyed the group, but actually had stronger memories of the group Brown formed after he left the Doughboys: "I liked music. I didn't know who they [the Doughboys and others] were at the time, when I was listening to them on the radio. One of my favorite bands was 'Milton Brown and the Brown-ies,' because they played a lot of jazz and a lot of popular stuff" (78–79).

Jim Boyd, who would join the Doughboys in 1938 and played with them off and on until his death, remembered being overwhelmed by Brown and his group when he saw them for the first time at the Labor Temple in downtown Dallas. "I went up the stairs to where they were playing. . . . And that Milton Brown was a good-lookin' rascal too! They had on brown suits with reversible vests. And I stood up there and looked at those boys and I thought they looked like a bunch of Greek gods! That was the finest-looking aggregation I had ever seen! I was really enthralled," Boyd said (Ginell, *Milton Brown*, 90).

Replacing the versatile Milton Brown was not an easy task. Wills auditioned 67 singers. The Doughboys required a vocalist who could handle styles including blues, traditional jazz, novelty songs, cowboy tunes, and, of course, popular songs. Finally, after two weeks, Wills discovered Tommy Duncan singing for tips at a root beer stand. Wills asked him if he could sing "I Ain't Got Nobody," and Duncan told Wills, sure he could. "If you can sing it the way I have in mind it should be sung, you've got a job," Wills replied. Obviously, Duncan sang the song to Wills' satisfaction, because he not only joined the Doughboys but went on to travel down many a highway with Wills as the lead vocalist of the Texas Playboys (Townsend, *San Antonio Rose*, 73).

Doughboy-to-be Kenneth Pitts said Duncan deserves a lot of credit not only for the Doughboys' continued success after Milton Brown left the group, but also Wills' later success. "A large contribution was the singing of Tommy Duncan," Pitts wrote. "He did not, in my opinion, have too much voice but there was a sound there that the untrained music listener found particularly attractive. The others in the ensemble [Doughboys and Playboys] added their individual parts, but not to as great an extent as that of Wills and Duncan" ("Light Crust," 1).

At about the same time that he found Tommy Duncan, Wills expanded the Doughboys by hiring Kermit Whalin to play steel guitar and bass, and rehired Arnspiger to play guitar. Bob paid part of Herman's salary out of his own earnings when O'Daniel resisted bringing Arnspiger back into the fold (Townsend, *San Antonio Rose*, 73).

Wills had seen Arnspiger walking the streets every day, and had occasionally given his old friend some loose change. Ruth Sheldon, who said Wills pushed Arnspiger out of the group because of his uninspired musicianship, wrote that Herman assured Wills that if he took him back, Arnspiger would never do anything to disappoint Wills again. Eventually, O'Daniel agreed to pay Arnspiger $12.50 per week (107).

It seems that O'Daniel had come to appreciate what Wills meant to Burrus Mill and the Light Crust Doughboys. He gave Bob a raise to $38 a week and told him to build the best band in the country, saying, "If it takes 17 men to do it right, hire them" (Townsend, *San Antonio Rose*, 75). But Wills' tenure as Doughboy was coming to an end.

The rift between Bob Wills and Lee O'Daniel began when Wills began pressing O'Daniel for higher salaries for the other band members. As he had done with Arnspiger, Wills would supplement their salaries with his own money. Also, Wills flew off the handle at O'Daniel when Wills' younger brother Johnnie Lee, a future band leader in his own right, appeared about to lose his job as a truck driver with Burrus Mill. A mill supervisor had threatened to fire the younger Wills when an elderly woman who ran a grocery store (and likely a Light Crust dealer) complained to the supervisor that Johnnie Lee owed her $4. When O'Daniel at first seemed reluctant to step in on Johnnie Lee's behalf, Wills angrily demanded that O'Daniel fire them both. "We can do as well as the truck drivers you've already laid off," Wills raged. O'Daniel then relented. But when Wills wanted to bring his brother into the band, O'Daniel again refused and this time refused to back down (Sheldon, 111).

He and the band still managed to play a few dances on the sly, but Wills, like Milton Brown, resented O'Daniel's no-dances edict. "Bob wanted to play dances," Marvin Montgomery related. "Milton Brown was playing at Crystal Springs and had his band going real good and was making more on Saturday night than Bob was making all week long." Montgomery said Wills' drinking habit became worse while playing the dances, and he began to miss a lot of jobs (Oral history, 96–97). Numerous incidents of too-much-booze had tried O'Daniel's patience, and he had warned the fiddler after failing to show for a broadcast, "One more time, Bob, you fire yourself" (Townsend, *San Antonio Rose*, 76).

Kenneth Pitts, who joined the Doughboys after Bob Wills left the band, wrote:

> After a couple of years, the group had established itself as one of the most popular in this area, and it was about this time that Bob Wills became very unhappy at the restrictions Mr. O'Daniel placed upon the band, restrictions which kept the group from achieving any sort of independence. They were not allowed to seek engagements on their own to play for dances or other entertainments or on the radio other than for Burrus Mill & Elevator Company. Part of these restrictions are understandable, but O'Daniel restricted them to the point that they were almost the 'property' of Burrus Mill. ("Light Crust," 1)

The matter came to a head in August 1933. Prohibition had just been repealed, and Wills and the other band members went out to celebrate at the many Fort Worth taverns. When Bob again failed to show for the broadcast the next day, O'Daniel sacked him, and replaced Wills with Clifford Gross (Sheldon, 111).

But O'Daniel asked Wills to stay on until the Doughboys completed work on a special broadcast O'Daniel had planned launching something he called the "Save Your Own Life Club." When the broadcast was done, Wills walked out without a word. But he returned to the studio to get his belongings as O'Daniel was speaking with the band. As Sheldon related the story, they fell silent when Wills entered the room:

"'Well, don't let me interrupt you,' Wills said. 'I just came back to get my clothes.'

O'Daniel replied, 'I was telling the boys that we'll have to carry on just as though you were still with us.'

'Why, of course. Why shouldn't you? I'm not going to bother you. You're a million dollar corporation. You don't have to make any explanations to man who ain't got nothin',' Wills responded bitterly."

It says a lot for Wills that when he was fired from the Doughboys, he took half of the group with him. The story is strongly reminiscent of the Biblical story of Ruth. Hearing the exchange between Wills and O'Daniel, Tommy Duncan and Kermit Whalin immediately decided to give up the comparative security of the Doughboys to join Wills in his next musical venture, whatever it might be. "Where do we go from here?" Duncan asked Wills. "What do you mean?" Wills replied. "I mean that I'm goin' with you. The reason you was fired was that you made trouble sticking up for us tryin' to get more money. You hired me, O'Daniel didn't. And I'm not leavin' you until you do fire me. Anywhere you go I'm goin'," Duncan said emotionally. Wills wanted to be sure Duncan and Whalin knew what they were doing. "You've got a job here. You're gettin' money that gives you a chance to eat and maybe feed me a hamburger once in a while. Let's just leave things like that," he said. But Duncan and Whalin had made their choice. Herman Arnspiger and Sleepy Johnson remained with O'Daniel as Doughboys, explaining to Wills that they felt it would be irresponsible to leave their secure positions (Sheldon, 112–13).

Wills and O'Daniel clashed over ownership of the Doughboys' car, upon which Wills had made an $80 payment. O'Daniel made the situation worse by sending Johnnie Lee to get the car from Bob. Finally, O'Daniel agreed to pay Wills $100 to settle the matter (Sheldon, 115).

O'Daniel dramatically admonished Wills, "You're taking these boys from a job where they make money . . . [to go] with you where they probably won't make a dime. This will go down in history against you, Bob." To which Wills replied, "It may go down in history, but it won't go down against me! . . . I've got somethin' to be proud of and those boys will get a break because I'll kill myself workin' to see that they do!" (Townsend, *San Antonio Rose*, 77)

Marvin Montgomery said there was more to the rift between Wills and O'Daniel than Wills' drinking. "Of course, Bob's father and mother were living out on O'Daniel's ranch at the time. All of that kind of stuff just got crossways . . ." (Oral history, 96–97). Wills' father John had been hit hard by the Depression. He lost his farm and was having a hard time consistently putting food on the table. The elder Wills was playing his fiddle while one of his daughters played guitar on street corners for tips. Bob moved the family into the rooming house where he and his wife Edna were living. But O'Daniel owned a farm near Fort Worth and consented to allow John Wills and his family to live there and raise crops and livestock. O'Daniel and the elder Wills clashed from the start. Apparently, John Wills felt O'Daniel spoke condescendingly to him. Finally, the elder Wills grabbed a three-foot wooden bar from a yoke used to hitch mules to a wagon, and went after O'Daniel, who high tailed it to the safety of his car. John and Emmaline left the farm and Bob Wills was gone from the Doughboys not long after that (Townsend, *San Antonio Rose*, 75–76).

Wills now felt responsible not only for himself and his family but also for his loyal band members. He was desperate to find work. The Doughboys had a big following in Waco, so Wills met with WACO manager Everett Stover. Before the end of the month, Wills' new band was going head-to-head with O'Daniel and the Light Crust Doughboys, playing at 12:30 P.M. each day on WACO in Waco. At first, he and his band were not paid, but he was sure that they'd soon find a sponsor and that the air time would help them land some dance jobs. A fireman friend of Wills, Bill Little, loaned Wills $25 and started booking dances for the band. At first the new band was called "The Playboys," and then, "Bob Wills and his Playboys." The name "Bob Wills and the Texas Playboys" came later (Sheldon, 113).

However, W. Lee O'Daniel was not yet through with Bob Wills. Now free to play all the dances they wanted, Wills and the Playboys set about the job of promoting themselves. The band's new manager, O.W. Mayo, printed flyers promoting a dance where the band would play. According to court documents, the flyers contained information "substantially as follows: Bob Wills and his Playboys, formerly the Light Crust Doughboys, will play a big dance in Whitney [Texas] Friday night, September 29th. Tune in station WACO at 12:30 each day. Admission 40 cents." However, the court documents also stated that another flyer read:

> "Bob Wills and his Light Crust Doughboys . . . Skeezix . . .
> Cameron, Texas, Saturday, September 30 . . . Dancing, 9 'til
> 12 . . . These Special Entertainers Have Been on the Air the
> Past Three Years from Ft. Worth . . . LOTS OF GOOD SING-
> ING . . . The Old and the Young Will Enjoy Them – Come!
> Gentlemen 40 cents, Ladies, 10 cents." (Court documents)

If, indeed, a flyer read "Bob Wills and his Light Crust Doughboys,"
it would seem that O'Daniel had a reasonable case against Wills.
Whatever the facts, O'Daniel and Burrus Mill sued Wills, Duncan,
and Whalin for $10,000 in damages, claiming that Wills' use of the
Doughboys' name had caused harm to Burrus Mill.

In addition, O'Daniel sued to stop Wills from using the familiar
Doughboys' theme song, whose lyrics Bob had changed to "We're
the Playboys from WACO." But Milton Brown's brother Roy Lee
said O'Daniel did not know that the savvy Milton had filed a copyright of the Doughboys theme. Brown gave Wills permission to use
the song, and O'Daniel dropped that part of the lawsuit. Milton and
his Brownies by that time had their own theme song, based on
Brown's composition, "Sunbonnet Sue" (Ginell, *Milton Brown*, 249).

Bob could not understand why O'Daniel was suing when he knew
that the band didn't have anything like $10,000. Wills hired two
young lawyers, Vernon Goodall and Harold J. Stafford, just out of
college to defend him, while O'Daniel was represented by well-es-
tablished attorneys from Dallas and Fort Worth (Sheldon, 119). But
O'Daniel lost the case in state district court when the judge ruled
that it was true enough that Wills and his band *were* formerly the
Light Crust Doughboys, and no harm had been caused to O'Daniel
and Burrus Mill. O'Daniel lost an appeal in the state court of civil
appeals, and then petitioned for a rehearing, which was denied
(Townsend, *San Antonio Rose*, 81–82).

Responding to complaints from listeners that they missed Wills'
trademark "hollers" during the Doughboys' broadcasts (apparently,
Bob became more outwardly exuberant after Milton Brown left the
group), O'Daniel got one of the remaining Doughboys to holler on
the air now and again. After Wills and his band won the case in

district court, he joked to his attorney, "O'Daniel sued me for stealing a name. Now I'm going to sue him for stealing my holler" (Townsend, *San Antonio Rose*, 82).

Bob Wills' tenure with the Light Crust Doughboys was short, especially compared to the band's history of more than 70 years. But it was crucial to the careers of both Wills and the Doughboys, and it laid the foundation for Texas to become a music center. "Between 1929 and 1933 Bob Wills made Fort Worth the cradle of western swing and western jazz," biographer Townsend wrote (77).

The departure of Wills from the Doughboys turned out to be good for the careers of both Wills and the band. But Wills did not instantly shoot by the Doughboys in popularity. "Bob, at that time, wasn't as big in Texas as the Doughboys, not by a long ways, and we didn't play for dances. We had the church people, *plus* the people who went to dances," Montgomery said (Oral history, 96–97). Wills' biographer, Townsend, acknowledged that the Doughboys achieved success in their own right without Wills in the group, "going on to even greater success" with a radio program that remained popular for another 20 years (77).

The bad blood between Wills and O'Daniel did not end when O'Daniel lost the court fight. "He had a vendetta against Bob when Bob left," Montgomery recalled. While biographer Sheldon wrote that Wills left Waco and WACO at the end of 1933 because the Central Texas cotton-picking season was over and Wills knew money would be scarce (Sheldon, 119), Marvin Montgomery knew a different story. "Bob had his band down in Waco [playing on WACO], and Pappy went down and told the radio station, 'I'll buy an hour of your time [daily] if you'll kick Bob off the air.' He did that, and they agreed. They kicked him off, and he [Wills] went to Oklahoma City. They did the same thing up there, and Bob was really getting discouraged by that time. His manager at the time called KVOO in Tulsa, and told them what was happening. They said, 'Well, come on up here, and we won't let Pappy take your time'" (Oral history, 96).

After Bob Wills and Milton Brown left the original group, the Doughboys went through a transitional period. In the new group, some members came and went quickly. Others would become fixtures. Clifford Gross, a Kentucky fiddler with a violent reputation who had made a name for himself with a group called the High Fliers, replaced Wills and stayed in the group for years until his temper caught up with him. Kenneth Pitts joined as a fiddler in 1934—bringing twin fiddles to the Doughboys for the first time—and would become a mainstay of the group.

Singer Leon Huff and guitarist Sleepy Johnson played with the Doughboys in the period after Wills and Brown left. Huff left the Doughboys to join the Hillbilly Boys and later sang with the Texas Playboys. Later still, he sang in the band led by Wills' brother, Johnnie Lee, before dying of an apparent heart attack at the age of 39 ("Leon Huff"). Johnson left the Doughboys and joined the Playboys. Ramon [pronounced like "Raymond"] "Snub" DeArman joined the group and soon left for Columbus, Ohio, to make electrical transcriptions for a cereal company, only to rejoin the Doughboys, where he stayed until the end of his tragically short life (Campbell, 9).

Leon McAuliffe, the legendary steel guitarist best known for his years with Bob Wills, joined the Light Crust Doughboys in October 1933. "O'Daniel wanted a steel guitar player, and so he got Leon, and Leon went to the World's Fair with them up in Chicago," Marvin Montgomery said. "He wasn't with them very long. He made a recording session with them during that period. But after awhile, O'Daniel decided he didn't want a steel guitar player, and he fired him." Late in 1934, O'Daniel asked McAuliffe to come back.

"Leon, of course, didn't want to come back," Montgomery said. "But Leon's mother said, go on, you'll be on the radio every day and everybody will get to know you. See, Leon was only 16 or 17 years old at the time. So, he came back with the Doughboys in February 1935. Then, he got word from Bob Wills that Bob wanted him to come up and join his band in Tulsa, and ol' Leon just took off, he didn't give notice or anything. Away they went. He got back at O'Daniel for firing him the first time." Montgomery said McAuliffe appeared as a guest on the Doughboys' radio program several times after World War II (Interview, January 3, 2001).

McAuliffe is one of the most respected of all the musicians to have played with the Doughboys. Doughboy Kenneth Pitts admired

McAuliffe's tune, "Steel Guitar Rag," which McAuliffe adapted from a tune called "Guitar Rag" by blues guitarist Sylvester Weaver. McAuliffe used Weaver's basic melody, but added a new bridge to the tune (Ginell, *Milton Brown*, xxvii; Ginell letter). Writing in a brief memoir on his music career, Pitts showed himself to be a skillful music critic. "Leon wrote the famous 'Steel Guitar Rag,' which I always considered to be a well-organized composition. . . . In its own way, the piece has just the right contrast with good 'highs' and 'lows,' simple harmony (chords) and three interesting internal tunes all of which combine to give the piece a real thrust." McAuliffe recorded "Steel Guitar Rag" with the Texas Playboys after he left the Light Crust Doughboys ("Light Crust," 1–2).

By 1935, O'Daniel himself was on the way out. "Jack Burrus [the son of Jack Perry Burrus, who founded Burrus Mill with his father William C. Burrus; Steen, 400], had a percentage deal with W. Lee 'Pappy' O'Daniel, where Pappy received so much money for every sack of flour he sold," Montgomery said.

> Pappy had the Light Crust Doughboys going and making more money than Burrus was making. Mr. Burrus was looking to get rid of Pappy.
>
> O'Daniel was taking the Doughboys up to Oklahoma City and playing a theater and maybe getting $1,500, which in those days was a stack of money. Pappy was keeping the money himself; he wasn't splitting it with the boys, and he wasn't turning it into the mill. Ol' Cliff [Gross, the fiddle player who took Bob Wills' place in the group]—"Doctor" we called him—went to Mr. Burrus and told him about it. That gave Burrus the chance, the excuse, to get rid of Pappy. . . . Pappy was also using workers from the mill to go down to his farm in Aledo to build barns and do different kinds of work on Burrus Mill time. . . . Burrus, said, "Pappy, get your stuff and go." He did. That was the way Pappy lost his job. (Oral history, 38–40; Schroeder, 100)

Despite the alleged shady behavior that cost O'Daniel his job, Montgomery charitably called the pitchman who would become the governor of Texas and a U.S. Senator "a good man" (Oral history, 38–40).

O'Daniel is remembered for campaigning for governor of Texas with the help of the Light Crust Doughboys. Of course, it never happened, although it's a natural mistake. Rather, he started a new band called the Hillbilly Boys. "All the people think it was the Light Crust Doughboys that helped the campaign," Montgomery wryly remembered. "We hardly ever tell 'em otherwise though, because it's good publicity" (Remick).

The legend of W. Lee O'Daniel and the Light Crust Doughboys/Hillbilly Boys remains strong. In 2000, the critically acclaimed movie, *O Brother, Where Art Thou?* borrowed extensively from the story. In the script, "Pappy O'Daniel" is the governor of Mississippi and hosts a radio show, "The Pappy O'Daniel Flour Hour" (the name partially borrowed from a popular radio blues program, "The King Biscuit Flour Hour"). At the climax of the movie, O'Daniel's re-election campaign is saved when he appears on stage and on a radio broadcast with a "hillbilly" band, the "Soggy Bottom Boys." One critic asked if the script's use of "pastiche" contributed to society losing its sense of history (Cook).

After leaving Burrus Mill, the resourceful O'Daniel quickly rebounded and started marketing his own product, Hillbilly Flour. Emblazoned on the sacks of Hillbilly Flour and spoken by a woman at the beginning of each radio program was the famous slogan for which O'Daniel is still remembered: "Pass the biscuits, Pappy." O'Daniel attached the folksy slogan to a traditional "hillbilly" song that he adapted for his own purposes. O'Daniel and the Hillbilly Boys performed on a WBAP radio show, just as he and the Doughboys had done (Caro, 696).

Listening to recordings of O'Daniel underscores how much society has changed since the 1930s. What attracted the largely rural Texas radio audience of the Depression era would surely escape most modern-day listeners. Texas observes San Jacinto Day on April 21, the date when the Texas army under Sam Houston routed Mexican

General Santa Anna's army in 1836. With the exception of Texas A&M University former students, who hold "musters" on April 21, most Texans today ignore the anniversary. But that was not so in 1937, when O'Daniel, without a trace of irony, in dramatic, theatrical tones, dedicated his show to the heroes of San Jacinto:

> Good afternoon, friends of the radio audience, this is W. Lee O'Daniel. . . . This song, "Will You Come to the Bower," should bring every red-blooded American to his feet. It was sung 101 years ago today just before the Battle of San Jacinto. We come today to do honor to those great Texans who fought for, and died for, our sake. . . . "Remember the Alamo! Remember the Alamo!" And today, we hear those cries as Santy-Anna [sic] heard them ringing in his ears as he was captured by Sam Houston. (Radio recordings)

The connection between the Doughboys and the Hillbilly Boys is not only because of O'Daniel's involvement with both groups. Several musicians served as members of each band at one time or another. At the time of the April 1937 program, the Hillbilly Boys included singer and guitarist Leon Huff, "The Texas Song Bird," who had played with the Doughboys before O'Daniel left Burrus Mill, and Carroll Hubbard, who would join the Doughboys after World War II. Former Doughboy and steel guitarist Kermit "The Love Bird" Whalin served more than one tenure with the Hillbilly Boys. (Whalin also played with Bob Wills and the Texas Playboys.) Guitarist and bass man Jim Boyd, who joined the Doughboys in 1938, joined O'Daniel's band in 1940. Other members of the Hillbilly Boys at the time of the San Jacinto Day program were bass player Wallace Griffin, singer and guitarist Curley Perrin, and O'Daniel's sons Mike on fiddle and Pat on tenor banjo. At various other times, the Hillbilly Boys also included female singer Kitty "Texas Rose" Williamson and accordionist Bundy Bratcher (Coffey, January 6, 2002 and February 20, 2002; Douglas and Miller, 107–8).

O'Daniel had somewhat dismissively referred to the original Light Crust Doughboys as a "hillbilly" band, and then he put the hillbilly tag on his new band, which often was confused with the Doughboys. But Marvin Montgomery said the Doughboys didn't consider themselves a hillbilly band: "No, they [the Doughboys] didn't call it hillbilly music. O'Daniel kind of started that when he named his band the 'Hillbilly Boys.' Up until that time, it was 'fiddle bands'" (Oral history, 124). The term "hillbilly music" came to be a kind of generic term that applied to almost all popular music with any connection at all to the South or Southwest. Milton Brown and the Musical Brownies, for all their refinement, were commonly called a hillbilly band, and many years later, when Elvis Presley first burst into the nation's consciousness, before the term "rock and roll" was in general usage, he was often referred to as a hillbilly singer (Guralnick).

Despite his less than perfect musical acumen, O'Daniel's popularity became so great that he began to think about politics. He asked the listeners to write and tell him if he should run for governor. A blind man asked him to run for the office, he said. By O'Daniel's account, he received more than 54,000 messages urging him to run. Only three said he shouldn't—and they said the job wasn't good enough for him, O'Daniel said (Caro, 698). On April 12, 1938, O'Daniel announced on the Hillbilly Boys' radio program that he was running to be the governor of Texas. He would run as the ultimate anti-politician, with the Ten Commandments as his platform (Douglas and Miller, 112). He sold himself as governor in the same way he sold Light Crust and Hillbilly flour, by crossing the state in a tour bus with his band. Biographers Douglas and Miller described a crowd waiting to hear O'Daniel and the group in the south Texas town of Rosenberg:

> More than an hour before scheduled time the usually quiet street was jammed. Wagons from adjoining communities had come in early. All sorts of motor cars chugged in to jumble the ill-managed traffic situation. Sacks of Hillbilly Flour, moved from store shelves, occupied prominent places on the sidewalks in honor of the expected visit. A happy, hopeful crowd, buzzing with light conversation, waited. (120)

A 1938 *Fort Worth Star-Telegram* article described a typical O'Daniel rally:

> The rally opens with hillbilly songs, then the candidate tells the crowd that the singing is over, and if anyone came just for the show he can leave. But no one does . . . "Beautiful Texas" is the theme song. . . . O'Daniel calls himself the candidate of the common people, but finds no fault with big business, corporations, and utilities . . . and advocates bringing more of them into the state. . . . Molly [O'Daniel's daughter] passes the collection plate, a miniature flour barrel. . . . No local dignitary introduces him. (McKay, 35–36)

Lyndon Johnson biographer Robert Caro quoted from "Machine Made," an article by Owen P. White in the September 18, 1957, edition of *Collier's* magazine. White described the crowd for an O'Daniel rally in the South Texas town of Raymondville:

> It was amazing. They [O'Daniel's audience] were fascinated. It was a typical summer day in the hottest part of Texas and there they stood, dripping sweat and drinking in [his] words. . . . Next to me . . . stood a young mother with her baby in her arms and her eyes glued to the face of the speaker. The baby squalled; she opened her dress and put the child to her breast without even looking at it. Every member of that outdoor congregation was equally attentive. (Caro, 702)

O'Daniel's appeal was especially strong to women. Some brought gifts to the stage at the Hillbilly Boys' appearances—boxes of fried chicken or homemade cakes. Others gave him symbolic tokens to help him fight his political foes—lariats, rabbits' feet, or paddles, to "spank" the professional politicians he derided. "Pour it on 'em, pour it on 'em," the crowds would shout (Fowler and Crawford, 124).

O'Daniel and the band played before a crowd of 26,000 in Houston, then the largest crowd ever for a Texas political rally. More than

15,000 turned out in a pasture outside the small North Central Texas town of Cleburne. O'Daniel often opened a rally with the crowd-pleasing line: "Folks, heretofore, I've always worked for an honest living—look at me now!" The opening musical selection would be O'Daniel's song, "My Million Dollar Smile." Before long, the Hillbilly Boys would break into "Them Hillbillies Are Politicians Now." O'Daniel had written new lyrics to an existing song, the improbably named, "Them Hill-billies Are Mountain Williams Now," recorded by the Hoosier Hot Shots in 1935 (Douglas and Miller, 112; Ginell letter):

> Been hangin' round the mountains all these years,
> Singin' songs about the train-wrecked engineers,
> They've been pavin' all the cities,
> With their pretty corn-fed ditties,
> And they've got the politicians all in tears.
> They come to town with their guitars,
> And now they're smokin' big cigars —
> Them hillbillies are politicians now.

Besides promoting the Ten Commandments, O'Daniel proposed a $30 per month pension for all Texans over the age of 65—a promise upon which he was not able to deliver (McKay, 233)—and promised to throw the "professional politicians" out of Austin. "If I am elected Governor, *we* will be the Governor of Texas—we meaning the common citizens, of which I am one," he proclaimed. He effortlessly shook off criticism that he had not paid his poll tax, and, therefore, could not vote in the election. "I didn't pay my poll tax because I was fed up with crooked politics in Austin and hadn't intended to vote for anyone this year," O'Daniel told adoring crowds (Caro, 701, 699).

In those days, the Republican party was exceedingly weak in Texas, and so his occupancy of the governor's mansion was all but assured when O'Daniel whipped 11 other candidates without a run-off in the Democratic primary on July 23, 1938. The *Fort Worth Press* wrote: "The O'Daniel election is a good lesson to smug officialdom.

It is a lesson in keeping in tune with the common human heart" (Douglas and Miller, 149–51).

O'Daniel biographer Seth Shepard McKay gave full credit for O'Daniel's remarkable victory to his popularity on radio, and traced his political success back to the Doughboys. The returns showed that the counties in which O'Daniel won a plurality of votes were those that had been receiving the Doughboys' and the Hillbilly Boys' radio broadcasts. Further, the counties in which O'Daniel won the largest pluralities were those closest to Fort Worth, where the impact of the Doughboys' program on KFJZ and, later, WBAP had been the greatest (49).

But, also, it is evident that O'Daniel won over some voters who were hearing him for the first time. Many Texans lived far away from the large cities and, for them, radio reception was unreliable. Also, many poor Texans could not afford radio in the Depression. As McKay quotes the 1938 *Fort Worth Star-Telegram* story: "A number of those interviewed said they did not own a radio, had never heard of O'Daniel and his Hillbillies on the air, and had never heard of O'Daniel until a week or so ago" (35).

The governor-elect took his gift for showmanship to Austin. O'Daniel took the oath of office before 60,000 people in the University of Texas football stadium, with the Hillbilly Boys, the UT band and the Texas A&M College band providing the musical accompaniment (Fowler and Crawford, 127).

O'Daniel continued to have stormy relations with the members of his band. "He wouldn't even let the musicians come in his front door if they came out to the house," Roy Lee Brown said. "He'd make 'em go around to the back door or the side door. O'Daniel had no use for the working man, he proved that over and over" (Interview). By the time he ran for re-election as governor in 1940, Kitty Williamson had left the band. Then, Leon Huff and Kermit Whalin suddenly quit the group, to O'Daniel's considerable chagrin. He announced on the radio: "This week the gang of professional politicians struck another blow at your governor, and two of the boys in our band were caught in their snare and induced to quit us without giving the usual notice. Not one word of discontent had been voiced by either of these boys to us, although we were together every day, and they had each just recently been given increased remuneration without their demanding it."

But Leon Huff disputed that he had received a pay boost and gave a statement to the *Wichita Falls News-Record* saying that he quit because O'Daniel had broken a pledge. "I worked for Mr. O'Daniel for eight years and he promised me a raise. He never gave it to me and I began to feel that I might be the next one on the list to get the ax," Huff wrote. He said he had to provide for his wife and two children and hoped the people of Texas would understand (McKay, 311–12).

Neither did all of the Light Crust Doughboys celebrate O'Daniel's success, despite Marvin Montgomery's allusion to O'Daniel as "a good man." "We weren't feeling too good about that [O'Daniel's political rise]. . . . We knew who he was," said Zeke Campbell. "He had the people pretty well fooled. I never did say anything bad about the man, because I never did work for him or anything. But I heard some pretty bad things about him from people who did work for him" (90).

Longtime Doughboy Kenneth Pitts joined the Doughboys in 1934, before O'Daniel's sudden departure. Many years later, his resentment toward O'Daniel remained strong:

> Even at times that we had nothing at all to do, O'Daniel made us stay around all day, I feel for no other reason than the fact that he was the type to "squeeze the last drop of blood." During these lax times, we would go across the street and shoot pool (five cents a game); sometimes we would practice individually and it was during these "devil's workshops" that I picked up the habit of smoking cigarettes because I had not previously taken part in that foolish pastime.
>
> In those days our audience would send us little gifts like cakes, boxes of cookies and that sort of thing, but practically all these Mr. O'Daniel took himself and they ended up at his home for his family to enjoy. He himself made more than all the band combined but he still had his hand out grabbing

even for these little tidbits. . . . I was still enamored with not having to do physical labor, seven days a week and felt quite fortunate. ("Light Crust," 3)

O'Daniel no doubt saw himself as the generous benefactor of his musical employees. He appointed Kermit Whalin, who was trained as a barber, the state barber inspector. But when O'Daniel became a U.S. Senator, he allegedly demanded that the Hillbilly Boys quit their state jobs and go to Washington with him, without telling them what their salaries would be. If they balked, they were immediately fired. Jim Boyd was evicted from his house, which was owned by the state. Although O'Daniel held a reception on the lawn of the Governor's Mansion for 5,000 people on the occasion of his daughter Molly's wedding (Biffle), members of the Hillbilly Boys felt they had been treated callously. Boyd claimed that he and his wife received an invitation to the wedding, but when they arrived at the church door, they were turned away (Townsend, "W. Lee O'Daniel").

But as the years went by, Boyd's feelings apparently healed somewhat. "He said O'Daniel was a little hard to work for and to get along with," Boyd's hunting partner Jay Streetman of Denton said, "but he [O'Daniel] treated him [Boyd] good. O'Daniel had places for Jim to hunt. Jim said O'Daniel was a tough guy, and a pretty self-centered man. But in his own way, he [O'Daniel] kind of took care of the people who worked for him" (Interview).

Even historian Charles R. Townsend, no apologist for O'Daniel, acknowledges that O'Daniel made a significant contribution to Texas music: "Aside from his politics and his personal qualities, O'Daniel was important in the music of Texas when it was in its formative years. Without his remarkable ability to promote and publicize, the innovative music of the Light Crust Doughboys might never have gained such vast popularity, and men like Bob Wills might have been known only in North and Central Texas. As governor, O'Daniel made the world aware that there was a distinctive Texas sound" (Townsend, "W. Lee O'Daniel").

Despite scrapes with his musicians and members of the state legislature, O'Daniel's popularity remained high. O'Daniel continued to broadcast a regular Sunday program on WBAP and the Texas Quality Network, and broadcast via transcription over a powerful Mexican border station, XEAW, in which he became part owner. O'Daniel's proposal for a 1.6 percent tax on all business transactions to pay for an old-age pension plan ran into stiff resistance from all quarters. But voters felt they knew O'Daniel from his radio program and liked him. "He's a good man," one voter said. "It ain't his fault he didn't do nothing." After his re-election as governor in 1940, O'Daniel invited all his supporters to a Texas-sized inauguration barbecue on the grounds of the Governor's Mansion in Austin. On his radio show, O'Daniel claimed to have personally slain a 900-pound buffalo in the Hill Country west of the capital, "brought in by the skilled hands and steady nerve of your governor," to supply meat for the wingding. Some 20,000 Texans accepted the governor's invitation, and they consumed 6,000 pounds of beef, 4,000 loaves of bread, and 1,000 pounds of potato chips, along with the buffalo (Fowler and Crawford, 129–30, 136–37).

Texas voters later elected O'Daniel to the U.S. Senate after Sen. Morris Sheppard died in April 1941. O'Daniel announced a special election would take place on June 28, but he did not immediately announce plans to run. Obviously not wanting to appoint someone who could strongly establish himself in the Senate and win election to a full term in 1942, O'Daniel named 87-year-old General Andrew Jackson Houston, the last surviving son of General Sam Houston, the hero of the Texas Revolution, to the post. Andrew Jackson Houston obligingly died two months after the appointment was announced. Urged to run for the Senate in a resolution passed by the state legislature (cynics say the move was made to ease O'Daniel out of Austin), the governor announced his plans to run for the Senate in a special election. In that election, O'Daniel defeated the young Lyndon Johnson, among others. Johnson, no political shrinking violet himself, tried to compete with O'Daniel's flair for flash with a six-piece Western swing band called the Patriots and a 285-pound female singer, Sophie Parker, "the Kate Smith of the South" (Fowler and Crawford, 141). But O'Daniel's established statewide popularity was too strong.

O'Daniel won election to a full six-year term in the senate in 1942, in a bitter campaign against former governors Dan Moody and James V. Allred. A runoff against Allred was necessary and O'Daniel won with 51 percent of the vote. But O'Daniel could not shake the rancor of the 1942 campaign. He feuded with the other Texas senator, Tom Connally, and rankled Democrats by voting with Republicans most of the time. As the election year of 1948 arrived, O'Daniel found his popularity fading, and polls showed him far behind former governor Coke Stevenson. He decided not to run again (McKay; Fowler and Crawford). The popularity of the Light Crust Doughboys would endure much longer.

"If you take Marvin, I'll break up the band!"

♩ ♪ ♫

The departure of three such towering figures as Bob Wills, Milton Brown, and W. Lee O'Daniel by all rights should have been the end of the Light Crust Doughboys. But at that time the Doughboys, besides being a band, were a corporate entity; simply put, they existed to promote Light Crust Flour and Burrus Mill. The name of "the Light Crust Doughboys" meant much more in the minds of Texas music lovers than the individual names of the band members. Bob Wills, Milton Brown and, especially, Lee O'Daniel, gained greater personal fame after leaving the Doughboys. The original band might have splintered, but the Light Crust Doughboys, whatever their makeup, still sold flour, and so Burrus

Mill kept the band going, long after the company sent O'Daniel packing.

In fact, it may be argued, the Doughboys enjoyed their greatest popularity without Wills, Brown, and O'Daniel. Many band members would come and go in the years and decades to come. They would create their own Doughboys legacy, in much the same way that new generations of athletes have added to the heritage of the New York Yankees or the Dallas Cowboys.

It was radio's "golden age." The Light Crust Doughboys would ride the crest of the wave that carried radio to the apex of its cultural importance in the heady years after World War II. But then that wave came crashing down, taking the Doughboys and many other radio stars with it. Almost overnight, television replaced radio in the nation's living rooms.

To understand the steadily growing popularity of the Doughboys, even after the departure of seemingly indispensable members of the group, remember that many parts of rural Texas in the early 1930s were, in effect, still mired in the 19th century. And so, while the Doughboys in the Milton Brown and Bob Wills years were certainly popular, in many parts of Texas they probably reached relatively few homes by radio:

> Because there was no electricity, the only radios in the Hill Country were the occasional crystal sets with earphones and poor reception. *Amos 'n' Andy, Lum 'n' Abner, Ma Perkins* [popular radio shows of the time]—theirs were voices familiar to most of America; it was a rare inhabitant of the Edwards Plateau who had heard them even once. (Caro, 512)

Even in big cities like Fort Worth, many people did not have radio. "When Milton left the Doughboys, [for] the first radio program with his [new] band, we had to go over to the neighbors to listen to it, because we didn't have a radio," Roy Lee Brown recalled. "Back then, times were so hard, maybe there'd be one or two radios in the whole block. If it was out in the country, they had these little old crystal sets. I've had many a person tell me they heard the Brownies on a crystal set. Couldn't but one person at a time listen to them [because they required headphones]" (Brown interview, December 21, 2001).

But, by the late 1930s, the urbanization of Texas was well underway, and radio could be found in almost every Texas home. In 1910, only 24 percent of Texans lived in cities of 2,500 or more. But by 1937, 18 percent of Texans lived in the state's five largest cities, Houston, Dallas, San Antonio, Fort Worth, and El Paso, and 30 percent lived in the state's 36 cities of 10,000 or more (McKay, 10). By the late 1930s, more Texans lived within the reach of broadcasting stations than early in the decade, and they were able to hear the Doughboys for the first time. More Texans also had access to radio receivers. For example, about 12 million American homes had radios in September 1930, just before the Doughboys took the air for the first time. But by September 1935, despite the economic ravages of the Great Depression, 22 million American homes, about two out of three households, were graced by radio. The average cost of a radio set had dropped from about $120 in 1929 to about $40 in 1935 (Bensman). It is not surprising, then, that the Light Crust Doughboys gained their greatest fame after the departure of Bob Wills, Milton Brown, and Lee O'Daniel.

Also, it is important to understand that the very nature of radio in the 1930s was different from what we know today. The standard radio-programming format then was more similar to today's television format of separate, distinct programs, one following the other, than the continuous flow of hit records that became familiar on radio beginning in the 1950s. Indeed, television directly derived its format from radio, and then commercial radio—still broadcasting almost exclusively on the AM band—was forced to change its approach to the "Top 40"-derived formats we are familiar with today. Radio listeners of the 1930s were accustomed to tuning in at a particular time to hear programs featuring their favorite singers and performers. Twelve-thirty every weekday afternoon became the time to tune in to the Doughboys. "I remember listening to them on the radio all the time," Jim Boyd's friend Jay Streetman, who grew up near Houston, said. "Particularly in the summertime, when we weren't in school, that was an everyday affair with us. We just didn't miss 'em. Even though I was young, that was just my kind of music" (Interview).

Radio as a medium grasped the fascination of its audience as television later would do. "I remember the first radio that my daddy bought," Jimmy Thomason of Waco, an early Doughboys fan, said. "You talk about having to hock the family jewels to get it, we did. I don't know what it cost, but I will never forget that thing. It didn't matter what we heard either. We just had to sit on one end and hear somebody else on the other" (Ginell, *Milton Brown*, 53). In many, many Texas homes, the most popular "somebody else" on the other end was the little fiddle band called the Light Crust Doughboys.

Nineteen-thirty-five was a pivotal year for the Light Crust Doughboys. It saw the end of the W. Lee O'Daniel era and the arrival of a new platoon of musicians, who would lead the Doughboys to new heights of popularity and success.

Marvin "Junior" Montgomery, banjo and guitar; Muryel "Zeke" Campbell, guitar; and Kenneth "Abner" Pitts, fiddle and accordion (who actually had joined the Doughboys in 1934 before O'Daniel's exit) stayed with the group during the entire period from 1935 to 1942. Guitarist and bass player Ramon "Snub" DeArman left the group for a time in 1935 and returned in 1937, replacing bass man Bert "Buddy" Dodson (Montgomery, "Doughboy recording sessions," 4). In 1937, J.W. "Knocky" Parker, joined the Doughboys to play piano and accordion. In 1941, Ted Druer briefly replaced Parker, followed by Frank Reneau (Montgomery, "Doughboy recording sessions," 17). In 1938, fiddler Clifford "Doctor" Gross and guitarist Dick "Bashful" Reinhart were replaced by Buck Buchanan and Jim Boyd, respectively (Jolesch; "Light Crust Doughboys: Picture Chart"). In 1939, Cecil Brower replaced Buchanan on fiddle, and in 1940 Joe Ferguson replaced Jim Boyd (who later would rejoin the group in the post-war period) on guitar and bass (Montgomery, "Doughboy recording sessions," 17). In 1941, J.B Brinkley joined the group as a guitarist and vocalist after the death of DeArman (Montgomery, "Doughboy recording sessions," 17). But it was the trio of Pitts, Campbell, and Montgomery who provided the anchor for the post-O'Daniel Doughboys.

Kenneth Pitts was born December 15, 1913, in San Simon, Arizona, and moved to Fort Worth in 1919 with his family. "We were living over on Terrell Street and I used to buy those little tin whistles down at Woolworth and play up a storm on those things," Pitts recalled. Later, Kenneth acquired an old cornet and taught himself to play some tunes on it. His mother and father took notice and decided to give him music lessons. Young Kenneth started taking violin lessons from a man who lived just around the corner, Wylbert Brown, no relation to Milton Brown. "In a year's time I was playing very complex tunes," Pitts recalled. "I used to play with the Lions Club and all those things" (Ginell, *Milton Brown*, 56–57).

Soon after he graduated from high school in 1931, Pitts formed a group called the Southern Melody Boys with another future Doughboy, Cecil Brower, who also took lessons from Wylbert Brown. Bob Wren on tenor banjo and Burk Reeder on guitar completed the group. When Reeder died of cancer, he was replaced by Hubert Barham on bass and Ramon DeArman on guitar. Because Pitts and Brower were trained musicians, the Southern Melody Boys played differently from most groups of the time. Pitts said he learned to play "fiddle" as opposed to "violin" while playing with Brower, but he and Cecil nevertheless played a sophisticated brand of music. "We didn't play hoedowns with the Southern Melody Boys, we played all popular music," Pitts recalled. "And played it in good violin style. We were quite well known in this part of the country for our duet work, Cecil and I. . . . I don't like to criticize the guys that grew up playing country music but frequently they don't play in tune. But Cecil and I played exactly right on pitch. All the time."

Pitts remembered that in the summer of 1931, after he graduated from high school, the Southern Melody Boys played at a root beer stand on Nashville Street in Fort Worth for about 50 cents a night. They also played at Ace's Root Beer on North Main where Bob Wills discovered Tommy Duncan. The Southern Melody Boys were good enough to attract the attention of someone from WBAP, which invited them to play on the air. The station didn't offer to pay them, but they played anyway, just for the experience and the exposure (Ginell, *Milton Brown*, 58–59).

The Southern Melody Boys became the first "string band" to feature improvised solos, inspired by jazz performers. Pitts reflected that the band didn't really know enough not to try to merge the styles of country and jazz. "In a way we should have left it alone because it wasn't the music for us," he said. "'Business in F' [a jazz standard] wasn't right for a fiddle band. 'Tiger Rag' was all right for us to play. Of course 'Sweet Jennie Lee' or 'Sweet Georgia Brown' lent themselves well to Cecil taking a chorus or me doing one."

Pitts remembered playing at "house dances" where the hosts would take up a collection for the band, usually not more than two or three dollars. But, Pitts said, that was good money in the Depression. He recalled the Southern Melody Boys making $4.50 each at a club in Dallas, where Dorothy Lamour, soon to hit it big in the Bing Crosby-Bob Hope "Road" movies, was singing.

But most of their gigs were less glamorous. Pitts remembered playing at a club where not a single customer would walk in the door for hours. "Then somebody would see somebody coming down the road and we'd say 'Strike up a tune! There's a car coming!' [laughs] Boy, times were hard then. My mother and I got down to the time when we didn't have any money or food in the house at all" (Ginell, *Milton Brown*, 59–60).

The Southern Melody Boys eventually played a regular program on KTAT in Fort Worth. A fan, Red Varner, from Waco recalled traveling to Fort Worth to see the group perform a live broadcast, and being impressed by their hospitality. Through a window, he and a friend stared wide-eyed into the studio, when Cecil Brower noticed them. "He made sure that we were comfortable, made sure we could see everything and everybody around the microphone," Varner said (Ginell, *Milton Brown*, 60).

Varner was as much impressed by the Southern Melody Boys' musical sophistication as he was by their congeniality. It was obvious that they were extremely well-prepared for their broadcast, Varner said. Pitts was known as the arranger of the Southern Melody Boys, Varner said. "He and Cecil worked on what was written until it flowed like the spoken lines of a fine actor who has the knack of sounding like he is ad-libbing just as he would in ordinary, everyday conversation," Varner recalled (Ginell, *Milton Brown*, 60–61).

Kenneth Pitts is given much of the credit for developing the twin-fiddle style that is so identified with Bob Wills. Pitts himself gave part of the credit for developing the twin-fiddle style to Brower. "In those days, fiddle bands had begun to use two fiddlers in order that they might play in harmony," Pitts wrote in a short unpublished memoir. "This was set in motion a great deal by a fiddle band Cecil Brower, my long time friend, and I had belonged to [the Melody Boys], doing some radio work (practically all free), for a couple of years after I graduated [from high school]. We had the knack of playing duet harmony quite well and we both produced a very good tone even young as we were and had become quite well known for our harmonizing, particularly our theme song 'La Golondrina,' arranged in waltz rhythm" ("Light Crust," 2).

The twin-fiddle style eventually became an important part of the increasingly sophisticated Light Crust Doughboy sound when Pitts joined the group. Despite the obvious talents of Bob Wills and Milton Brown, the Doughboys' penchant for musical innovation actually accelerated after Wills and Brown left the band. Doughboy Zeke Campbell said Kenneth Pitts deserved much of the credit. "They [the Doughboys] were one of the first bands that had two fiddles in it, one playing harmony to the other. It was just about the only band around here that had two fiddles," Campbell said. "They were doing that when I came over here—Ken Pitts and Cliff Gross. Gross played lead, and Ken played the harmony. It was distinctive in that way" (Oral history, 82). Later, as fiddlers came and went, Pitts played lead with Buck Buchanan playing harmony, and when Cecil Brower replaced Buchanan, Brower played the lead and Pitts returned to playing harmony (Montgomery, "Doughboy recording sessions," 1, 9, 11).

As innovative as the Southern Melody Boys were, financial pressures eventually forced the group to disband. Brower joined Milton Brown's Musical Brownies in early 1933. It represented a major step up for Brower, because while the Southern Melody Boys were barely scraping by, Milton Brown's band had quickly become one of the Southwest's most popular musical acts after Milton left the Doughboys. Pitts said he never made more than $10 in a week while playing with Brower. In fact, the Southern Melody Boys sometimes played for fun as much as anything. "I remember when [Franklin] Roosevelt got nominated by the Democrats for president, we had a big party with lots of beer drinking and carrying on," Pitts remembered. "Then we had a wild party and picnic on Labor Day in '32 at Oakland Park." Pitts had supplemented his small income by playing on a classical music program four times a week on KTAT. But when Brower joined Milton Brown, Pitts was discouraged. He actually gave up on being a professional musician for a time, and took a job as a church janitor (Ginell, *Milton Brown*, 87–88).

But in 1934, Pitts' big break finally came. For a time, he had played with then-Doughboy Sleepy Johnson in a "for fun" dance band. "When Sleepy heard Mr. O'Daniel (he called him 'the old man') talking about getting an additional fiddle, Sleepy persuaded O'Daniel to have me down for an audition and I got the job. My starting salary was $15 a week" ("Light Crust," 2).

♩ ♪ ♪

William Muryel "Zeke" Campbell joined the Doughboys only days before Marvin Montgomery. Born in Marietta, Oklahoma, April 29, 1914, the son of the town blacksmith, Campbell's early childhood was not especially musical. "I never had a musical instrument in my hand as long as I lived up there [Oklahoma]," he recalled, "except for an autoharp that my grandmother bought for a cousin of mine. I used to fool with that a little bit, but I never had an opportunity to play a musical instrument until I moved to Texas" (2).

Will and Dolly Campbell briefly moved their family to Texas in 1923, returned to Marietta, and then moved to Cockrell Hill, a suburb of Dallas, in 1929. There, he was surrounded by musical relatives. "My mother's folks were all musical," he reminisced. "My aunt was talented; an uncle of mine played the mandolin; my mother's sister played some kind of instrument. My dad bought my brother a guitar and me an old fiddle from Sears Roebuck. That's how I got started" (4).

In Cockrell Hill, Muryel met a neighbor, Jake Wright, who was an excellent guitar player. "He was about the best around there," Campbell recalled. "I got acquainted with him. Instead of playing the fiddle, I branched off on the guitar and got to playing. I didn't even have a guitar of my own. An uncle of mine loaned me his and I learned to play on that" (4).

After graduating from Sunset High School in 1931, at the beginning of the Depression, young Muryel did what he could to earn a little money for himself and his family, picking cotton, baling hay, harvesting grain (3–4). But he continued to practice on his guitar. Eventually, Muryel was playing in front of audiences, on the air and in person. He played for a time with Raymond Hall and the Rhythm Rascals on KGKB in Tyler. They also played at dances throughout East Texas, sometimes playing for a percentage of the gate, sometimes not covering their expenses. But his big break came while informally playing with his friend Jake. "He [Jake] had a friend who lived up at Lake Dallas [now Lewisville Lake] and took care of [Burrus Mill president] Jack Burrus' property on the north side of Lake Dallas," Campbell recalled. "This fellow's name was [Bill] Blagg. Jake and I used to go up to his place there on the weekends and take out guitars and play. He'd have all the neighbors come in from around the country and listen to us play. He told Jack Burrus about us" (5).

"I was sitting there at home one Sunday with my folks. I was living with them, my dad and mother and brothers. Bill Blagg drove down to the house with a letter from Jack Burrus, addressed to Eddie Dunn [who had replaced W. Lee O'Daniel as the announcer of the Doughboys]. It said, 'Eddie, there are a couple of guys who are kind of handy with a guitar.' I remember the wording of it. It said, 'Give them a tryout'" (8).

Muryel and Jake drove to the old Burrus Mill building at Jennings Street and Lancaster in Fort Worth in Muryel's $50 1927 Oldsmobile the next day. Both boys played for awhile with the Doughboys. The next day, October 15, 1935, Muryel was asked to join the group. For whatever reason, Jake Wright was not invited. Many years later, in retirement, Campbell and his brother Chilton played again with Jake Wright, just for fun, until Wright died in 1995 (Campbell, 9, 53).

"I started out making $22.50 a week, which in 1935 was pretty good money," Campbell remembered. "Nobody had a job back in those days. I finally got up to making $30 a week before it was over with" (25).

Marvin Montgomery was an Iowa farm boy who "never learned to milk a cow." Born in Rinard, Iowa, a town of 160 people, on March 7, 1913, as Marvin Dooley Wetter, his musical career began when he won a ukulele as an award for delivering newspapers. "I got me a little chord book. I've still got that book. . . . It said, 'Learn the Ukulele in Five Easy Lessons.' My mother, every time she would go to Fort Dodge, Kansas, would bring back some sheet music. I'd learn to play the chords along with her [as she played on piano]. Then she got this banjo for my brother and I picked it up" (Oral history, 9).

Marvin's father Charles Henry Wetter "gambled" on the grain market. "One day we would be rich, and the next day he wouldn't have anything," he remembered. His parents divorced when Marvin was 13. "I've been on my own since then," he said.

"I always wanted to be in show business or to be a musician, in my heart," Montgomery recalled. "I called my cousins, and I got kazoos. I organized little orchestras with those kids playing the kazoos. None of them could carry a tune. . . . Out in the old barn, where my grandfather kept his car, I built a little stage in there and had a little show. Charlie Chaplin was the big guy then, and I would be Charlie Chaplin and do these little shows" (Oral history, 10).

Music was very important in the Wetter family, and especially to Marvin, who showed his commanding presence as a musical leader at an early age. "When I was about five or six years old, and my brother was four, one Christmas we worked on a song to play at church. My mother played the piano. I forget what the song was. My brother was supposed to sing one line. They stood us up on this piano bench to sing for the Methodist church. We rehearsed that song and during rehearsal, my brother just goofed off and wouldn't sing his line right. Sure enough, that night when we were doing the Christmas program at the church, he missed his line, and I slapped him. Boy, I felt bad about that. . . . In the back of my mind, I've always had a guilty conscience about that incident. I was the serious one about music" (Oral history, 2).

In high school, during the early days of the Depression, Marvin played in a dance band with his mother Mabel, and for a time traveled from town to town with a piano-tuner cousin, passing the hat or playing for a dozen eggs. In 1933, a traveling tent show from Texas came to Ames, Iowa. Marvin won second place in an amateur contest playing the banjo. He played "The World is Waiting for the Sunrise." "This little gal won the five dollars [first place]. She was about five years old and did a tap dance. I won the three dollars. That was enough to eat for two weeks" (Oral history, 2).

The manager of the tent show from Jacksonville, Texas, J. Doug Morgan, was impressed by Marvin's banjo virtuosity. "About two weeks later, after I entered that contest, J. Doug sent me a telegram and said, 'Can you join the show down in Grinnell, Iowa?' My grandfather carried me down, and we saw the tent. He dumped me out with my suitcase and my banjo, and I've been on the road ever since" (Oral history, 20).

Soon after, Marvin Wetter became Marvin Montgomery. An official with the show, Neal Helvey, said "Wetter" would not look good on a marquee. "At that time, Robert Montgomery, the movie star, was real famous. I said, 'I like ol' Robert Montgomery.' . . . So I became 'Marvin Montgomery: The Boy with Two Voices and the Fastest-Playing Banjo Player in the World.'" Two voices? "Oh, I used to do a thing where I would sing, 'Carolina Moon Keep Shining,' in a normal voice, and then I would sing it higher" (Oral history, 30–31). Later, in the Doughboys, Marvin would take the "little-girl parts" in skits that the band performed (Oral history, 32).

Playing with the Texas tent show, Montgomery became homesick for Iowa and his money took him as far as Dallas. "I had $30 saved up. . . . I bought a ticket, and it got me to Dallas on the train. I got into Dallas about four o' clock in the morning." He walked to the Adolphus Hotel knowing that Blackie Simmons and His Blue Jackets performed an early-morning show on KRLD, which was located in the hotel. "He was rehearsing for his program. I said, 'I'm a banjo player and a guitar player,' and I picked up a guitar and did a few things. I stayed for the program, and he said, 'Are you looking for a job?' I said, 'I sure am.' I was broke. I had spent all my money for my train ticket." Simmons told Montgomery that the manager of KRLD needed a guitar player for a party that night. "That night, the piano player picked me up, and we went out to the Dallas Country Club, of all places. It was a stag party, and I'd never seen a stag party. This gal took off things she didn't even have on. We played the music, and I was cross-eyed looking at the girl" (Oral history, 33). Suddenly, Marvin was not homesick for Iowa anymore.

The piano player at the party told Montgomery that a fiddle band called the Wanderers who played on *The Early Birds* program on WFAA needed a banjo player, and Marvin went to audition. "I played a few licks on the banjo, and they said, 'Well, play with us on the program this morning.'" Later, the Wanderers invited Marvin to play a show with them. "They said, 'Come on, we'll try you out. We're going down to Kilgore tonight and play at the Casa Linda Ballroom.' . . . I made $12. . . . I became an important part of the group. I took care of the money and everything else. I made out [planned] the programs for the radio show and that stuff real quick [after joining]" (Oral history, 35).

As an aspiring high-school musician, Knocky Parker was a big fan of both Milton Brown and the Wanderers. "They were both very good. I think I liked the Wanderers better," Parker recalled, "[because of] Marvin, I guess. I was wild about Marvin's work" (Interview).

Marvin Montgomery officially joined the Light Crust Doughboys on October 22, 1935, after Burrus Mill fired W. Lee O'Daniel, and was with the group for the rest of his life. "Mr. Burrus hired Eddie Dunn [the WFAA 'Early Birds' program announcer] to take Pappy's place," Montgomery said. The Wanderers, including Montgomery, played on the Early Birds show. Dunn essentially brought the Wanderers with him to Burrus Mill.

"The Doughboys then had nine musicians," Montgomery recalled. "Eddie wanted to upgrade the band, and he wanted Bert Dodson and Dick Reinhart [members of the Wanderers] to come over and join. They were both singers, and Dick played the guitar, and Bert played the bass. Mr. Dodson [Bert's father and the Wanderers' manager] said, 'If you take Marvin, I'll break up the band. I'm tired of riding around in that old station wagon [playing dances] every night anyway.' Eddie said, 'Okay, I'll take three of them,' so Eddie fired six of the guys in the Doughboys and kept three. With us three, we had a six-piece band" (Oral history, 40–41).

Just prior to what amounted to a merger between the Wanderers and the Doughboys, the Light Crust Doughboys' membership, as cited by Zeke Campbell, included Campbell on guitar and vocals, fiddlers Kenneth Pitts and Clifford Gross (all of whom survived the change), guitarist Bruce "Roscoe" Pierce (who later would join the Doughboys again in their post-war "Flying X Ranchboys" television incarnation), bass player Hubert Barham, banjo player Doc Eastwood, accordionist Matt Welch and singer Leonard Grider (10). If there was a ninth man, as Montgomery held, Campbell didn't name him. In his comprehensive listing of the recording sessions of the Doughboys, Marvin Montgomery wrote, "I have been unable to find a picture of this group. [Bruce] Pierce states that they were Doughboys for such a short time, no picture was made" ("Doughboy recording sessions," 22).

New Doughboys master of ceremonies Eddie Dunn had grown up in Waco, where he started in radio while still in high school. He had gone to work for WFAA in 1928 while attending Southern Methodist University in Dallas. Besides serving as the master of ceremonies of the "Early Birds" program, Dunn had broadcast Texas League baseball games, Southwest Conference football games, and wrote and acted in a children's program ("Dunn—biography").

A Doughboys' custom that began with O'Daniel continued after he left to pursue his political career. When O'Daniel fired Bob Wills, he hit upon the idea of giving the members of the Doughboys generic nicknames, so that as the inevitable personnel changes continued, they would be less apparent to the public. "Part of the formula for the Doughboys' enormous popularity was personalizing the band," Janis Stout, the daughter of longtime Doughboy Kenneth Pitts, wrote. "Each player had an established personality, and they all had nicknames – Dad was 'Abner,' Marvin Montgomery, 'Junior,' Muryel Campbell, 'Zeke.' People followed them like friends of the family" ("Light Crust Doughboys were on," 5).

Montgomery said one reason for the nicknames was O'Daniel's ego. "'Pappy' [O'Daniel] never wanted anyone to get more popular than him. I replaced a guy called Junior so when I took his place they called me Junior. Same thing with the guy named Bashful. Dick Reinhart inherited the nickname of 'Bashful.' There were five or six different 'Bashfuls' in the group," Montgomery recalled (Remick; Oral history, 58).

Kenneth Pitts agreed that the nicknames were a way for O'Daniel to keep the individual members of the group in line. "He'd take whatever stand would promote O'Daniel," Pitts said. "He didn't want you to amount to anything." Pitts' nickname of "Abner," like the others, was an O'Daniel creation, Pitts said. "He just reached up and grabbed the name, and stuck it on the back of my neck" (Interview, May 27, 1986).

Of course, the Doughboys continued to promote the Burrus Mill and Light Crust Flour. "If they had a rodeo or fair, where there was going to be a lot of people, that would be our main object," Montgomery remembered. "In the meantime, we might stop in a town or two and play on the square for 20 or 30 minutes, too" (Oral history, 97–98).

"In the 1930s, after O'Daniel left, we were just as popular in Texas as the Beatles became in the 1960s," Montgomery said. "We would announce on the radio that we were going to be in Hillsboro at 10:00

tomorrow morning at the square to play a 15- or 20-minute program. Boy, there would be 10,000 people there, everybody in town plus a lot more people would show up. All we had to do was announce it on the air" (Oral history, 95).

The radio broadcasts allowed the Doughboys to build their vast following. The main attraction of the broadcasts was, of course, the Doughboys' music. But the purpose of the program was to sell Light Crust Flour. Housewives then bought flour in large containers, and used a lot of it. No short cuts—cake mixes, muffin mixes and so on—were yet widely available (Gray, 211). The Doughboys' program was produced by an advertising agency, J. Walter Thompson, as were the majority of radio programs in the pre-television, pre-Top 40 era. After Dunn joined the program, the emphasis on O'Daniel-style fatherly advice and "old-folks-at-home"-type tunes noticeably declined. But the program definitely retained a folksy quality. Eddie Dunn's first program as the Doughboys' announcer on May 22, 1935, featured this easy-going pitch for Light Crust, following a performance of the fiddle standard, "Sally Goodin":

> We received a letter the other day from the Sorrels twins of Fort Worth. I imagine only one of them wrote the letter, but we're glad to see they both signed it, giving double force to the letter—and here's what it said: "We have been using Light Crust Flour for years and have heard you folks tell of the difference of using it and a cheap flour but we just didn't realize the big difference until our money got a little short and we tried buying a sack of cheap flour. The first time mother made biscuits with it, we got up from the table with our faces so long they could almost be used for hoe handles. But now she is using good old Light Crust Flour again and our faces are not long anymore, but always smiling and believe us, there'll be no more cheap flour for the Sorrels family." Well, that letter speaks for itself—and we've always heard that two heads are better than one—so that message from the Sorrels twins is something we can all think about. ("Eddie Dunn's first")

Listening to recordings of the Dunn-era Doughboys program, it is apparent that Eddie Dunn—speaking in a friendly, well-modulated baritone — introduced a lighter, mainstream show-business style to the show. After the traditional greeting, "And the Light Crust Doughboys are on the air!" followed by the Doughboys rollicking theme, Dunn would make a quick plug for the sponsor: "By the way, let me spell 'Burrus' for you . . . The Burrus Mill and Elevator Company. It's spelled 'B-U-R-R-U-S'—Burrus Mill and Elevator Company, the maker of Light Crust." Then a snappy introduction to the first tune: "Bashful sings the first number today. It's the good ol' favorite, 'Dinah.'" The Doughboys themselves did not speak, unless it was off-mike in good-natured reaction to one of Dunn's announcements. Between numbers, Dunn would provide a transition. "That was the opening number on the program today, Bashful, it was, singing for us, 'Dinah.' And next, another old favorite, dating back probably to those same days when 'Dinah' was all the rage. This one's called the 'Limehouse Blues.' It's an instrumental number featuring each one of the six Light Crust Doughboys, with fiddles, guitars, banjos, bass fiddles and most everything they can find. Go ahead, boys, with the old 'Limehouse Blues.'"

Dunn brought some of Bob Hope's joshing, knowing style to his role as master of ceremonies, seemingly winking at the audience as he delivered a pitch for Light Crust:

> Once in a great while, a person using Light Crust gets the blues. That may sound amazing to you, [voice rising] it may be a revelation, boys, to think that I would go on record here on the air as saying that sort of thing [off-mike, mock exclamations of disbelief]. But, it's true, friends, that once in a while a person using Light Crust Flour will get the blues. And you now why? Because she runs out of Light Crust before she's made as many of those good ol' biscuits that everybody wants [off-mike, noisy, confounded reactions]. Ha, ha! I knew I'd get you on that. (Radio recording)

On occasion, the Doughboys would take on fictional identities for a comic number. For example, "Grandpappy" and "Dan and Nan," the hired man and hired girl from the farm, performed "The Preacher and the Bear." It was one of Marvin Montgomery's novelty tunes, about a minister being pursued by a hungry beast ("Oh, Lord, if you can't help me, for heaven's sake don't help that bear").

Dunn (to "Dan:") Will you say hello to all the folks in the radio audience?

"Dan" (in a dull monotone): Hello to all of the folks in the radio audience.

Dunn: That's the boy. That's "Dan," friends, you can understand that he certainly is going places someday. We don't know where, but he's going places, and it won't be long.

Like O'Daniel, Dunn would sometimes reach for the heartstrings with a recitation. On August 16, 1935, after the fatal air crash of beloved humorist Will Rogers and aviator Wiley Post, a poem that Dunn wrote and read in tribute drew 56,000 requests for copies. Burrus Mill hired 12 women to handle the mail:

> Today the world is sad and blue,
> Mourning the loss of those great two.
> Beggars and kings have raised a toast
> To our Will Rogers and Wiley Post! . . .
> American hearts have all been smashed!
> "Will Rogers and Wiley Post have crashed"!
> In every land they had a friend
> But they died alone at earth's far end.
> Wiley has taken his last long flight;
> He'll be at his Maker's airport tonight.
> Will Rogers' alarm clock has rung its last—
> His time is up; his program past!
> No more, Will, shall we hear of your capers;
> Now all WE'LL know is what WE read in the papers. (Dunn, "In memory of ...")

Another O'Daniel tradition, the theme program, continued after he was gone. On January 27, 1937, Eddie Dunn and the Doughboys celebrated the arrival of a baby born to Dick "Bashful" Reinhart and his wife Juanita. In the cozy style of Depression-era radio, Dunn introduced the Doughboys' version of "My Blue Heaven:"

> Now folks, if there are any of you listening whose home happens to be blessed with 5 or 6 or 7 or 8 or more chillun, you might be wondering just why we're making all this fuss over one little teensy, ninecy baby . . . here's why . . . that sort of thing just don't happen very often with the Light Crust Doughboys—as a matter of fact, this is the first time in the six years they're been on the air, that a baby has been born to any of the Light Crust Doughboys—and so that's why we are doubly proud of Bashful today—good old Papa Bashful—but you know, I guess since the song first came out years ago, Bashful has sung this number a hundred times or more . . . but I wonder if he ever gave much thought to HIM being able to sing it and really mean it . . . I'm thinking of "My Blue Heaven"—let's have it right now. ("Bashful's Baby")

Other songs in the program included "That Little Boy of Mine" and "Sleep Baby Sleep."

Despite the decidedly traditional nature of the songs in the program described above, the Doughboys' new personnel brought an increasingly complex sound to the group. Dick Reinhart introduced a guitar style heavily influenced by black music to the Doughboys. Montgomery said Reinhart was one of the earliest white musicians to seriously study the styles of black players and learn their songs. "If he had made a record by himself on guitar, you'd probably think he was a black guy. He'd do 'Matchbox Blues,' and 'Gulf Coast Blues,'" Montgomery said (Govenar and Brakefield, 144).

In trips to the downtown Dallas district of bars and music clubs frequented by Reinhart, Marvin Montgomery was introduced to African-American blues. Reinhart would invite Marvin to go with him to the black music clubs on Elm Street, in the area called Deep

Ellum. Often, they'd be the only white people in the place. "These guys knew Dick, and when he'd come in they'd wave him over and he'd take his guitar," Montgomery said. In the black clubs, Marvin saw the guitar played with a bottleneck slide for the first time. "They'd lay the guitar down flat in their lap and take that slide up and down [the neck]," Montgomery said. "They'd have an old-six-string guitar all beat up and scratched up. I never did see a real good instrument" (Govenar and Brakefield, 143–44).

But, like many talented people, Reinhart could be difficult. "He was one of those musicians—you don't find many of them anymore, and if you do, I ignore them—who think there is only one way to play a song. There is only one set of chords that will work on a song, like, 'The Birth of the Blues.' . . . His way was the only way, if it was ever to be played. He was always telling us what chords to play. That's a minor thing now, but it used to be a big argument" (Oral history, 107).

Montgomery believed the Doughboys played a major role in bringing the style of black musicians to a wider audience in Texas and the Southwest. "Once we did a song on the Doughboys program, everybody did it. . . . Every other band started playing it. Like 'South,' every other band picked up on that real quick. 'Trouble in Mind' and several of those songs that Dick learned from those guys, we started doing them, and first thing you knew, everybody else was recording them and doing them, too" (Oral history, 111).

Even when the Doughboys went on the road, they sought out the company of black players, as when they went to Little Rock each year to play in the Arkansas State Fair. "We'd get through at the fair about nine o' clock at night, and Knocky [Parker], Zeke and myself would go down to this black club and jam with them," Marvin said. "I'd take my banjo there. They knew we were in town, these black people, and we would go down there and jam until one or two o' clock in the morning" (Oral history, 116).

Zeke Campbell said the integration of Montgomery, Reinhart and Dodson into the group changed the Doughboys' sound in a major way. "I think—and I've always said this—that bringing Dick Reinhart, Marvin Montgomery and Bert Dodson over here kind of influenced the turn-around in the type of music the Doughboys played. We got to playing jazz, stuff like 'Limehouse Blues.' They [the Wanderers] were a dance band, and we [the Doughboys] weren't. They kind of played a rhythmic style and a lot of jazz stuff. I think it was kind of a novelty in those days. There weren't a lot of bands like us. At that time, there were quite a few groups on radio, but I think the Doughboys were different. You could listen to them [the Doughboys] and tell they were pretty well-rehearsed or organized" (79).

When the Doughboys jammed together, they usually ventured into jazz, Montgomery said. He said the Wanderers also enjoyed experimenting with jazz, and so did Milton Brown and the Brownies, Bob Wills and the Texas Playboys, and most of the other fiddle bands of the day. "Swing jazz was new and made us all want to try it," Montgomery said (Govenar and Brakefield, 149).

"We'd listen to Dixieland, Mexican, and jazz records, then copy them. We'd dig for those records anywhere we could find them. We'd let the electric guitar play the trumpet part and have the banjo do the drum. Then we'd put twin fiddles playing the lead. We didn't call it Texas Swing back then, but we knew the sound was more jazz than Nashville. We just called that kind of playing 'getting hot around the lead,'" Montgomery reflected (Gilchriest, 90).

One of Marvin Montgomery's closest friends and musical accomplices over the years, Ed Bernet, considered the Doughboys trailblazers. "The Doughboys were leaders, right on the cutting edge of Western swing with Bob Wills," Bernet said. "They used fiddles to play music written for horns. They borrowed both music and musicians from other styles and adapted them to swing." Bernet is a Dallas musician and the former owner of a club called "The Levee" where Montgomery became a featured performer in the 1960s. He and Marvin also owned the Sumet recording studio in Dallas (Smith, 18).

Campbell reflected: "It [the Doughboys' music] had a distinctive rhythm to it. You can listen to some of those records we made, and they've all got that same beat." He partly attributed the Doughboys' sound of that era to the use of "slap-style bass," where the player of an acoustic bass "slaps" the strings. "We didn't have drums like Bob

Wills did. Marvin's banjo contributed a lot to the rhythmic style we had" (81).

But rhythm is a relative thing; at least it was in Marvin Montgomery's view. Montgomery described the Wanderers as "a hot fiddle band," and coming from a band that was more rhythmic, he did not see the Doughboys as having an especially strong beat. In his view, the Doughboys played less "dance music" and more "listening music." The Doughboys, he said, played a lot of hymns, cowboy songs, and slow waltzes, such as "Home on the Range" and "Red River Valley," in addition to the jazzier numbers, taking away some of the edge from their music (Govenar and Brakefield, 144–45).

Still, a latter-day booking agent for the Light Crust Doughboys, Will Schotte, agreed with Campbell that the group's bass style had a lot to do with its distinctive sound. "Just from listening to people talk, they still talk about that 'slap-style bass.' Usually, the bass is not what you would call a featured instrument in any ensemble, so there is something different that they did that really carries through" (81).

The Doughboys sometimes employed a distinctive guitar sound. "We had a little three-guitar deal—Marvin, Dick [Reinhart] and I. Marvin played tenor guitar," Campbell said. "He'd play lead, and Dick and I would play harmony. There wasn't anybody else doing anything like that. . . . We didn't use any amplifiers. It was just acoustic guitars. We would just get up in front of the microphone" (83–84).

Later, electric guitars would become part of the Doughboy sound. In fact, the Fender electric, so identified with rock, received a tremendous boost from Western swing, which, of course, was pioneered in part by the Doughboys.

"Zeke didn't get an electric guitar until after we got back from California [after making a movie] in the fall of 1936," Marvin recalled. "That's the first time we had electric guitar on our programs. When Leon McAuliffe started on steel guitar it was still just a little thing you laid in your lap, with no amplifier on it. Things changed" (Interview, Jan. 3, 2001). Western swing historian Kevin Coffey, who has written articles on the music for *The Journal of Country Music* and the *Fort Worth Star-Telegram*, among others, commented that, in fact, Zeke Campbell became a trailblazer. "Zeke Campbell was one of the most important and exciting of early electric guitarists, quite influential," he wrote (Personal communication, July 29, 2001).

By unanimous consent, Marvin Montgomery's developing virtuosity on the banjo contributed heavily to the Doughboys' sound. "People who listen to a lot of banjo hear his distinctive style and say, 'That's Marvin [Montgomery].' Nobody else plays it that way . . . real fast single-string, plus chord solos. . . and he didn't learn it from anybody," Ed Bernet said (Smith, 18). Alan B. Govenar and Jay F. Brakefield, in their book, *Deep Ellum and Central Track*, wrote that Montgomery's playing style changed somewhat when he joined the Doughboys. With the Wanderers, he had played mainly rhythm, but with the Doughboys he started playing more solo banjo. His technique changed, too. Influenced by vaudeville musicians who switched from violin to banjo, the resourceful Marvin said he tuned his banjo like a viola and fingered it the same as a violin, but he pitched the banjo a fifth lower. "This came out so vaudeville musicians could switch from violin to banjo," Montgomery said. "When Dixieland jazz got popular in the 1920s and earlier, a lot of fiddle players began to lose their jobs and they started playing the banjo" (Govenar and Brakefield, 145).

Even though the Doughboys' music increasingly reflected the influence of jazz and blues, the group made a powerful impression on a later generation of country performers. Some of the country music stars of the 1960s gladly credited the Light Crust Doughboys as an influence. Jimmy Dean, a West Texas native who became a major star with "Big Bad John," invited Marvin Montgomery and the Levee Singers from The Levee club to perform the Light Crust Doughboys theme on his ABC television show in the early 1960s. "Jimmy said that back in those days when he was growing up he would have given the shirt off his back to be a Light Crust Doughboy" (Oral history, 173).

Latter-day Doughboy Art Greenhaw observed: "You'll see CDs now, like Roger Miller has a three-CD set out. It mentions how Roger grew up listening to the Light Crust Doughboys. Roger Miller was in Ray Price's band for awhile, and Ray Price counts the Light Crust Doughboys as really influential on him" (Montgomery, Oral history, 174).

Historian Kevin Coffey sees the Doughboys' influence as profound. Coffey believes Milton Brown's Musical Brownies may have been the first true Western swing band, but he said by the mid-1930s the Doughboys were among the best:

> With additions by 1937 like Marvin Montgomery (tenor banjo), Kenneth Pitts (fiddle), Zeke Campbell (electric guitar), and Knocky Parker (piano), they were innovative and, more importantly, set a musical standard both in solo work and in ensemble work and arrangements that were ahead of their time. They were, from the time Montgomery, Dick Reinhart and Bert Dodson joined the band in 1935, simply an impeccable musical group, in technical and creative terms. And their sophisticated arrangements looked forward to the postwar slickness of West coast performers like Spade Cooley and others, while the Doughboys' mid-1930s contemporaries were still sounding a few years out of date. (Personal communication, July 29, 2001)

Prominent in the lore of the Light Crust Doughboys is the image of grassroots musicians traveling the back roads of a still mostly agrarian Texas, performing on small-town squares for appreciative crowds of hard-working fans, who turned out in droves to hear the boys whose lunchtime performances they enjoyed on the radio every day. That image belongs in part to W. Lee O'Daniel's Hillbilly Boys, but the Hillbilly Boys never would have existed if not for the Light Crust Doughboys. And the Doughboys certainly traveled many more miles down the two-lane blacktops of Texas than the relatively short-lived Hillbilly Boys, several of whom were members of the Doughboys at one time or another. At the center of the Doughboys' traveling-band persona is the bus that served the group so well for so long.

Under W. Lee O'Daniel, the Doughboys had traveled in a customized car. But just before Marvin Montgomery joined the Doughboys, O'Daniel had acquired a new tour bus that was to stay with them for two decades. The bus cost more than $50,000 in 1935

(Campbell, 90). The Doughboys would perform on a sizable back porch built into the bus, similar to the train-caboose platforms used by politicians on whistle-stop campaigns. Marvin Montgomery and Knocky Parker recalled sitting on the platform and jamming together on banjo and accordian while the bus was speeding down the road (Schreyer).

Kenneth Pitts' daughter Janis Stout recalled that on a few occasions the Doughboys and the Hillbilly Boys showed up in the same town at the same time. "O'Daniel must have felt pretty low when he saw his wonderful bus sitting there inaccessible," she wrote. "One of those times, though, just one, when his own sound equipment failed, he got to use the bus." Stout had happy childhood memories of the bus. She recalled a custom chess board with holes carved in it so that the pieces could be held secure while the bus traveled down the highway. "What could have happened, I wonder, to that chess set and board?" she asked. "It seems like a thing we would have kept" ("Light Crust Doughboys were on," 8).

The Doughboys used it for the first time on their trip to California to make *Oh Susanna* with Gene Autry. "We took turns driving it," Zeke Campbell recalled. "I never did drive it, but Dick Reinhart and Bert Dodson took turns driving. We drove the bus out there, and we got stymied out in Arizona. There was a port of entry [truck inspection and weight station] out there. Some little policeman figured we had stolen the bus or something, and he stopped us and wouldn't let us through. Luckily, Eddie Dunn was coming behind us. He drove his own car. He bought himself a brand-new Packard at that time, and he drove it out there. He told the guy everything was okay. They finally let us go" (26–27).

Joe Ferguson, who joined the group in 1940, recalled another encounter with a big Hollywood star that involved the Doughboys' bus. The cast of the movie *The Westerner* flew in to Fort Worth for the premier of the film. The Doughboys and the cast of the movie made several stops around Fort Worth that day. "They had us [the Doughboys and their bus] out at Meacham Field. When they brought the actors off the airplane, like Gary Cooper, they came up onto the bus and said a little stuff over the PA system we had on the bus. In fact, I furnished Gary Cooper smokes all the time he was here, from the airport to the coliseum. He would get behind the bass fiddle, wherever we got, and he would bum cigarettes. I was smoking Bull Durham myself, and he liked to roll them. So, I just handed it back to him, which was one of the highlights of my career, you might say (laughter). Gary Cooper followed you around and bummed cigarettes all day" (Oral history, 29).

"It was a white bus, custom-made [by the White Motor Co. in Oklahoma]. . . . It was quite a bus. It carried 12 people, with captain's seats. Then it had the built-in 110-watt generator. We had a built-in public address set with big speakers built right in the back of the bus, and we put it [the bus] by the big stage. That was the reason Jerry Stewart, our engineer, went with us, because he ran the sound" (43–44).

Campbell remembered, "It had all the equipment on it. It had broadcast equipment, a public-address system, and everything— right on the bus. It had its own power. They could start that motor up, and we had our own power. We didn't even have to hook into local power if we didn't want to" (24).

"Lots of times, they would just tie into the telephone line [for the Doughboys' daily 12:30 P.M. broadcast]," Montgomery recalled. "If we were playing out in West Texas at Odessa or someplace, he would hook it into a telephone line, and we would do our broadcast direct from the back of that bus" (Oral history, 43–45). The cost of a telephone line for a live broadcast from the bus was enough that the Doughboys didn't do it very often. Montgomery said a chamber of commerce or some other sponsor would sometimes pay for the cost of the line in order to enjoy the publicity of a live broadcast originating from its town or business (Interview, May 28, 2001).

Campbell recalled: "They would book us out at some dealer, in some town that was just starting to handle Light Crust Flour. They'd send us there, and we'd put our show on there. . . . We got to traveling a lot. It seemed like the further along it got, the more we traveled. I got to where I was kind of tired of it, after I got a family. It was a lot of fun when I was single. After I was married and had two children, it got to where it wasn't much fun" (69–70).

Campbell remembered the convenience of being able to perform from the back of the bus. "It was big enough for all of us to stand on," he said. "It was kind of crowded, but we could all stand back there and play. We'd pull into town and pull up to the town square and just unload. We played to as high as 15,000 people up in Arkansas. . . . We played Hot Springs, Jonesboro, Pine Bluff, and Little Rock. A lot of times, we'd go up to Little Rock and stay for quite a while. We'd put a program on up there and stay. That was always enjoyable to go up there. The people always treated us real hospitably. I always enjoyed going to Arkansas" (24, 78).

The Doughboys frequently would play for their fans on downtown squares. "Sometimes they had a radio station there [on the square], and we would put a radio program on," Campbell recalled. " We would play where the most people could gather. It was always well-advertised. We'd play downtown in these small towns."

Ferguson said the performances sometimes took the form of street dances, even though the Doughboys were not known as a dance band. "If they wanted to dance, they could sure dance," Ferguson said. "It wasn't a paid dance. I'll put it that way. They were all free. You can take a pasture full of people, and somebody will do something [dance]" (40).

In the days before touring rock bands set an impressive standard for debauchery, the traveling Doughboys were relatively tame. But they did have their hell raisers. Zeke Campbell made references to liquor stores and bordellos in remembering the Doughboys touring days. "I didn't partake of it, myself. I was a married man, and I didn't believe in that kind of stuff," Campbell hastened to add. He and Marvin Montgomery became roommates on the road. "That's the reason we kind of got to rooming together, because some of these other guys were a bit wild. The first thing they'd do was to take off looking for a woman when they got into town. That was against my beliefs. . . . We [Campbell and Montgomery] didn't drink, you know, and most of the other guys drank. They went their way, and we'd go ours when we got out on the road" (77, 64).

"I did a little hugging and kissing, but I was afraid of a social disease," Marvin wryly recalled. "Of course, we had all kinds of chances with these little 16-year-old girls." Montgomery remembered one Doughboy who would proposition young women in the bluntest possible way. "He'd be successful about one out of four times, I'd say," Marvin said (Oral history, 119). Joe Ferguson, who inherited the nickname "Bashful" when he joined the group, recalled, "Those ol' girls would be on the back of that bus, and they would say, 'You don't look bashful to me!'"(66).

Campbell said the Doughboys traveled in style. "One thing about it, we stayed in the best hotels. They [Burrus Mill] furnished all of our clothes and paid for our cleaning and everything. They furnished all of our meals while we were out on the road. They [the Doughboys] went first class. . . . We usually stayed in the best hotels and ate in the best restaurants. We just generally lived a pretty good life for those days. There were a lot of people wanting our job, I know that. A lot of these musicians would have given anything to have a job with us. It didn't pay a whole lot of money back in those days, compared to salaries today, but back then it was pretty good, back in the 1930s. We hadn't recovered from the Depression yet" (25, 70).

As Ferguson remembered it, times on the tour bus were pretty mild. "We would try to play a little poker on the way in the bus," he said. "I played from here to Corpus Christi, and never won a pot [laughter]. Low stakes, penny ante. Nobody was getting rich, I'll tell you that for sure" (38–39).

New members of the Doughboys were subject to a wet initiation. "When we had a new guy, and he needed to take a leak, we'd tell him to go off the back of the bus, and it'd fly back in his face," Montgomery chortled. "We got quite a few guys with that" (Interview, May 28, 2001).

Sometimes the Doughboys would run into trouble even when they were on their best behavior. "I remember one time we played in San Antonio," Campbell recalled. "We went out on a Mexican-American picnic out at a park someplace and put on a program. We were all sunburned so bad we could hardly play. We had been fishing down at Corpus Christi and had pulled our clothes off. We got blistered, and it liked to have [nearly] killed us all" (90).

A similar misfortune befell another Doughboy. "I remember that we went to Galveston, and J.B. Brinkley was a player on the guitar then," Ferguson said. "He rolled his pants up and got on top of the cabin of this boat we were on. He got sunburned, and he couldn't put his shoes on. We played a dance that night back up in Texas somewhere, and it was a street dance. He didn't have his shoes on, and he was miserable, all sunburned" (39).

The Doughboys touring bus stayed with the group into the 1950s, Marvin Montgomery said. In 1951 or 1952, the Doughboys performed in a tour of Big State movie theaters. "They had a whole group of theaters that covered East Texas, down around Beaumont, on over to Sugar Land and South Texas," Montgomery said. "We played every one of those theaters, some of them three days and nights. We'd come home on Saturday night, and Monday, we'd make transcriptions for the Dixie Network, and then we'd go out again" (Interview, Jan. 3, 2001).

"We'd drive that bus up in front of each theater where we were going to be playing," Marvin said. "They would park it there for advertising, while we were playing. We played in Beaumont, Orange, and all over East Texas [on a theater tour], clear around to Sugar Land. . . . We'd drive that bus out to the school and play for the kids. We'd just pull up in front of the school, and they'd let the kids out, and we'd play off the back of the bus. That was the last time we drove it" (Oral history, 146).

Burrus Mill finally gave the bus to the American Legion chapter in Fort Worth, Montgomery said. The Legion used the bus in parades until the Fort Worth Stock Show changed its rules and no longer permitted motorized vehicles in its big annual parade. A member of the Doughboys at that time, J.B. Brinkley, bought the bus for $300 from the American Legion, and sold the electronic equipment in the bus to recording studio owner Clifford Herring for the same amount, Marvin Montgomery said.

Montgomery remembered the bus with great fondness. "The last time I drove it, it had over 200,000 miles on it, which I made every one. . . . The last time I saw it, it was sitting up on a hill over in Fort Worth, up above Herring's studio," Marvin recalled wistfully. "It was just falling apart. I wish that I had got a hold of it. Later on, this guy who has the [transportation] museum in Fort Worth, called me and wanted to know if I could find it. He wanted to put it in that museum. . . . I called everybody I knew . . . I sure wish I could have found it for him, because if he had it down there, it would be there yet" (Oral history, 146–48).

One of the major perks of being a member of the Light Crust Doughboys was free clothing. "They [Burrus Mill] furnished all the clothes that we wore, all the uniforms, including the shoes some-times," Montgomery recalled (Oral history, 113). The pre-war Doughboys rarely dressed in cowboy fashion, latter-day Doughboy Art Greenhaw said. "Of course, they wore some [Western] hats for the movies, but back then, the string bands would wear suits, dap-per-type stuff. . . . The Brownies and the Doughboys would wear ties and suits" (Montgomery oral history, 128). Marvin added: "The shirts had the name 'Light Crust Doughboys' embroidered on the back. There was a little emblem. . . . The emblem had the 'Light Crust Doughboys' and then our [individual-group-member] name underneath. We had different trousers. We had little bellhop jackets on in some of those pictures. They were cut off like bellhop jackets. They had sweaters and stuff we didn't use on the [radio] program, but we wore them when we traveled" (Oral history, 128).

At one time, the Doughboys wore caps that resembled policemen's caps. On at least one occasion, it kept them from getting good ser-vice. It was during the days of Bonnie and Clyde. "Cliff Gross and I pulled up at a gas station in West Dallas," Montgomery recalled. "We were wearing our Doughboys' caps. Raymond Hamilton's daddy was working at the station [Hamilton was a member of Bonnie and Clyde's gang.] He wouldn't wait on us because he thought we were policemen" (Interview, May 28, 2001).

It is remarkable how important the Doughboys considered the clothing provided to them by Burrus Mill, considering that they couldn't very well have worn the clothing for many occasions other than their performances. At least they didn't have to buy work clothes. It was, of course, the middle of the Depression. Kenneth Pitts said: "One big fringe benefit (they were not so-called in those days) was that the company furnished us high-grade navy-blue slacks, tailor-made white shirts with the lettering 'Light Crust Doughboys' across the back with a music lyre on the front of the shirt, nice ties, a big sweater-style jacket with lettering and a very dressy blue sweater with lettering—all of this real quality clothing. Not only that, the company furnished all the cleaning, pressing and laundering of these uniforms. Oh, yes, there was a military-style cap that topped out the uniform. This all seemed quite luxurious" ("Light Crust," 2)

The Light Crust Doughboys were full-time employees of Burrus Mill. Zeke Campbell said the Doughboys had a routine like any other group of working people. "Marvin, Cecil Brower and I would usually ride together. We'd meet over at Marvin's house. He lived there in Riverside [a Fort Worth neighborhood], and we'd go in one of our cars. We'd take one car, and we'd drive out there. . . . We'd get there about 9:00 in the morning [at Burrus Mill in Saginaw]," he recalled. "We'd rehearse on what we were going to do. We had it pretty well down, what we were going to do. . . . We were kind of a family. We just stayed together and played together and traveled together. We were just like a family. We were real close. We visited each other's homes, and we knew each other's problems. We were really close" (71, 68, 85).

Joe Ferguson had similar memories of the daily routine. "We showed up early enough to rehearse and make a [transcribed] program for the week following, and then we'd do our regular [live] program. We were busy from nine or ten o' clock right on up until noon, when we'd come on. After that, we might have some stuff that we wanted to work on, but not too often did we have to do anything after the program was over. It was pretty well cut and dried. Heck, everybody had done it before and knew what we were going to do. If the personnel changed, then it took a little longer. It was real nice" (64–65).

Ferguson remembered that the transcribed programs were closely coordinated with the live broadcasts. "We would make the programs a week in advance. . . . Our coverage [daily broadcast] here at WBAP was live, and we had made that program the week before and sent it to these other stations. They played it at the same time we were playing live up here" (37).

Campbell remembered: "We had our own studios. Of course, we would make a transcription of the show that was going to be sent to all these other stations [on the Texas Quality Network]. It [the transcription] would be [broadcast] on the same day our program would be on [WBAP] here. We'd send it ahead of time. By the time we'd get around to doing the program here [live, at Burrus Mill], we had already done it and sent it out. When we went on the air here, we'd already rehearsed it and put it on transcriptions and sent it to these other stations. . . .That was our typical day. After we got through with our program, we were off for the day" (68–69). However, Kenneth Pitts remembered that, at least for a time, the Doughboys played a second daily radio program. "We prepared a program which we also played on station KTAT at around 6:30 P.M. in the evening," he wrote ("Light Crust," 3).

Marvin Montgomery said when he joined the Doughboys the group performed its daily show from the Blackstone Hotel in downtown Fort Worth, the site of the WBAP studios. Later, Burrus Mill set up a studio for the Doughboys in what had been O'Daniel's office. "They set up a little booth for the equipment, with glass around it," he recalled. "In 1936, we moved out to the new [Burrus] mill, out at Saginaw. We had our own studio up on the second floor of the office building. We could seat about 200 people, and we would have about 200 people out there every day" (Oral history, 41–42, 61).

Pitts recalled that the Doughboys' recording facilities were first-rate. "We were rather at the vanguard of the recording process at that time in that we were the first in this area to have the facilities for recording an entire 15-minute program on an acetate disc which was of good enough quality to be sent to a radio station, WWL in New

Orleans, where it was played nightly. A similar arrangement was possible when the technology advanced to the point where these programs could be copied—a similar arrangement was concluded with station KARK, Little Rock; [apparently, KWKH], Shreveport; and KVOO, Tulsa. If circumstances made it impossible on some occasion to use a copy of the program in a particular location, we would make a special 'cut' for that station. . . . So you can see O'Daniel and Burrus Mill were getting a great deal from us in terms of musical service" ("Light Crust," 3).

Marvin Montgomery said the transcriptions of the 1930s were crude compared to modern recordings. "They would run for 15 minutes," he said. "It was a disc about this big [indicates a circumference about equal to a large pizza], and, of course, the radio stations all had turntables [to play the large discs]. They were made of acetate and aluminum-based [material]. You could only play them four or five times, they were real soft" (Interview, March 21, 2001). While Marvin remembered the transcriptions playing at 15 revolutions per minute, historians say most were recorded at 33 1/3 rpm (Martini).

Zeke Campbell said recording the transcriptions meant that the Doughboys sometimes got to hear themselves on the air. "Of course, if we were out of town, we would play our transcription here [in Fort Worth] on the radio," Campbell said. "A lot of times, we listened to it wherever we happened to be. We'd listen to ourselves on the radio. . . . No matter where we were in Texas, we could always pick it up [on WBAP]. It was a strong station" (70, 75).

Knocky Parker felt that, among Texas "hillbilly" musicians in the Depression, the Doughboys held an elevated status. "We were sponsored by a flour company, and didn't have to hustle," Knocky reflected. "We didn't play dances, except occasionally when we wanted to, not as the Doughboys, but as side jobs. Little groups of us would go out when we wanted to. We didn't have to do anything for a living but play that one, 15-minute program a day, That's all we played. We were on the staff [of Burrus Mill]. We were on the payroll there. We were regarded as a little bit, perhaps, above a person that had to get in there and hustle a few bucks, you know" (Oral history, 7, reel two).

Off for the day by 1 P.M., Campbell had plenty of leisure time, quite a change from the early days when Lee O'Daniel required the boys to put in a full day at the mill. "Well, I would go home, and I would go fishing a lot. I had an aunt that lived over there on the north side. She liked to fish, and my wife and I would go pick her up. We would go out to the lake, and we would fish. We spent a lot of time going up to her [Campbell's wife's] folks in Oklahoma. We'd go on weekends. I always enjoyed going up there on the farm" (71).

Kenneth Pitts, who started with the group during the O'Daniel era, remembered his Doughboys days with a mixture of ecstasy and bitterness. "Of course, life to me seemed like a 'basket picnic' because the job I had come from was hard, the most menial labor (janitor of a church) and lasted seven days each week (for $13 per). I had little time for playing and development in music, no lessons, of course. So being daily and full-time occupied with music, even though it was only country-style music, seemed like the garden of Eden. . . . Of course, we were being exploited in a big way. But in those days, one did not raise his voice or complain, since it was quite the privilege to even have a job at all, much less one on which you were doing what you enjoyed and did not have to work like a horse" ("Light Crust," 2–3).

Marvin Montgomery did not harbor as much resentment in later years as Pitts did, but his memories were similar. "As far as finance, it was all the same. We all made the same amount all the time," Montgomery said. "We never did get a raise [from Burrus Mill]. Oh, we got one raise toward the end. We made $25 a week, and later, maybe it became $30. . . . I think maybe Kenneth Pitts was making $30 because he was doing the programming most of the time" (Oral history, 113).

The Texas music scene of the 1930s, as today, was a close-knit community. The bands were very interested in what the other bands were doing. "We listened to these different bands from around that we knew," Zeke Campbell said. "We'd listen to Adolph Hofner if we happened to be down around San Antonio. We listened to [Milton Brown and] the 'Brownies.' They were still on [the radio] for a while before Milton Brown got killed" (28).

The Doughboys story has from time to time been tinged with tragedy. On a Sunday evening, April 12, 1936, a 16-year-old girl, Katherine "Katy" Prehoditch slipped away from her home, without the knowledge of her parents, and went to the Crystal Springs dance hall with two friends, one of whom was Idell Rotosky. Idell was a friend, and later the wife, of Fred Calhoun, a member of the Musical Brownies. Later, Katy, Idell and Fred went to the Oasis club, where they met up with Milton. Fred asked Milton if he would take Katy home, and Milton agreed. They drove on State Highway 199, the Jacksboro Highway. Sometime after midnight, April 13, there was an accident (Ginell, *Milton Brown*, 195–196, 265). Weldon Massey, a night manager at the Rockwood Motel on the Jacksboro Highway, was sitting in his car outside the motel listening to the radio, and happened to be looking in the direction of Brown's car as it approached a curve. Massey said the headlights of the car started "quivering.... Then it rose a little and seemed like it flipped over to the right. In my mind, it looked like it hit a guy wire, took 'em off the ground, and then flipped over" (Ginell, *Milton Brown*, 196–97).

Milton's friend Calhoun later said:

> I know what happened to him [Brown] as well as anything in the world. He went to sleep. A lot of times, we'd take our cars on dances. We'd get tired of the bus and we'd drive our own cars up to Denton or Gainesville or somewhere. He'd always want me to drive him in his car, because he couldn't stay awake. He'd start out driving, and we wouldn't get two or three miles. We'd be talking about the band or something, and he'd say, "Fred, I'm getting so sleepy, you'll have to drive." (Ginell, *Milton Brown*, 199)

Roy Lee Brown agreed that Milton probably fell asleep. "He bought himself one of the first recliners," Roy Lee said. "It had a button you'd punch and it'd lean back, you know. He'd come home and sit down in that chair and lean back, and be talking to you, and you'd ask him a question, and he never would answer. He'd be asleep. He lost a lot of sleep [because of his work schedule], but I think he had narcolepsy." Roy Lee said Milton's appendix had burst when he was 12 years old, and doctors told the Brown family that could have caused a tendency for Milton to suffer from chronic drowsiness.

Roy Lee is convinced that alcohol played no part in the accident. "I know he wasn't drinking that night. According to what Ocie [Stockard] and Derwood and some more people came to us and said, they said they'd offered him a drink, and he said, no, he'd been sick at his stomach and didn't want to drink anything," Roy Lee said (Interview). Cary Ginell, Brown's biographer, wrote in a footnote to the chapter on Milton's death, that he was convinced from his research that there was no evidence of intoxication or recklessness in the accident. "Nor was it in Milton Brown's nature to be capable of such irresponsible actions," Ginell wrote (265).

Milton Brown was not dead, but Katy Prehoditch was. "This girl is dead, but we'd better get him to the hospital," Massey heard someone say. A passing taxi picked up Brown and took him to Methodist Hospital in Fort Worth. Katy was taken to the same hospital by ambulance and pronounced dead at 3:45 A.M. Milton was conscious and doctors at first thought he would survive. But he had a punctured right lung and developed pneumonia. By Tuesday, his condition was declining. "The first inkling we had that he might die was when the doctor ordered an oxygen tent for him," Milton's brother Roy Lee said. "Back then, when someone got pneumonia, they rarely ever got over it. When they got that oxygen tent out I heard Dad say, 'Oh, I sure hate to see that thing'" (Ginell, *Milton Brown*, 200).

An article in the *Fort Worth Star-Telegram* reported: "Yesterday afternoon, he looked up and smiled as his doctor entered the room. 'How about a cigaret [sic], doc?' he asked. 'Why, you'll burn my oxygen tent up, Milton,' the physician jokingly replied. 'Later perhaps.' But he never got that cigaret [sic]" ("Auto Injuries").

The funeral for Katy Prehoditch took place on Tuesday, April 14. Calhoun said, "Katy was a real nice girl. My wife [Idell] knew her real well from their church. She wasn't any one-nighter or nothing like that. . . . Milton told me later before he died, 'That sure was a nice little girl.' He just hated to hear that she died." Roy Lee Brown said Milton and his wife of about a year, Mary Helen, had divorced the month before. "A lot of people didn't know that," Roy Lee said. "They thought he was out running around, you know, although he was just taking that girl home. There was no romantic stuff there." Mary Helen Hames Brown later twice married Bob Wills. Milton left a baby son, Buster Lee Brown (Ginell, *Milton Brown*, 201, 221; Brown interview).

Milton Brown died on Saturday, April 18, 1936. He was 32. The *Star-Telegram* reported: "In a dying delirium, Milton Brown thought of his Musical Brownies. And he sang, like he did every day on the radio. He called the names of towns where they played, according to Miss Nell Stringer, his nurse. This morning, he mumbled a song. Miss Stringer caught a few lines—'Goodby Ma and Goodby Pa'" ("Auto Injuries").

Before he died, Brown asked Calhoun and other members of the Brownies to play their scheduled dates without him. On the Texas Quality Network, W. Lee O'Daniel eulogized his former employee. "I can remember only one time that I saw tears in Milton's eyes. That was when he was singing for me and I asked him to dedicate a song to his mother." O'Daniel and the Hillbilly Boys dedicated two songs to Milton, "That Silver-Haired Mother of Mine" and a song Brown had written for his infant son, "Our Baby Boy." Some Fort Worth radio stations observed a minute of silence in honor of his passing (Ginell, *Milton Brown*, 202–3). The *Star-Telegram* commented: "In Milton Brown's death, Texas' ranking fiddle band lost its leader" ("Auto Injuries").

"I was with Bob [Wills] when Milton died," remembered Joe Ferguson, who then was a member of the Texas Playboys. "We were going from Tulsa to Enid, Oklahoma. . . . We heard it on the radio, that Milton Brown had killed himself [in a car accident]. He had one heck of a good [lineup of] personnel in his band. If he had stayed alive, he might have been great. Whether he had the charisma that Bob had or not, that is the difference, as far as I'm concerned" (67). Roy Lee Brown said Milton was planning to leave North Texas at the time of his death. "He was fixing to go to Houston," Roy Lee said. "I've got a letter he wrote to the station [KPRC]. He was fixing to leave this part of the country." Roy Lee, of course, believes his brother's fame eventually would have spread far beyond the Southwest (Interview).

The *Fort Worth Press* estimated that 3,000 people attended Brown's funeral. The *Fort Worth Star-Telegram* put the number at 3,500. In any case, Roy Lee Brown remembered that people came from all over North Texas. "The people who lived near the cemetery had to take down their pasture fences so that everybody would have a place to park," Roy Lee recalled (Ginell, *Milton Brown*, 266).

Milton Brown's death was a terrible blow to the close-knit Texas music fraternity, but, with bitter irony, his passing gave a big career break to the Light Crust Doughboys.

Prior to his death, Milton Brown had negotiated a contract with Republic Pictures for himself and the Brownies to appear in the Gene Autry movie, *Oh Susanna*. After Milton died, Republic hired the Doughboys in his place (Ginell, *Milton Brown*, 209–10). Autry told author Mickey Herskowitz, in the book *Back in the Saddle Again*: "With *Oh Susanna* we began what was to become a policy for most of the movies I did at Republic: employing various country music groups, usually regional, with at least some radio fame. The Light Crust Doughboys were first, out of Fort Worth" (Ginell, *Milton Brown*, 210).

A brief Fort Worth newspaper article announced the group's good fortune: "The Burrus Mill Doughboys, pop radio artists, Sunday will miss their first broadcast since they began performing six years ago, when they leave for Hollywood to make their bow on the screen" ("Doughboys to miss").

"'Uncle Art' Satherley of Columbia Records recommended that we go," Montgomery said. "He was the fellow who was the A&R

man for Columbia who made our records for us. He produced them, so he recommended to Republic Pictures that they use the Light Crust Doughboys. We were the first, regular, well-known group to be in a musical Western. . . . Of course, later on Bob Wills and a lot of guys got into it, but we were the first ones" (Oral history, 46–47).

Brown's brother Derwood carried on for his brother as the leader of the Brownies, and, conceivably, the band still could have performed in *Oh Susanna*. But, at that point, the Brownies, being a dance band, could not afford to go to California for several weeks, at the relatively small fees Republic offered. "The Brownies were an independent band," Roy Lee Brown said. "They didn't have a Burrus Mill backing them. The Doughboys could go out there and still get their weekly salary. But the Brownies, if they gave up their dance job, they didn't get anything." Burrus Mill, of course, was delighted with the exposure the Doughboys' appearance in a popular Gene Autry movie would bring (Interview).

Marvin Montgomery has fond memories of performing in the movie. "This was before the days of tape recording, so they recorded our music first. It was on film. RCA had a big truck, and they brought it around. When we actually did the picture, they had a truck going ahead of us with a little speaker, playing our music. We just pretended we were playing. Otherwise, I wouldn't be sitting on a horse, playing banjo. I would fall off.

"I fell off, anyhow, practically. I went to get on this horse, and this ol' Hollywood cowboy, he was holding the horse. I put the wrong foot in the stirrup and started up, and I realized I was getting on the horse backwards. They said, 'Here's a kid from Texas who doesn't even how to get on a horse!'" (Oral history, 53).

Production on the movie ended on July 18, 1936. Reviewers were not especially kind to *Oh Susanna*. The headline of the *New York Times* review said, "Song stuff is cowboys yodeling and hillbilly whining. Too much of it." But the opinion of the *New York Times* mattered even less in Texas and the Southwest then than it does today, and the movie was highly successful with Autry's loyal audience (Ginell, *Milton Brown*, 267). To see the Doughboys performing in *Oh Susanna* is to understand more completely their immense appeal to audiences in the 1930s. Not only are they expert musically, but they are exuberant, energetic performers, with sunny smiles and engaging personalities. Playing for the guests at a ranch barbecue in spiffy Western outfits, it is as if the Great Depression was only a rumor.

Still, in his self-effacing, forthright way, Kenneth Pitts was dismissive of *Oh Susanna*. Asked if announcer Eddie Dunn was in the movie, Pitts wryly replied, "Yes, doing nothing. We all did nothing. It was not anything to be proud of. . . . Those movies were not much. Republic was just cashing in on the fact that our name was pretty well known."

But Pitts did enjoy California. "Back then, I thought it was all right. There weren't so many people there. Looked like a pretty good place. But, good night, there's so many people there now, where would you put your feet down?" Pitts remembered going to a movie premier at Grauman's Chinese Theatre in the Doughboys' bus with Marvin Montgomery and Bert Dodson.

In true Hollywood style, Pitts said Republic replaced the Doughboys' singing voices in *Oh Susanna* with more "professional" voices, while maintaining their instrumental performances. "They dubbed in voices for us," Pitts recalled. "I was strumming a mandolin. Man, I had a fine voice [laughing]. It was almost operatic, which was entirely out of place. It would have been better if they'd let me sing, and I couldn't sing. But it would have been more genuine than having some real sophisticated voice singing" (Interview).

The movies may have had a greater impact musically than they did as films. "I still run into people all the time who say, 'I used to listen to you when I was little kid,'" Marvin said. "I'm surprised how many banjo players I influenced by their seeing me in that movie, *Oh Susanna*. This one guy said, 'I was nine years old and I went to see that movie 10 times just to see you play "Tiger Rag"'" (Interview, Jan. 3, 2001).

Montgomery and the Doughboys worked with and became friendly with several Hollywood stars. Autry, the popular singing cowboy, came to visit the group at its Burrus Mills recording studio.

"He became a friend, and we took him out to the house for a chicken dinner and all that stuff," Montgomery recalled. While they were in California, the group performed with Bing Crosby on his radio show (Oral history, 52, 61).

The Doughboys went to California as ambassadors for the state of Texas, then celebrating its centennial. A newspaper article hailed their return: "Texas can expect an influx of visitors from the west coast this summer. . . . The Doughboys made this trip in a special bus built for them by their sponsors. They had it loaded down with literature furnished them by offices of the Fort Worth Frontier Centennial and other celebrations. Pamphlets were distributed and posters displayed wherever they stopped to entertain" ("Doughboys return").

Part of the Doughboys' second movie with Gene Autry, *The Big Show*, was filmed at the site of the Texas Centennial celebration, Dallas' new Fair Park. There, Marvin made friends with Roy Rogers, then a young, upcoming Western singer himself with the Sons of the Pioneers. He was then known as Leonard "Len" Slye, his name from birth.

Montgomery tells a story about young Len Slye that contrasts sharply with the image of Roy Rogers, the man who would later become the wholesome hero to millions of American boys and girls. Because Slye had a tendency to prowl the city streets at night and get into trouble, Republic Pictures executives locked him in his room at the Adolphus Hotel in Dallas. But, while Montgomery waited outside his door, Slye would climb over the transom and he and Marvin would then hit the funky clubs in Dallas' Deep Ellum district (Oral history, 56–57).

Montgomery fondly remembered playing at the Texas Centennial. "Right down where Big Tex [the giant cowboy figure that greets State Fair of Texas visitors] is, they had a building that was built in a U-shape. It had a glass front all the way around, and each room was a different radio station. There would be three or four live programs on at one time. . . . We did a lot of our broadcasts from there. . . . It was a happy time" (Oral history, 49).

The Light Crust Doughboys' movie career was a brief one. But as musicians, they were just hitting their stride.

"Seems to me I heard a piano player"

The Light Crust Doughboys had begun as a "fiddle" band, with two acoustic guitars and a single fiddle. Over the years, their sound and style steadily grew larger and more sophisticated. At the beginning of 1937, the Doughboys sound became "complete" when they added pianist John William "Knocky" Parker, Jr., to their lineup. Parker's arrival cemented the Doughboys' move to a jazzier, bluesier style of playing, and, symbolically at least, represented the band's arrival at its pre-war musical and professional peak. Despite his importance to the band, Knocky was its youngest member.

Parker's style fit perfectly with Marvin Montgomery's playing. "The banjo was a big influence on me because you could have all this movement, and you can have slurred notes. In my own style . . . there's a wild banjo quality there. . . . In piano, I do the same that this little old banjo did, because Marvin Montgomery was a tremendous, tremendous virtuoso. . . . [He] was one of the greatest banjo pickers of all time, anywhere" (Oral history, 4, reel two; 7, reel one).

Knocky Parker showed remarkable musical aptitude from a very early age. He learned to play from piano rolls. "I was four years old," he remembered. "Mama was on the phone one time, and she heard something. But she knew this wasn't exactly the roll because it wasn't quite as full as that. . . . I was playing the piano, the same little piece we had on the roll. . . . Kids play with toys, you know, and they tear down bicycles and put them back together. Well, my world was the player piano rolls." Soon thereafter, his parents took him to play at church camp meetings around Central Texas (Oral history, 1–2, reel one; Interview).

Unlike most of the other Doughboys' nicknames, Parker's nickname was for real. He said he had been "Knocky" for as long as he could remember. "They [Knocky's family] claimed I was playing the piano and the top was up, and I'm banging away on it, and a hammer flies out and hits me on the eyebrow, and they had to take some stitches or something. Now, I can't believe that" (Interview).

Like Dick Reinhart and Montgomery, Parker was strongly impressed by the style of black musicians. Knocky said his first real music teachers were black blues players he met on trips to Dallas with his father between 1925 and 1928. Knocky's dad would go to the black music clubs in Dallas (unbeknownst to Knocky's mother) looking for men to work on the family's cotton farm. Knocky, already fascinated with music, would sit down at a piano and the musicians, seeing the boy's eagerness, would sit down with him.

"We would play four hands on the piano," he recalled. "So there'd be my left hand, his left hand, my right hand, his right; and move all over the piano, playing all kinds of ways and variations. I'd try to copy everything they did, you see. They would laugh and show me everything they played. . . . The music was great. I was getting the finest training that you could possibly get anywhere from all these wild people. . . . I worshipped these people, respected them, admired them. I was just a little kid, and they saw this [admiration] in me, and they were very kind, generous and loving and careful that I was treated right. . . . They'd drink [liquor] and bring me ice cream." Knocky remembered taking naps on the beds of "ladies of the evening." Parker said, as a boy, he once met legendary blues guitarist Blind Lemon Jefferson at one of the clubs (Oral history, 2–3, reel one; Interview).

Besides being a powerful influence on his own development, Parker agreed that the Dallas black blues scene strongly influenced the Doughboys' sound, even more than jazz. "The Negro blues in Dallas," he said in 1963, "more even than New Orleans, was a focal point. . . . Leadbelly and Blind Lemon, and all, coming from there is one of the influences that makes us different. . . . We were somewhat close also to the Gulf of Mexico and New Orleans. That gives us a difference from the other people, and, I think, that makes us a little bit better, and I treasure this very much" (Oral history, 8, reel three).

Before joining the Doughboys at the age of 18, Knocky Parker played with Bill Boyd's Cowboy Ramblers (Boyd's brother and future Doughboy Jim was a guitarist in the group) and Blackie Simmons and his Blue Jackets. Knocky was playing Bill Boyd's group before he was out of high school. He joined Blackie Simmons when he was 16 and had just graduated. "They advertised me as a 12-year-old piano player because I was real small, green—green as a gourd—and inexperienced. . . . Country, country, country. Rice and hay all over me." He remembered playing honky tonks with Simmons. "We used to play such things as bathing suit dances in cheap dives. And brother, when you play a bathing suit dance in a cheap dive, you've got something indeed. . . . They got a big kick out of these improper places we played because I was so naïve" (Oral history, 4–6, reel one). But Knocky soon earned the respect of the other musicians. "He was a great showman and a fantastic musician," a member of the Blue Jackets, banjoist Sam Graves, said (Ginell, *Milton Brown*, 211). Historian Kevin Coffey noted: "Knocky Parker was a great and creative pianist, who later attracted a lot of attention as a ragtime and 'legit' jazz player" (Personal communication, July 29, 2001).

Parker told an interviewer many years after leaving the Doughboys, "There's a strong West Texas, harder, harsh attack in my playing that makes it, I think, singular. [It's a] free-wheeling, daredevil type of thing that comes with the Doughboys. I think this is always with me" (Oral history, 8, reel three).

Marvin Montgomery's first meeting with Knocky in 1934 was very nearly their only meeting. "He was running across the street from the Adolphus Hotel to the Baker, where the Wanderers broadcast, and got struck by a car," Montgomery recalled. "Didn't hurt him very bad. That's where I got acquainted with him, and I'm responsible for him playing with the Doughboys" (Govenar and Brakefield, 146).

Zeke Campbell said Knocky Parker joined the Doughboys after informally playing with the group at one of their appearances. "We went down to Trinity University," Campbell recalled. "It was down in Waxahachie at that time. There was a kid down there named 'Knocky' Parker, who played piano. He knew some of the Doughboys. He knew Dick Reinhart and Marvin Montgomery and Bert Dodson from coming up to Dallas. He was going to school down there at Trinity University. He sat in and played with us. He was on the piano while we were down there, and we put on a program. . . . Lo and behold, he came up here looking for a job. He just got out of school; he just walked off and left the school and came up to get a job. They [Burrus Mill] hired him and that made seven of us" (Oral history, 11).

Knocky remembered playing several times on the Doughboys' radio program in an on-the-air audition around Christmas of 1936. He recalled announcer Eddie Dunn joking with the listening audience, "'Seems to me I heard a piano player.' And somebody [a Doughboy] would say, 'Oh no, that's just the banjo player. He sounds like that sometimes,' and the audience never did know any better." He joined the group as a regular member in January 1937 (Oral history, 5, reel one).

Knocky Parker had made up his mind to join the Light Crust Doughboys. "They were regarded as tops in the hillbilly field, all up and down the country," he said. "[Hillbilly groups] were the only jobs available for a poor white boy who couldn't read music, but could play" (Oral history, 7, reel one). The teenage prodigy's determination to join the Doughboys has become part of the group's legend. Parker grew up in the country, near the town of Palmer. "Knocky Parker had been so determined to join the Doughboys that when he came down with measles right before his audition date, the family hid his shoes to keep him home in bed and he tried to walk it barefoot," wrote Kenneth Pitts' daughter Janis Stout. "They went after him and got him back and got him well, and he hit the Fort Worth musical scene full force" (Stout, "Light Crust," 6).

Knocky was certainly a young man to be reckoned with. Ultimately, he earned a doctoral degree in English, and served for many years on the faculty of the University of South Florida. "Right up until he died in 1986 he played a wild, rhythmic style so raunchy he sometimes hit the keys with his elbows, just as he had played when he joined the Doughboys," Stout said. "Marvin said in later years that he would travel anywhere anytime to play music with Knocky Parker—which tells you a lot about both of them" ("Light Crust," 6).

Late in his life, Marvin Montgomery spoke more enthusiastically about Knocky Parker than any other musician. "Knocky was the guy who really influenced the Doughboys and some of the music we played," Montgomery said, "because he would get these Bob Crosby Dixieland things, 'South Rampart Street Parade' and those things" (Oral history, 121). Parker introduced black blues numbers to the Doughboys' repertoire. "Knocky could play them just as good as they could, and we played them on the air," Montgomery said. "We recorded them. All the boogie-woogie and blues things. Knocky could play stride and a variety of other styles." Montgomery said the Doughboys played tunes such as "Dallas Blues," "Beale Street Mama," "Memphis Blues," and "St. Louis Blues" in their live performances thanks to Parker, although they did not record those particular tunes (Govenar and Brakefield, 147–48).

Montgomery would arrange the tunes Parker brought to the group in the Doughboys' style. "He'd bring the record to me, and I'd write it out with a guitar playing the lead," Marvin said. "Zeke Campbell would play the trumpet parts on guitar, and we always had two fiddles. The fiddles would play the clarinet and the trombone parts. I'd write three-part harmony, and every once in while, four-part harmony. . . . When we went [out of town] on the bus, the piano player [Knocky] had to play accordion, because we couldn't put a piano on that bus very well" (Oral history, 121).

Just as musicians frequently came and went in the Doughboys, so did announcers. By 1937, Eddie Dunn had left the group to return to WFAA ("Dunn — biography"). Marvin Montgomery recalled: "The Mill auditioned several different people including Harley Sadler from Sweetwater, Texas. Sadler was the owner of a tent show which played all over Texas. He wanted $1,000 a week and the job only paid $125. In the meantime, for several weeks, each member of the Doughboys took turns acting as announcer—that was a disaster" ("Light Crust Doughboys announcers"). The announcer/manager who succeeded Dunn was Larry Rowell, who came to Texas from Chicago, the headquarters of advertising agency J. Walter Thompson, which produced the program for Burrus Mill. Rowell tried to take the Doughboys in a new direction. "He had an idea of doing a little skit," Campbell said (26).

Marvin Montgomery remembered the soap opera phase with little affection. "They sent the script down from Chicago. They didn't know any more about Texas than I did at the time" (Interview, Jan. 3, 2001).

The Doughboys' ill-fated detour into melodrama was announced in the June 6, 1937, edition of the *Fort Worth Star-Telegram*, in a story detailing the arrival of Rowell:

> Larry Rowell, a bright young man from the West, has introduced continuity and sound effects. From now on the seven Doughboys will have speaking parts, becoming definite characters, and participate in a story revolving around Ripple Creek [a fictional rural community]. . . . Clifford Gross, the character heretofore known as "Doctor," becomes Jeremiah

Holly, a lovable old farmer with whom the boys are vacationing. "Mr. Holly" is a peaceable, philosophical soul, and he's been showing the boys a grand time on his farm, but now, suddenly, a dark cloud has been cast over his sunny life. "Mr. Zimmer," a city slicker, had entered the picture. Mr. Zimmer is a viper, boding the Doughboys no good. . . . The music will not be discontinued, never fear. Plenty of the snappy rhythm long associated with the Doughboys will be continued. Listeners all over the Southwest consider them the finest fiddle group on the air. ("Doughboys make change")

"There were so many soap operas on the radio at that time, so he had the idea of doing a kind of little soap opera or skit," Campbell said. "It just finally went away. People got to writing in such complaints about it that they finally just took it off. They let Larry Rowell go. That's when Parker Willson came down, about that time. They [the Doughboys] went back to their old format" (26).

Montgomery remembered that the "soap opera" format was nearly the end of the Doughboys. "They had regular scripts that they sent down from Chicago. We'd get to play the [Light Crust Doughboys] theme song and maybe a breakdown. That was all. The rest of it would be talking about things: 'We're going to have a barn dance out to Red's farm tonight, out in his barn.' . . . Finally, Burrus caught on, and they canned ol' Larry, and that's when we got Parker Willson. That saved our lives" (Oral history, 117). The soap-opera experiment lasted only from June to August 1937.

Parker Willson returned to Texas from Chicago and became the Doughboys' new announcer. Willson rivaled W. Lee O'Daniel himself as the listeners' favorite Doughboys' master of ceremonies. "Parker was our most popular emcee," Marvin said. "He was real popular. He was a good-looking guy. The poor guy died of bone cancer [in 1962]" (Oral history, 113).

Willson was a Taylor, Texas, native, and a University of Texas graduate. He worked for a time at WBAP as an announcer, and then went on to Chicago, where he worked for NBC as a radio announcer and actor. He once filled in, apparently quite ably, for Orson Welles in a radio play, and another time portrayed Will Rogers. Willson performed in radio plays with movie stars Constance Bennett and Robert Montgomery, Marvin (Wetter) Montgomery's boyhood hero (W. Jolesch; Lawson). A September 1937 *Fort Worth Star-Telegram* article heralded his arrival: "Six feet tall, flashing eyes, dark wavy hair, Clark Gable shoulders, a winning smile, a hearty laugh. . . . If television were here, a lot of damsels around Fort Worth and West Texas would be glued to their radio sets each weekday at 12:30 P.M. . . . Reason: Parker O. Willson, new master of ceremonies with the Light Crust Doughboys." Willson told the newspaper he had been homesick: "[I returned] because I like it better. Texas, after all, is my home, and I understand the sons and daughters of the Lone Star State" (Lawson).

Willson also sang with the Doughboys, as did several of the emcees, in "a rich baritone voice" ("WFAA, KGKO, WBAP"). Willson usually sang as part of a trio or quartet on novelty songs, such as Marvin Montgomery's "We Must Have Beer" and "I Want A Waitress." He also was adept at providing sound effects. On Doughboys' novelty numbers such as "She Gave Me the Bird," Willson sang the bird's part, and on "We Found Her Little Pussy Cat," Willson provided the voice of the cat. On at least one song, "In Ole' Oklahoma," Willson sang the lead (Montgomery, "Doughboy recording sessions," 11, 20).

Upon Parker Willson's arrival, the Doughboys became involved in another soap opera, this time, thankfully, not their own. "Your Home Town" featured Willson and Ora Martin, who also was heard on the radio show "Backstage Wife." The 42 transcribed episodes of the show were produced by the J. Walter Thompson Advertising Agency at the Burrus Mill studio. It required the inclusion of "hillbilly music," hence, the Light Crust Doughboys. A newspaper article reported: "In [producer L.E.] Jacobson's opinion, the best hillbilly band in the country is known to WBAP listeners as the Light Crust Doughboys" ("Radio Feature").

Just as O'Daniel had been the man in charge of the Doughboys during the early years of the group, Willson and the announcers who succeeded him also functioned as managers. "They more or less were the boss of us," Zeke Campbell recalled. "They told us what to do. The announcer was the boss. We'd go out on these trips and he [the manager] arranged everything" (24–25).

During the Parker Willson years, the Doughboys featured a "mascot," Charles Burton. His real name was Wilson, but Parker Willson did not want listeners to think Charles was his son. When he joined the program, he was only 12 years old. He sang with the group on the Monday, Wednesday, and Friday programs, and went on tour with the Doughboys during the summer months. Charles Burton was the lead singer on three Doughboy recordings, "Beautiful Ohio," "If I Didn't Care," and "Mary Lou." Young Charles stayed with the group for about two years, and then, when his voice changed, he was replaced by an 11-year-old girl, "Dolores Jo" Clancy, who performed with the Doughboys until the original radio show left the air in 1942 (Jolesch; Remick; Montgomery, "Doughboy recording sessions," 6, 7, 11, 19).

The movie star and cowboy singer Tex Ritter was a friend of Willson's from their University of Texas days. "Any time he was in running distance, he would come on the program," Marvin Montgomery said. Ritter, a Country Music Hall of Fame member, performed "Boll Weevil" among other popular tunes on the Doughboys' radio show. "He was a good guy, a smart guy. He went to law school at UT" (Interview, May 28, 2001).

Sometimes the guests on the program were members of the Doughboys' own families. Kenneth Pitts' daughter, Janis Stout, recalled performing on the show herself. "I remember sitting there while they went through the show and being real quiet, then being hushed when I forgot—a fifteen minute show seemed so long," she wrote. "And then settling myself on the piano bench and saying something into the microphone when Parker Willson asked me a question, trying, no doubt, to make this cute. And then I played my little piece, and then there was the closing theme and the red ON THE AIR went off and I could talk again" ("Light Crust," 5).

But Marvin Montgomery recalled that all was not necessarily as it seemed on the Doughboys wholesome, jolly radio program. "On the air you were one big happy family, but not always off it. We would be singing hymns and the breath on some of them would knock you over. But the clean ones are still alive and the others are dead," Marvin ruefully remembered in the early 1980s (Remick).

Joe Frank Ferguson, though, said the drinking was never very bad. "I couldn't put up with that," he said. "No way could I put with a drunk performer. . . . 'Snub' [Ramon DeArman] and J.B. [Brinkley, who replaced DeArman] would nip every once in awhile, but that was on their own time. It wasn't on the job or anything like that. Even I took a drink of beer or something every once in awhile myself, but not on the job" (Oral history, 42).

With any group of talented, ambitious young men traveling and performing together, drunk or not, tempers are bound to flare. But one incident on the Doughboys' bus nearly got out of hand. Marvin remembered an incident involving Clifford Gross, the fiddle player who replaced Bob Wills in the Doughboys. The Doughboys were performing a skit involving a moonshine jug. Someone put black goo from a melted acetate in the jug, and it ran out on Gross' shirt. Gross took offense, and later on the bus, he pulled a switchblade knife and held it to Parker Willson's throat. "We were scared," Marvin said. "Dick Reinhart started talking to Gross—they were kind of buddy buddy—and he talked him out of hurting Parker. Gross finally pulled the knife away. He sat in the back of the bus, mumbling all the way home. The next morning, when we go out at nine o' clock, he had already been there and got all of his clothes and his instruments. That's the last [time] that he was with the Doughboys. He knew he was through" (Oral history, 82, 84–85).

At about the same time, Dick Reinhart left the Doughboys. "Reinhart . . . left because Burrus Mill hired Parker Willson as MC and boss instead of him. Reinhart joined Gross and they formed the Universal Cowboys for Universal Flour Mills." Later, Reinhart went to California and played on Gene Autry's radio program, "Melody Ranch" (Montgomery, "Doughboy recording sessions," 8; Ginell, *Milton Brown*, 260).

Knocky Parker remembered that Reinhart's expert guitar playing was vital to the arrangements. "He was one of the first ones, before amplified guitar, to play the trombone part [in an arrangement]," Parker said. "And even with amplified guitar, he would turn his [amp] down not too loud, and still play a little trombone [piece] in the bass [strings of the guitar]. Very much the role of the trombonist. Terrific, terrific guy and a very fine instrumentalist" (Oral history, 8, reel one; 5, reel two).

In Marvin Montgomery's 1989 discography of the Light Crust Doughboys recordings he was less generous than usual in commenting on the abilities of Clifford Gross: "On a lot of the [recorded] songs Gross did not play due to the fact that he couldn't read music and was a slow learner. On the recording sessions, we didn't like to waste time waiting for him to learn a song and so Pitts (who acted as leader on the sessions) would leave him out—Gross would go to the corner and sulk." But in a letter from Kenneth Pitts to Montgomery at the time Marvin wrote the discography, Pitts noted that Gross later returned to Louisville, Kentucky, and was successful in starting his own band (Montgomery, "Doughboy recording sessions," 2, 22).

The departure of Dick Reinhart brought Jim Boyd into the Doughboys. "He [Boyd] was just a knockout," Knocky Parker said. "Old Jim Boyd played very well—very, very well" (Oral history, 6, reel one). Boyd, born in 1914, and his older brother Bill, born four years earlier, grew up in Fannin County in North Texas, and began playing country music on the radio in Greenville, Texas, in 1926. By 1933, they had moved to Dallas and formed the Cowboy Ramblers, a group that was strongly influenced by Milton Brown and his Musical Brownies. The Cowboy Ramblers, like most Western groups, weren't cowboys at all. But Jim did his best to promote a realistic image. For one photo session, he applied cow manure to one of his boots (Govenar and Brakefield, 158, 162).

Modern-day Doughboy Art Greenhaw was an admirer of Jim Boyd's. "He was a pioneering rhythm guitarist in the famous Texas Swing style of 'moving' chord forms. That is, he would change the chord or chord inversion with every couple of beats," Greenhaw said. "Jim's singing style was mighty fine. Like Rick Nelson, he could sing a beautiful ballad with his pleasing tenor voice, and yet he could also sing an up-tempo song, but make it effortless and smooth. He could make a rocker sound like a smooth ballad that you could pat your feet and snap your fingers to. He could sing any type of material and sing it well" (Personal communication, Dec. 30, 2001).

Boyd, who played bass and guitar in his on-and-off career with the Doughboys that continued into the 1990s, receives credit from some researchers with what may be the first recorded use of an electric guitar. It occurred in a September 1935 session with the group Roy Newman and His Boys, who played on Dallas radio station WRR. They recorded "Shine On Harvest Moon," "Corrine, Corrina" and "Hot Dog Stomp" (Govenar and Brakefield, 160; Broadbent, 13).

The Doughboys, directly or indirectly, play a significant role in the history of the electric guitar. Zeke Campbell, of course, was an early and influential practitioner of amplified guitar picking. Although the Light Crust Doughboys are not mentioned by name, two names that figure prominently in Doughboy history, Leon McAuliffe and Hank Thompson, are credited in *The Fender Book: A Complete History of Fender Electric Guitars:*

> It was Western swing, a lively dance music that grew up in Texas dancehalls during the 1930s and 1940s, that popularized the electric guitar in the U.S., at first primarily, though not exclusively, with steel guitars. Many of its steel players used Fender electrics, notably Noel Boggs with Spade Cooley and Leon McAuliffe with Bob Wills, and well as some "Spanish" guitarists like Telecaster-wielding Bill Carson with Hank Thompson's Brazos Valley Boys. (Bacon and Day, 19)

Milton Brown's biographer Cary Ginell notes that McAuliffe played an amplified steel guitar in a recording session with Bob Wills the same week that Jim Boyd made his historic recordings with Roy Newman. A member of Brown's band, Bob Dunn, introduced the amplified steel guitar (Ginell letter; Ginell, *Milton Brown*, xxvii; Govenar and Brakefield, 153).

When Cliff Gross left the Doughboys after giving Parker Willson the scare of his life, Robert "Buck" Buchanan came into the group as Kenneth Pitts' partner on the fiddle. Buchanan was a natural partner for Pitts, having studied under Pitts' old violin teacher Wylbert Brown in Fort Worth. He had played for a time with Milton Brown's Brownies, along with guitarist Lefty Perkins, who would join a later incarnation of the Doughboys. "Buck was one hell of a harmony man," Perkins said. "He could double-stop that fiddle and make it sound like three or four fiddles. Johnny [Borowski] would play lead and Buck would play both second and third harmony behind him." Kenneth Pitts also was an accomplished "double-stop" player (Montgomery, "Doughboy recording sessions," 8; Ginell, *Milton Brown*, 213, 57–58). "Buck was very inventive and very knowledgeable in music. He was well schooled and a good musician," Pitts said. But Buck Buchanan stayed with the Doughboys only a short time, from late 1938 to mid-1939. "Buck was there long enough that we played over at the Dallas [Texas State] Fair while Buck was on the job," Pitts recalled. "We used to go over there and broadcast every day from a booth the mill had. But it wasn't long after that that Cecil [Brower] came back, and Parker [Willson] picked him up and let Buck go" (Interview, May 27, 1986).

If Buck Buchanan seemed a great partner for Kenneth Pitts, his replacement was an even better match. Cecil Brower, Pitts' old partner in the Southern Rhythm Boys, had played with Milton Brown's Brownies and Ted Fio Rito's orchestra in New York City before returning to Texas. When Knocky Parker was interviewed in 1963, he called Brower "one of the first jazz violinists. . . . [He] is now the leading hillbilly violinist in Nashville. Most of his time is spent recording, just playing some wild background cadenzas behind any singer at all. Terrific, terrific musician" (Oral history, 1, reel two). Brower played fiddle for country music stars Red Foley and Jimmy Dean, among others (Ginell, *Milton Brown*, 223).

Brower had been born near Bowie in Northwest Texas, and had moved with his family to California as a child. Then the family moved back to Texas, settling in Fort Worth in 1924. Cecil's father, a police detective, was determined that his son would learn to play a musical instrument. And so, he too received formal violin lessons from Wylbert Brown. Brown remembered that he taught Pitts and Brower the classical method of bow handling, giving them an edge on most "hillbilly" fiddlers, who, Brown said, "had no technique in bowing at all." Pitts and Brower were both prize pupils. "Those two were so talented, they could have picked up anything I taught them and played it," Brown said. "Cecil was a lot more spunky than Kenneth, and I taught him to use the 'tremolo mute.'" The tremolo mute was a small spring with a ball bearing attached to it. Placed on the bridge of the fiddle, it would produce a "vibrating sound like it was being played under water," Wylbert Brown said (Ginell, *Milton Brown*, 57–58).

Marvin Montgomery said Brower, like most of the Doughboys, was strongly influenced by jazz and the big bands. "Cecil Brower would listen to a hot clarinet chorus by Benny Goodman and we would copy it almost note for note on the fiddle," Montgomery said (Govenar and Brakefield, 149).

As a testimony to Brower's talent, Doughboys fan Red Varner recalled a transcendent moment that Cecil created when he was playing with Milton Brown. Varner said he did not recall the tune Brower was playing, but said it did not matter what it was:

> At some point in the solo, Cecil played a passage that affected everyone on the dance floor. I think everyone responded in his or her own way to that fleeting sound that was not likely to be heard again. But one old boy out there on that floor could not contain himself. His roar of complete, absolute, uncompromising, and joyous approval and appreciation completed the frosting on the cake, but must have deafened his dancing partner. I would bet that they heard that shout ten blocks away.

Years after hearing Brower's fleeting musical passage, Varner was nearly moved to poetry: "How often are we affected by the song of a bird? Does the bird know that his song was heard and noticed?" (Ginell, *Milton Brown*, 105).

For many years after their departure from the Doughboys, W. Lee O'Daniel and Bob Wills continued to exert a strong influence on the group, for better or worse. Near the end of 1939, O'Daniel lured Jim Boyd away from the Doughboys to play with the governor's Hillbilly Boys in his 1940 run for re-election. Wills then, as if to offset the move of his old nemesis, provided the Doughboys with a first-rate replacement.

"He found out Jim Boyd was going to leave the Light Crust Doughboys and go to work for W. Lee O'Daniel," Joe Frank Ferguson recalled. Ferguson had learned to play bass from Wills' bassist "Son" Lansford and Leon McAuliffe. "Bob said, 'They're going to need a bass player. I know you don't like that saxophone [which Ferguson also had learned and was then playing in the Texas Playboys]. Why don't you go down and audition for it? If they like you, you'll have a good job down there. If you don't like it, and the situation is not the way you like it, come on back. You've got a job here anytime you want it" (9). As Marvin Montgomery observed, "Joe Frank Ferguson is the only musician to come from the Bob Wills band to the Doughboys. All the other musicians left the Doughboys to join Wills" ("Doughboy recording sessions," 14).

Ferguson said his first paying job with the Light Crust Doughboys was on January 1, 1940. "I did play with them on New Year's Eve. We weren't supposed to play, but we played a private party on New Year's Eve of 1939, so I can say I was with the Light Crust Doughboys in 1939. . . . I really enjoyed the Doughboys gig." Joe took Boyd's nickname of "Bashful" (9).

The story of how Ferguson became a professional musician and eventually a Doughboy is magical. In early 1936, he had entered a singing contest at a club in Tulsa and, after weeks of competition, finally won first prize.

> I missed my bus back home and had to stay all night, so to have something to do the next morning until bus time, I went to KVOO radio station. There was a lady there by the name

of Lydia White, who was playing some hymns on the organ there in one of the studios. I had my face up against the glass, listening to it and watching her. She saw me standing out there, and she motioned me to come in the studio. I went in the studio, and she asked me if I sang hymns or anything. I said, "Yes, and I love to listen to them." She said, "What else do you do?" I said, "Well, I like pop tunes." We played a couple of tunes and sang them. She said, "Say, we have a 'Staff Frolic' [radio program] in the afternoon at the radio station. I believe I can get you on there if you want to stay and do it."

Ferguson stayed and sang on the program. About 20 minutes after it was over, Bob Wills called the station. He had heard Ferguson singing, and said he wanted to talk to Joe the next morning. After their meeting, Wills hired Joe Frank to join the Texas Playboys (4–5).

Late in his life, Joe Ferguson was asked if he thought that, over the years, he had become a good bass player. "No, technically not. That is, musically not, but rhythm, yes," he replied. "I had a knack. Very few people knew what it was that was making it go [his bass playing] like it did. . . . I had a knack of accenting a four-beat, but your best swing music is in a two-beat. When you get into a four-beat, then you get into a faster, or more subtle, swing-type thing. I would still accent the two-beat bit in there."

Ferguson played the same bass instrument during all his years with the Texas Playboys and Light Crust Doughboys. Bob Wills purchased the bass when Ferguson joined the Playboys. "Bob went down to the Jennings Music Store in Tulsa and bought a Juzek upright bass and two Super 400 guitars," Ferguson recalled. "He gave one of them to Herman Arnspiger and one of them to Eldon Shamblin, and the bass to me." Ferguson said Wills showed the same generosity with the bass he had shown in letting Ferguson join the Doughboys. "When I came down here with the Light Crust Doughboys, I used their bass. O.W. Mayo, Bob's manager, said, 'You can't use that [Doughboys] bass to go out on these other jobs [Ferguson played other gigs outside the Doughboys]. I'm going to send you your bass from here. We'll just get this other kid [Ferguson's replacement] another bass.' They sent me that Juzek down here then. I think I owed Bob $34 or something like that when I left up there. He said he would even forget about that [chuckles]. They sent me the bass and didn't charge me for it." Ferguson said he used the bass on the Doughboys radio shows, and played a different bass on the road. In 1996, Ferguson donated the bass to the Country Music Hall of Fame in Nashville, as part of an exhibit on Western swing that included the Light Crust Doughboys (70, 81–82).

While most of the music played by the early Doughboys is lost to posterity, the post-Wills/Brown Doughboys recorded frequently. Between 1936 and 1941 the Doughboys recorded 156 songs, of which 128 were commercially released (Montgomery, "Doughboy record-ing sessions," 21). Montgomery said of the 1930s recording sessions: "We'd have maybe two or three sessions recording everything we knew, like maybe 20 songs or something" (Interview, March 21, 2001).

At a time when the recording industry was much more regional in nature, the Doughboys' records, boosted by the group's radio program, out sold all other fiddle bands in the Dallas-Fort Worth area, historian Charles R. Townsend wrote (Display). Historian Kevin Coffey observed, "The Doughboys best recordings of the late '30s in particular are among the best and jazziest in Western swing history" (July 29, 2001).

The Doughboys recorded for Columbia's subsidiary labels Vocalion and Okeh under the direction of "Uncle Art" Satherley, the legendary English record producer (Montgomery, Oral history, 65). Satherley is one of the giant figures in the history of country music. He was inducted into the Country Music Hall of Fame in 1971. He was the first to record Bob Wills and the Texas Playboys. Satherley also recorded Gene Autry's first big hit, "That Silver-Haired Daddy of Mine." He discovered and recorded many other Hall of Fame artists: Roy Acuff, Tex Ritter, Red Foley, the Original Carter Family, Bill Monroe, the Sons of the Pioneers, Lefty Frizzell, Marty Robbins,

Little Jimmy Dickens, Floyd Tillman, Lester Flatt and Earl Scruggs, and Roy Rogers (F. White, 105–6).

But, listening to the Doughboys' recordings of the period, it is striking how little in common they have with the sound that we today call "country." The jazz and swing influence is obvious. The Doughboys' most frequent lead vocalist in the mid- to late-'30s was Dick Reinhart. Reinhart's suave tenor vocals, influenced by Milton Brown, would not have been out of place on any of the big-band recordings of the day, as on the driving "Just Once Too Often." On the later recordings, after Reinhart left the band, Jim Boyd sang lead on many of the tunes, also in a confident tenor voice that conveyed a slightly more ironic tone than Reinhart's, as on the raunchy "Thousand Mile Blues." The Doughboys recorded the song in Boyd's first session with the group, November 30, 1938. (Boyd's brother Bill and his Cowboy Ramblers had earlier recorded the song.) Later in the period, Ramon DeArman and Joe Ferguson took on more of the vocal duties, and the recordings from 1940 and 1941 feature more harmony singing, with DeArman and Pitts being joined by Kenneth Pitts and announcer Parker Willson. Later, J.B. Brinkley's voice replaced DeArman's.

The Doughboys' style on the recordings is similar to the better-known work of Bob Wills and the Texas Playboys, but, of course, the Playboys, with horns and drums, had a fuller sound than the Doughboys with their small group. The Doughboys generally exhibit a grittier, earthier sound than the Playboys. They were a very tight band.

On their recordings, Dick Reinhart on guitar, Marvin Montgomery on banjo and Bert Dodson and, later, Ramon DeArman on bass provide a relentless rhythm, despite the absence of drums. The lively twin fiddles of Kenneth Pitts and Clifford Gross (with Buck Buchanan and Cecil Brower later succeeding Gross) frequently take the lead, but rollicking piano, and sometimes accordion, solos by Knocky Parker, high-spirited banjo solos by Montgomery, and elegant electric-guitar breaks by Zeke Campbell are just about as frequent.

Art Greenhaw says the playing of Knocky Parker and Marvin Montgomery stands out on the early recordings. "You hear some wonderfully unorthodox piano playing by Knocky, who had creative, jazz-oriented fingering techniques and would strike the piano percussively with his elbows and the palms of his hands, on occasion," Greenhaw said.

"The banjo is highly unique the way Smokey [Marvin] plays it, with power chords, moving constantly up and down the neck and lightning-fast combinations of single note and chord banjo solos," Greenhaw commented (Personal communication, Feb. 19, 2002).

The Doughboys showed considerable aptitude for the blues. Jim Boyd, especially, seemed to have a feel for the indigenous Southern music as the vocalist on "Thousand Mile Blues," among others. "Thousand Mile Blues" begins with a sprightly twin-fiddle intro by Pitts and Buchanan, before Buchanan takes off on a smart solo. Zeke Campbell's electric guitar solo is more influenced by melodic jazz than the raw, elemental style of rural black blues. Marvin Montgomery breaks into a raucous kazoo solo.

On "Thousand Mile Blues," Knocky Parker's piano provides a strongly rhythmic background, but on his own composition "Mama Gets What She Wants," recorded June 15, 1939, the influence of Parker's youth spent in the black honky-tonks of downtown Dallas is more than apparent. He opens the recording with a bawdy, roadhouse-style piano solo. Boyd sings Parker's lyric with lusty confidence at the top of his tenor voice:

My love is great and hard to satisfy . . .
Whatever mama wants, I certainly qualify.

Parker's yells are clearly heard in the background. "He felt so good about the way Boyd was singing his song, he couldn't hold it in," wrote Marvin Montgomery ("Doughboy recording sessions," 13).

Greenhaw sees the strong influence of the blues on the Doughboys' playing on their '30s recordings. "You hear much bending of the strings in the playing of Zeke and Dick which is characteristic of their blues influences and the Doughboys' association with Deep Ellum and other black musicians. The guitar tone is fairly full and rich considering the tiny amplifiers of the times and the limited microphones (in some cases, one mike for everything)," Greenhaw observed (Feb. 19, 2002).

As with many popular recordings from the period, the emphasis on the Doughboys' recordings is as much on the playing as the singing, with the vocals often not beginning until the middle of the record. Or sometimes the group would take extended instrumental breaks in the middle of the recording. Most of the recordings are uptempo and high-spirited, with Marvin's shouts of "Yeah, man!" (a trademark until his dying day) very evident, among others' exclamations. Sometimes the band changes pace with a slower, blues-influenced number such as "Sitting on Top of the World" (not the pop tune by the same name), but almost never slows down for a purely melodic ballad. The Doughboys would perform slower, more traditional songs on their radio program, but on their recordings the rhythm is almost always at the forefront.

Many of the recordings are strictly instrumental. One of these is the jazzy "Mama Won't Let Me," composed by Zeke Campbell, Knocky Parker, and Marvin Montgomery, although Montgomery modestly averred, "I wrote the fiddle parts only." Recorded June 15, 1939, it features a solid bass line performed by Boyd with Parker and Campbell playing off one another on piano and electric guitar before Pitts and Brower step forward for a twin-fiddle break. "Little Rock Get-À-Way," recorded the previous day, is a *tour-de-force* of piano prowess for Parker, although Campbell on guitar and the twin fiddles of Pitts and Brower also get in their licks. "Avalon" was popularized by the Paul Whiteman Orchestra's recording in 1928, which featured a whistling-saw-like solo and an otherwise tricked-up, full-orchestra arrangement. The Doughboys' version of the catchy melody, recorded June 12, 1937, was more straightforward, very much in the Western-swing style, with the twin fiddles of Cliff Gross and Pitts leading off the track. Pitts and Knocky Parker contribute a "four-hands" piano solo, with Pitts on the bass end of the keyboard and Parker on the high end. Marvin Montgomery chips in one of his distinctive tenor banjo runs. Ramon DeArman's enthusiastic shouts are heard throughout the recording. Parker returns for a solo on his accordion as the recording comes to an abrupt, but clean, end (Montgomery, "Doughboy recording sessions," 12; "Paul Whiteman").

The camaraderie that contributed to the Doughboys' excellent ensemble sound was apparent one weekend afternoon at Marvin Montgomery's house as they were working out some new numbers. "I have a scratchy recording they made that afternoon on somebody's home equipment," Stout recalled. "There they are, talking over the numbers they were trying out, planning who would come in when for a solo, cutting up, laughing. Their sessions must all have been a good deal like that" ("Light Crust," 7).

For his part, Knocky Parker staunchly maintained that, as musicians, the Doughboys were second to no other Western swing band of the day, not even the vaunted Playboys. "We had better soloists than [Bob Wills] had," he said. "I suppose [having] this large orchestra was because he did not have outstanding soloists. He had [singer] Tommy [Duncan]. . . . We had [well-known] names, even then. . . . On the [Doughboys] records, it specified who was playing solos, you know. So and so on the piano. Bob Wills never did have that. . . . We were just, really, better musicians. When we were playing we didn't need drums at all or anything. . . . I don't think Bob Wills would agree with this, but I think that all the Doughboys would. . . . We could go against anybody" (Oral history, 7, reel two).

Of course, the Playboys had the advantage of Wills' great songwriting talent. The Doughboys usually recorded well-known standards or less well-known songs they picked up from other performers. Knocky Parker said the Doughboys mostly selected their own material, rather than having Art Satherley choose songs for them (Oral history, 1, reel three). But the Doughboys themselves were capable of writing songs. Zeke Campbell wrote "Dirty Dish Rag Blues." Knocky Parker wrote "Mama Gets What She Wants." Frank Reneau, the pianist who replaced Parker, wrote the instrumental "Slufoot on the Levee." Kenneth Pitts, Campbell, and Parker wrote "She's Too Young (to Play with the Boys)" and "Mean, Mean Mama (from Meana)," and Pitts wrote lyrics to the old fiddle breakdown "Cripple Creek." But, by far, the most prolific composer and lyricist among the group was Montgomery. The Doughboys recorded 34 songs written by Montgomery, four of which were unreleased (Montgomery, "Doughboy recording sessions," 21), but these tended to be novelty numbers, such as "Cross-eyed Cowboy from Abilene" or "We Must Have Beer."

"I wrote these terrible songs and I couldn't get anyone else to sing them, so I had to sing them myself," Montgomery later wrote in his self-deprecating style. "In hindsight, I think that if I'd been serious about my song writing, instead of doing the off-beat stuff, I might have come up with something worth listening to" ("Doughboy recording sessions," 3, 13). Kenneth Pitts' daughter Janis Stout remembered many other comic Doughboy songs, such as "Three Shif'less Skonks" and "The Preacher and the Bear." "As far as I can tell, the only money they made off this kind of stuff, or any of their records, was a fee for the recording session itself," Stout said. "If there were royalties, they couldn't have been much" ("Light Crust," 7).

The trademark Western-swing twin-fiddle style can be heard on many Doughboy recordings, yet Zeke Campbell felt that many of the Doughboys' recordings from the period did not reflect the band's live-radio sound. "Of course, on our recordings we didn't have a whole lot of that [the twin-fiddle style]. We started playing jazz stuff, and that was just usually one fiddle. On the Doughboy programs on the air, we generally played two fiddles. . . . Generally, on a recording, we'd play stuff that would go on the juke boxes, to dance to" (82–83).

The record business was different then. Sales to jukebox operators were important, and the Doughboys concentrated on that market. Radio (and the Depression) hit the recording industry hard. In 1927, about 104 million recordings and one million phonographs were manufactured. But by 1932, only six million records and 40,000 record players per year were produced. By the end of the 1930s, the recording industry had rebounded, thanks in no small part to coin-operated phonographs, or jukeboxes. About 400,000 jukeboxes were blasting popular music in restaurants, bars, and clubs, and they accounted for half of the 75 million records pressed (Rasmussen, 2).

The jukeboxes reached a working-class audience that preferred the Doughboys' style of music. "As coin men quickly realized in the

1930s, coin-operated phonographs were almost ideally designed to reach and satisfy audiences who preferred 'hillbilly,' 'Western,' and blues music," researcher Chris Rasmussen wrote. Up to this point, the recording companies had concentrated on marketing conventional popular music, but the jukeboxes helped to focus attention on the previously neglected market for such home-grown, rootsy music (2–3).

The Doughboys and others recorded songs that were not intended to be played on the radio, but could be played on honky-tonk jukeboxes. One of these was a Marvin Montgomery novelty tune, the provocatively named—even by today's standards—"Pussy, Pussy, Pussy" (Montgomery Oral history, 105, 194). "Uncle Art Satherley was looking for danceable, jukebox type of songs and we were giving him the stuff that we played on our daily radio programs," Marvin Montgomery wrote. "I think the reason Uncle Art took so many of my songs was because I was writing trash that we could never play on the air but which the jukebox operators liked, such as 'Pussy, Pussy, Pussy,' 'You Got What I Want,' 'Baby, Give Me Some of That,' 'She Gave Me the Bird,' etc." ("Doughboy recording sessions," 21).

Obviously, there is curiosity about a song with the title of "Pussy, Pussy, Pussy." Recorded on November 30, 1938, "Pussy, Pussy, Pussy" begins with a simple piano vamp by Knocky Parker. Then Marvin Montgomery, in falsetto, squeaks, "Say, fellers, I lost my little pussy cat. Will you help me find it?" Kenneth Pitts, Jim Boyd, Ramon DeArman, and Montgomery then join in a unison chorus, "Of course, of course, of course, of course, come on, gang, let's call it. . . . Here pussy, pussy, pussy, pussy, pussy, pussy, pussy, Where can you be?"

As you might surmise, a certain amount of alcohol was imbibed during the recording session. "I remember the session where we did 'Pussy, Pussy, Pussy,'" Marvin said. "It was over here in Dallas, at a warehouse where Brunswick Records, which was part of Columbia then, stored records and stuff. They had [electric] fans and stuff running. Some of the guys were down to their underwear. In those days, a lot of drinking went on those sessions. . . . 'Uncle Art' never did bring it to us, but he didn't mind the guys drinking. When we recorded that song, to me, that was one of the best sessions we ever had" (Oral history, 72–73). "Pussy, Pussy, Pussy" may be gimmicky, but it features a highly polished electric-guitar break by Zeke Campbell, a masterful piano run by Parker, and a fine swing fiddle break by Buck Buchanan, who had recently replaced Clifford Gross.

The record sold well as far away as New York, despite the understandable absence of radio airplay. "Knocky [Parker] went up to see ol' Fats Waller [the jazz pianist], the black guy who was real popular and wrote a lot of good music. He went to Fats and said, 'I'm Knocky Parker with the Light Crust Doughboys from Fort Worth, Texas.' Fats said, 'Oh, you were the boys who put out 'Pussy, Pussy, Pussy.' . . . There was nothing wrong [risqué] with the words. It's just the title. It's about a little girl who lost her pussycat and wanted the boys to help find the cat. The last cat they found, I say [in Marvin's "little-girl" voice], 'My pussy has no stripes. Besides, it ain't never smelled like that. Call my cat, boys, call my pussy.' It means they found a skunk, in other words" (Oral history, 130).

Montgomery reflected, "I don't know where I got the idea for that song. It's only got two chords. We had three chords and took one of them out. I was trying to write songs that I thought the jukeboxes would take, and they took that one. I wrote several songs along that line. I wrote quite a few cat songs. I finally did one called, 'We Found Our Little Pussycat.' . . . We did 'The Three Little Kittens,' 'The Tom Cat Rag.' I wrote quite a few cat songs, and I never did like cats. But my wife [Kathleen] did" (Oral history, 130).

Despite Marvin Montgomery's explanation, Knocky Parker said the refrain of "Pussy, Pussy, Pussy" was "unmistakable as to symbolism. . . . It did sell enormously on the juke boxes. People would see that name there, and this is enough for a nickel anytime. . . . People would get drunk, and start, you know, chanting the obscene words to this song, and feed that thing with nickels." In fact, Parker found double entendres in other Doughboy songs, such as "Dirty Dish Rag Blues," recorded by the Doughboys on November 10, 1938 and written by Zeke Campbell (Oral history, 5, reel one; 9, reel two). A traditional blues tune, Jim Boyd sang the melody. If "Dirty Dish

Rag Blues" is at all off-color, it's in the title's vague suggestion of menstruation:

> I went to wash my dishes,
> And the rag wasn't in the pan . . .
> Now I found that dirty dishrag in the garbage can.
> Now my gal left me, ran off with another man . . .
> Feel like that dishrag, laying in the garbage can.

But then, the obvious suggestiveness of "Pussy, Pussy, Pussy" is also mainly in the title of the song. In those days, that was enough. If the Doughboys ever sang a truly suggestive lyric, it was "Thousand Mile Blues," recorded the same day as "Dirty Dish Rag Blues":

> I've got a gal, built like a hog,
> When she starts to wiggle, she hollers, "Oh, you dog!"

Many, many years later, Montgomery was stunned to find that the Doughboys' recording of "Pussy, Pussy, Pussy" had been included in the soundtrack to the Demi Moore movie, *Striptease*. The novelty song is briefly used in a scene featuring a dancer in a cat outfit. The movie's closing credits list Marvin Montgomery as the composer and the Light Crust Doughboys as the performers. Finally, Marvin, the song's composer, received a payment. "They thought I was dead," he said wryly (Tarrant; Interview, May 3, 2001).

"Did You Ever Hear a String Band Swing?" was the first of Marvin Montgomery's songs to be recorded by the Doughboys. Recorded April 5, 1936, on the second day of the Doughboys' first post-Wills and Brown session, "Did You Ever Hear a String Band Swing?" is a jaunty, Dixieland-style tune in Montgomery's characteristic jesting style. Marvin takes the lead vocal, with Kenneth Pitts, Dick Reinhart, Bert Dodson and Clifford Gross performing a unison chorus in the style of many big-band recordings of the day.

As with most of the Doughboys' recordings, the arrangement allows plenty of room for instrumental solos. The tune features rhymed interplay between the Doughboys before each one takes an instrumental break and, two years before "Pussy, Pussy, Pussy," a feline reference. It works better on the recording than on the printed page:

> (Marvin, to "Abner" Pitts) Hi, there Ab, come on over here,
> There's music from that fiddle we all want to hear.
> ("Abner") Aw, now boys, I can't play my fiddle,
> 'cause hi, diddle, diddle, there's a cat in the fiddle.
> (Marvin) Aw, we don't mind that, 'cause if you play flat,
> we'll blame it on the cat. . . .
> (Marvin to Bert "Buddy" Dodson) All right now, Buddy, don't hide your face,
> Come on over here and slap that bass,
> ("Buddy") Aw now, fellers, I can't play the bass,
> Unless Zeke takes his guitar and sets me a pace.
> (Marvin) Well, you begin, we'll bring Zeke in, he has his gee-tar with him. . . .

Marvin estimated he wrote at least a thousand songs over the years (Oral history, 183). He reckoned his most successful composition was "It's Your Worry Now," a song recorded by the Doughboys and Denver Darling (a country singer best known as the co-composer of "Choo Choo Ch' Boogie"), among others:

> I don't care 'cause it's your worry now,
> You'll find out you were unfair to me,
> I gave all my love to you; now what more was I to do?
> I don't care 'cause it's your worry now.

"It's Your Worry Now" was recorded February 27, 1941, at the WBAP studios in Fort Worth's Blackstone Hotel. It features a simple arrangement of Zeke Campbell on guitar and the fiddles of Kenneth Pitts and Cecil Brower, with a vocal by J.B. Brinkley, who had recently joined the band (Montgomery, "Doughboy recording sessions," 18).

"We were playing in Conway, Arkansas, and I was walking down the street with Knocky Parker. I heard this little black girl. She was walking along with a black boy, and she said to him, 'It's your worry now.' I don't know what she meant, but that's what she said. . . . I've often wondered what he had to worry about. . . . I wrote that down and came home and wrote a song called, 'It's Your Worry Now.' It was one of the few songs that I wrote that wasn't trying to be funny. . . . I was trying to get songs off the beaten path. . . . If I had gone along like those guys who wrote regular country songs . . . I wouldn't be sitting here today. I'd be dead. . . . I would probably have gone the route that most of those guys went. They got the big head and drank a lot and smoked marijuana and all that stuff. They can't handle it. It messed them up pretty bad" (Oral history, 194–195; "Doughboy recording sessions," 18).

Of course, many of the Doughboys' 1930s-era songs are obscure today. But some are well-known, mainly through recordings by other, better-known artists. For example, "I'm a Ding-Dong Daddy from Dumas," the first song the Doughboys recorded under the guidance of Art Satherley at their initial session together in Fort Worth on April 4, 1936, was a standard at the time. It had been recorded by Louis Armstrong in 1930, and later was recorded by Bob Wills, Benny Goodman, and Phil Harris, among others. Armstrong's recording features his small jazz band playing the melody as an ensemble and as soloists for more than a minute before the great Satchmo's unmistakable voice is heard. But the Doughboys' version begins with a quick 24-second ensemble play-through of the melody before Dick Reinhart begins his self-assured reading of Texan Phil Baxter's lyric, inspired by a night spent in the small Texas Panhandle town of Dumas. The recording features acoustic-guitar solos by Zeke Campbell and Dick Reinhart, one of Marvin Montgomery's unmistakable banjo breaks, and what Montgomery called "a hot fiddle solo" by Kenneth Pitts.

The bouncy "Dusky Stevedore," recorded by the Doughboys June 12, 1937, had also previously been recorded by Louis Armstrong in 1933. The twin fiddles of Cliff Gross and Kenneth Pitts take the lead that is carried by Armstrong's trumpet in the earlier recording. Montgomery comes in later with a joyous banjo solo, and Parker takes a lively turn on the accordion. Reinhart and Ramon DeArman per-

form a rare vocal duet (Montgomery, "Doughboy recording sessions," 1, 5; "Louis Armstrong"). Despite being recorded by
Armstrong, one of the great figures in African-American history, the
lyrics of "Dusky Stevedore" would not pass the test of political cor-
rectness today:

> My dusky brow is wet,
> I doesn't mind the sweat,
> Of shoveling all the day long.

The Doughboys recorded their version of "(New) Jeep's Blues,"
the popular Duke Ellington tune, on November 30, 1938, not long
after Ellington had recorded the number himself. One of the
Doughboys' slower recordings, it is a good example of how the
Doughboys could take a jazz or big-band number and convert it
into their own style. While Duke Ellington recorded "Jeep's Blues"
as a full-fledged big-band number, the Doughboys give it a strong
Western-swing flavor. The Doughboys' recording is dominated by
the twin fiddles of Kenneth Pitts and Buck Buchanan. The tune features one of Zeke Campbell's most soulful, bluesy electric-guitar
solos, and another of Knocky Parker's Deep Ellum-style piano runs
(Montgomery, "Doughboy recording sessions," 9; "Complete Compositions").

The Doughboys' song choices were not always as stylish, to modern ears, as the songs of Louis Armstrong and Duke Ellington. They
recorded such 1930s standards as "My Buddy" and "Tea for Two,"
both still heard occasionally today, though usually thought of as
hopelessly corny.

"My Buddy," a sentimental popular tune written by Gus Kahn
and Walter Donaldson in 1922, had been made popular by Al Jolson.
No doubt it reminded many people of young men who did not return home from World War I. Buddy Clark made a popular recording of the song in 1930 with a weeping organ accompaniment. "My
Buddy" received the Western treatment from the Doughboys, with
twin fiddles by Cliff Gross and Kenneth Pitts, and a vocal trio of
Bert Dodson, Dick Reinhart, and Pitts singing the sad lyrics. The

Doughboys recorded it on May 26, 1936, while in Los Angeles filming *Oh Susanna* ("The Beat;" "Melody Lane;" Montgomery, "Doughboy recording sessions," 20).

Even by the 1930s, "Tea for Two" had become so overly familiar that it was a target for send-ups by groups like The Comedian Harmonists. But the old Tin Pan Alley chestnut by Vincent Youmans and Irving Caesar had also been recorded by such great jazz pianists as Art Tatum in 1923, and, more recently, Willie "The Lion" Smith in January 1939. It is likely that these versions inspired Knocky Parker and the Doughboys to record their instrumental version of the tune on June 14, 1939 ("Primarily A Cappella;" "Major Jazz;" "Willie 'The Lion;'" Montgomery, "Doughboy recording sessions," 11).

Obviously by their use of the Armstrong tunes, the Doughboys took considerable inspiration from Dixieland. Art Greenhaw said Montgomery, with his banjo virtuosity, brought a strong Dixieland influence to the Doughboys (February 19, 2002). "The Birth of the Blues" was a Dixieland-style number recorded by the Doughboys May 14, 1938. It features an insistent rhythm guitar and jaunty vocal from Dick Reinhart and a stylish electric guitar solo by Zeke Campbell. "Waiting on the Robert E. Lee," recorded on the same day, was already at least 25 years old when the Doughboys recorded the tune, and is one of the best-known Dixieland songs. The Doughboys' rendition opens with the twin fiddles of Cliff Gross and Kenneth Pitts establishing the melody before Reinhart begins his vocal. It features one of Knocky Parker's occasional accordion solos and a rare solo appearance by Pitts on piano, although strictly in a support role. Pitts apparently laid down his fiddle after the introduction, and sat down in front of the keyboard. Campbell contributes an intricate electric-guitar solo (Montgomery, "Doughboy recording sessions," 7, 8).

"Slow Down, Mr. Brown," a lively tune with a bouncy-Dixieland quality—apparently not a particularly well-known tune at the time it was recorded on May 14, 1938—has somehow earned a strange sort of immortality. The listeners of Louisville, Kentucky, public radio station WFPK voted the Doughboys' version of "Slow Down, Mr. Brown" as one of the "2,001 best songs of all-time," placing the song at number 1,048 on the list, between "Riot in Cell Block #9" by Wanda Jackson and "West End Blues" by Louis Armstrong. To show the range of material on the list, the listeners chose John Lennon's "Imagine" as the top song. "Slow Down, Mr. Brown" begins with Cliff Gross' and Kenneth Pitts' twin fiddles establishing the melody, and features an exuberant Dick Reinhart vocal, and a jumping piano solo by Knocky Parker. Ramon DeArman can be heard shouting encouragement to the band throughout the recording ("WFPK 2001;" Montgomery, "Doughboy recording sessions," 7).

Montgomery recalled making records when the master recordings were literally made of wax. "One of my first sessions they used a disc about this thick [indicates about one inch] of bees' wax. They'd tell you, 'If you make a mistake, don't quit unless we [the technicians] stop.' The minute they got one made, they'd put it in a big box, I guess they used some kind of ice, and when they got six of 'em [individual recordings] they'd send them up to the plant up in Connecticut to have 'em processed. They didn't even play them here. It was a one-time play thing [the discs would wear out quickly]. They just had to go by the ear. 'That's a good one. That's one we'll send up there.' That's the reason you hear a lot of mistakes on those old records" (Interview, March 21, 2001).

The Doughboys missed out on a hit or two in their time, including "Beer Barrel Polka." "We didn't record that. 'Uncle Art' wanted us to, and we should have. He sent the [demo] record down, but we didn't think it would go. About a year later, it was the biggest thing going [as a hit by the Andrews Sisters]" (Oral history, 105).

The Doughboys later played "Beer Barrel Polka" on the air, but called it "Roll Out the Barrel," because they were not permitted to make references to beer. "Yes, there was a lot of that stuff," Campbell laughed. "Radio was pretty clean in those days. 'Pistol Packin' Mama' had the line 'drinkin' beer in a cabaret.' They wouldn't even put that on the air" (83).

In his commentary on the Doughboys' recording career, Marvin Montgomery noted that most of the Doughboys were multi-talented musicians who could play more than one instrument if necessary. For example, when Ramon DeArman returned to the group in 1938, he and Jim Boyd shared the bass playing and rhythm guitar duties for the Doughboys. "You can identify DeArman's bass playing because he slapped it more than Boyd—also he was inclined to play a lot of backward bass," Montgomery said. "Example: Play a C chord in 2/4 time [and] you should play C then G—DeArman would reverse the rule and play G then C. Hence the term 'backward bass.' This was very upsetting to some of the musicians in the band, most especially Knocky Parker" ("Doughboy recording sessions," 8). But, later in his life, Knocky remembered DeArman fondly, and as a talented musician. "Ramon did not have the technique that Bert Dodson had, or that Jim Boyd had. And he would compensate for it with a swashbuckling slapping, I suppose. As a rhythm guitarist, Ramon was outstanding, very outstanding. He had rhythmic prowess" (Interview).

Current Doughboy Art Greenhaw says DeArman's bass playing was ahead of its time. "You hear some slapping of the bass violin which has been so identified with rockabilly music and Sun Studios in the mid-1950s," Greenhaw noted. "Keep in mind, the Doughboys were slapping bass for rhythmic effects 20 years earlier" (February 19, 2002).

Montgomery said the Doughboys made their best pre-war recordings in 1938–39. "That was when we made our best records, when Knocky [Parker] was playing piano" (Oral history, 113). Montgomery identified the June 14, 1939, session as the best recording session ever for the pre-war Doughboys. "We recorded in the old Brunswick Warehouse with no air conditioning and it was hot. We played with our shirts off and I suspect the bottle was passed around a few times among some of the band members as well as the boss man [Parker Willson]—why hide it—Willson, Brower, DeArman and [Art Satherley's associate] Don Law and maybe a swag or two by Boyd." In this day-long session, the Doughboys recorded "Let's Make Believe We're Sweethearts," "Thinking of You," "If I Didn't Care," "Mary Lou," "In Ol' Oklahoma," "Tea for Two," "Little Rock Get-a-way," and "The Cattle Call." They recorded the Marvin Montgomery compositions "She Gave Me the Bird," "Three Naughty Kittens," "We Must Have Beer," "The Texas Song of Pride," and the follow-up to the notorious "Pussy, Pussy, Pussy," "We Found Her Little Pussy Cat." They also recorded the Montgomery song, "Old November Moon," which was not released.

The day after what Montgomery calls the Doughboys best-ever session, they made what he said was their worst recording, on a song called "All Because of Lovin' You." "This is the worst performance of any song we had recorded so far. The Doughboys always played the same chords at the same time up until this song. I don't know how the mixed-up chords and bass got by Uncle Art and Pitts. Campbell and Pitts had the best ears in the band—not counting [Knocky] Parker" ("Doughboy recording sessions," 10–12).

Zeke Campbell considered fiddler Kenneth Pitts to be the group's musical leader in those days. Pitts generally decided on the tunes the Doughboys would play for a performance. "He would look back over old programs. He kept a record. . . . He'd look back and see we played something two months ago, and he'd say maybe it was time to play it again. He'd put it on, although maybe not in the same position. He was the one who arranged all the music" (85).

Pitts said that his role as arranger grew gradually after he joined the Doughboys from the Southern Melody Boys. Pitts' seriousness as a musician is apparent. "I, of course, did not know all the selections this new group knew and it was at this time that I began to write down melodies so that I might keep going properly when we were on the air," Pitts wrote. "Also, if I did not readily conceive of a proper duet harmony, after one of the other fellows had played or sung a melody to me, I would write out the duet harmony. This then led to, at times, writing out trios, and even sometimes quartets for vocal performance. From this continued experience, my ability to arrange for all sorts of groups began to develop" ("Light Crust," 2).

Pitts was not easily satisfied, with others or with himself. When Marvin Montgomery wrote his extensive discography of the Light Crust Doughboys in the late 1980s, he asked Kenneth Pitts to listen to a tape containing the recordings and then write his observations. You only need to see the Doughboys performing "Tiger Rag" in *Oh Susanna* to know Pitts could be as energetic as any of the Doughboys. But his writing reflects a brooding, self-critical side. Pitts later taught music in the Fort Worth schools, and his letter to Montgomery was characteristically professorial in tone:

> My first general observation of this entire effort is that the band might have been better off under the leadership of someone other than me. I failed in many instances to exhibit any imagination and foresight musically. All I wanted was to hear what I thought was good from a group with the ability that group had. My judgment business-wise and in the matter of dealing with other people was very minus. I needed to be much more 'political' that I was. On the other hand, I realize that it is easy to make great 'hindsights' about anything.

Pitts continued with an unsparing assessment of the Doughboys' recordings:

> My second general observation is that Mr. Satherley should have really taken us to task as to repertoire and style on the recordings. Possibly he was trying to let our natural inclinations lead us to some sound that would have been distinctive. As it was, the only distinctive sounds we had were Zeke Campbell, you [Montgomery], Knocky Parker and the twin-fiddle sound. But none of these four ever seemed to get together and really jell. However, I don't want these acid criticisms to be interpreted to mean the entire effort was a complete loss. (Montgomery, "Doughboy recording sessions," 21)

Kenneth Pitts wasn't indifferent to the Doughboys' recordings in particular; rather, he did not take any popular music very seriously. "All this country, and dance band, and popular music is just a way of making a living," he said. Pitts said he was more interested in the music he played in an informal string quartet. "We used to meet regularly for seven or eight years, and we practiced about four years before we ever put on a concert. When we put on the concert, it was good, I'll tell you. It's not that country music is not good. . . . It should be simple music. Of course, it's degenerated into a bunch of nothing" (Interview).

Pitts' somber professionalism was complemented by Montgomery's more exuberant nature. While Pitts was the Doughboys' primary arranger, Marvin handled the more offbeat material, of course, providing some of it himself. "He wrote a lot of tunes," Campbell said. "We got to playing a lot of stuff in harmony, a guitar lead, and fiddles playing in harmony. Marvin would write a lot of arrangements and stuff. We got to doing a lot of Dixieland stuff" (85).

The Light Crust Doughboys' foray into gospel music in the modern era was by no means their first experience with religious music. For a time, the group was doing two radio programs per week, Tuesday and Thursday, consisting entirely of religious songs. Willson received a fan letter praising the religious-music programs:

> Dear Mr. Parker [sic],
> I'm asking for the lovely song you sung on your religious program. Since I do not know the name, [I] will quote a few lines: "May God watch over thee and me, While we are apart one from the other . . ." I love your religious programs, and also have used Light Crust for some time, and I am, so my husband said, the "champion biscuit maker." (Kinney)

In a March 1941 session, the Doughboys cut some religious recordings. At the time, the Doughboys were featuring a vocal quartet made up of Joe Ferguson, J.B. Brinkley, Kenneth Pitts, and Parker Willson. "Parker Willson talked Uncle Art into letting the quartet do some religious songs," Marvin wrote in his Doughboys' discography. "Frank Reneau played the piano. Campbell and I went home." The songs were "Salvation Has Been Brought Down," "I Shall See Him By and By," "I Know I'll See Mother Again," and "Beyond the Clouds," which were not released. "These songs would never get on the juke boxes (our biggest market at that time); hence, Uncle Art was reluctant to release them," Montgomery wrote. "Besides, the

Chuck Wagon Gang and the Stamps-Baxter Quartets had that market sewed up" ("Doughboy recording sessions," 20).

As musicians, the Light Crust Doughboys often found work outside the Burrus Mill framework. The Doughboys, or most of the band, transcribed a daily radio program for "Crazy Water Crystals." Crazy Water Crystals were boiled down from the mineral water that came from the Crazy Woman Spring in Mineral Wells, a small city west of Fort Worth, which was then a major resort because of its natural springs. The spring water was promoted as a natural laxative and general promoter of good health. The crystals were stirred into regular tap water. Carr Collins, an insurance executive from Dallas and a key supporter and adviser to Lee O'Daniel, and Collins' brother Hal owned the company. Hal was the announcer for the radio program. This was a typical, subtly nuanced pitch for Crazy Crystals: "When I was a kid, I used to have a shotgun, and when that shotgun got clogged up, I used to take me a ramrod and give it a good cleaning. Now, Crazy Water does the same for you. When you get clogged up, Crazy Water is just like that ramrod" (Fowler and Crawford, 97).

The group performed anonymously on the Crazy Crystals program. "We didn't have any vocalists [on the program]," Knocky Parker recalled. "Everything was instrumental . . . [Playing the program on the air] They would tone down the music there, and put in an ad. Then, they'd bring up the music, tone it down again, and put in another ad. . . . They thought if we didn't have any vocals, there'd be no identification with the group, but anybody with any knowledge of the music could identify who it was, that banjo especially. This was Marvin Montgomery, no doubt. The tunes, the same arrangements, and everything. The name was something they cooked up, I have no idea [what it was]" (Oral history, 4, reel 3).

In fact, the group was given a different name for morning, noon, and night programs. In Parker's memory, the group would record 21 programs, seven for the morning, seven for noontime, and seven for late night, and play different styles for each. "In the morning—

wake up stuff, wake up, arise, alert songs . . . [for the nighttime program] the violins playing dreamy, dreamy music. ... Then, in the noonday program, we'd be a little bit freer," Knocky said. Parker remembered that a "stalwart faithful," not all of the Doughboys, participated in making the program (Oral history, 6, reel two; 4, reel three). The Crazy Crystals program was broadcast on WBAP and many other stations, including XEAW, a Mexican border station, which Carr Collins partly owned (Fowler and Crawford, 104).

Montgomery said the group recorded in the basement of the Crazy Hotel, owned by the Collinses. They were each paid a whole dollar for every program. "He [Carr Collins] had an orchestra, but he also wanted country music," Marvin remembered. "It was really loose, and we would holler. So, one night, I went to the mike and said, 'Mr. Collins, do you know what the old hen said when she laid the square egg?' He said, 'No.' I said, 'Ouch!' After that program, he really jumped on me. 'I don't want any jokes like that on this program.' That was really a bad joke in those days." Montgomery explained that recordings were still being made on acetate discs, each disc cost two or three dollars, and it was not possible to record over what had already been recorded (Schroeder, 101).

Knocky Parker recalled, "He [Carr Collins] had a quantity of big discs. . . . Big 15-minute, 16-inch discs. Slapped these discs on, and we'd start playing. . . . Slap on a record, we'd play 15 minutes; slap on another one . . . and then groggily going home, and work the next day" (Oral history, 4, reel three; 6, reel three).

Marvin remembered that Dizzy Dean, the St. Louis Cardinals pitcher and folk hero, later a beloved baseball broadcaster, visited Mineral Wells in the winter, and would sit in on the Doughboys radio sessions (Schroeder, 101).

Parker said the Doughboys, or part of the group, also recorded programs twice per week for Buck Brand Work Clothes in Fort Worth. "A fellow would say, 'Buck Brand Work Clothes wear like leather,' and then we'd play 'Leather Britches,' for the theme song." The band members received $3.50 apiece for each Buck Brand program. Anonymously recording the sponsored programs actually enhanced the Doughboys' reputation with other musicians, Knocky said. "This gave us the status of a staff band, and this was above the other groups, the Bill Boyds even, and Roy Newman" (Oral history, 4–5, reel three).

Similarly, the Doughboys' commercial recording experience was not strictly limited to their own discs. They sometimes served as session men on the recordings of other performers. For example, in 1937, Marvin Montgomery, Knocky Parker, Kenneth Pitts, and Zeke Campbell played on recording sessions for the Cowboy Ramblers, featuring brothers Bill and Jim Boyd, before Jim joined the Doughboys. The Cowboy Ramblers basically featured a traditional country string-band sound, but the Doughboys brought a Western-swing style to the Cowboy Ramblers' recordings (Govenar and Brakefield, 158). Knocky Parker said that the sessions with Bill Boyd were not as enjoyable as the Doughboys sessions because of the producer, Eli Oberstein. "He wasn't kind and friendly, the way that Don [Law] and Art were," Parker said. "We didn't joke, [or] have any camaraderie at all." Knocky said Boyd paid off his musicians on the recording sessions with suits he received from an advertiser on his radio program (Oral history, 9, reel two).

The Doughboys crossed paths again with Bob Wills for an historic recording session. On April 16, 1940, the Doughboys and the Texas Playboys both had sessions scheduled at the same studio, with the Playboys going first. Doughboy Joe Ferguson recalled that the session took place at the Blackstone Hotel in Fort Worth, although some remembered it being at the Burrus Mill studio. "I always remembered it being down at the Blackstone Hotel, because Zeke Campbell's guitar always picked up the police radio signals through his amp [laughs]. When Bob's band came out of the studio, Bob saw me and said, 'Hey, go get your horn. I've got something we're going to do.' That was when we made the 'New San Antonio Rose' and 'Big Beaver.' I'm in the horn section on the 'New San Antonio Rose' that they put the words to, and I'm in the horn section on 'Big Beaver'" (27–28).

Ferguson, who played with both the Doughboys and the Playboys, was asked what was the main difference in the two bands. "No drums [in the Doughboys]," he quickly responded. "The lack of a rhythm section. We still had the guitar and piano and banjo.

The only thing lacking was the drums." Ferguson agreed with the notion that the Texas Playboys were a dance band, while the Light Crust Doughboys made music mainly for listening pleasure, the Doughboys' rhythmic recordings notwithstanding (36–37).

The band's outside musical activities were not limited to radio shows and recording sessions. Ferguson said he played in a big band at the Hotel Texas, and on the Saturday midnight show at the Worth Theater while he was with the Doughboys. "I had too much going for me," he said ruefully (57). Marvin said he and other members of the Doughboys, like Bob Wills and Milton Brown before them, on occasion moonlighted by playing dances. In 1937, Montgomery, Reinhart, and Pitts played in a group representing Southern Select Beer, the "Southern Selectors." Two women, steel guitar player Vida Mae Spoon, and accordionist Gail Whitney, also played in the group. In a single evening, Montgomery said they might play in five Fort Worth honky tonks. "We were playing seven nights a week, five honky tonks a night, five hours a night, making $15 a week," Marvin said with a laugh (Interview, January 3, 2001). And for a time, they had a 15-minute show on KTAT in Fort Worth at 6:30 P.M. Monday through Saturday (Southern Selector). But it soon came to an end. "J. Paul Smith, the general manager of Burrus Mill, called us in after our picture appeared in the newspaper. He told us: 'You boys are going to have to decide who you want to play with, a beer company or a flour company.' So, naturally, we quit that job in a hurry" (Oral history, 99–100; Interview, Jan. 3, 2001).

The early 1940s were a time of tumult throughout the entire world, and so it was for the Light Crust Doughboys. Union membership, or lack of it, increasingly became an issue. For an April 24, 1940, recording session at the Doughboys' Burrus Mill radio studio in Saginaw, several regular members of the band had to be replaced by union members. "All of the major record labels had just signed contracts with the American Federation of Musicians and could not record non-union musicians. At that period in time, Local 72, American Federation of Musicians did not seem to want country-and-western musicians in their union, although Kenneth Pitts, Knocky Parker and I were attending Texas Christian University at the time as part-time students studying every music class available and probably knew more about music history, etc. than a good percentage of the union members," Marvin Montgomery wrote.

"[Cecil] Brower, having traveled with Ted Fio Rito's orchestra belonged to the Los Angeles local. Joe Ferguson came off the Bob Wills band and was a member of the Tulsa local [Brower and Ferguson were allowed to play on the session]," Montgomery wrote. "I had belonged to the AFM local in Newton, Iowa, before I came to Texas, but was not a member at the time of the session. Uncle Art decided to let me play on the session anyhow as there was not a union banjo player available. I don't know whether he listed me as playing on the session or not. I suppose that if the AFM had found out that Uncle Art had done such a dastardly deed as to let a non-union banjo player play with union musicians on a recording session they would have taken him out and hung him by his thumbs. But until now this fact has never been written down.

"And so, for this session only, some of the regular Doughboys had to be replaced by union pickers. Leroy Millican replaced [Zeke] Campbell on electric [guitar]. Babe Wright faced up to the piano in Parker's place. Paul Waggoner picked the rhythm guitar. . . . Singing and arranging was not yet controlled by the union and so Pitts, DeArman, Willson and Campbell could get in on the singing. Also Pitts wrote all the lead parts for the electric guitar to make the band sound as much like the Doughboys as possible" ("Doughboy recording sessions," 15).

Montgomery wrote that few people noticed that the "real" Doughboys were not playing on the recordings. Of the song "Alice Blue Gown," Montgomery wrote: "Up to now [in the union session] the piano was not featured on a solo due to the fact Willson and Uncle Art were afraid that people would realize that it was not Knocky Parker playing. But unto this day, none of the music historians, or anybody else has ever questioned me on who the musicians were on this session. It seems Pitts did a good job arranging the music in the Doughboy fashion regardless of the players. And we non-union musicians, who swore on a stack of old broken Doughboy 78s to keep the secret from our radio fans, did—until now!" ("Doughboy recording sessions," 16).

Ironically, the session produced the Doughboys biggest-selling record, the instrumental "South," which Montgomery estimated sold about 50,000 copies (Oral history, 105). "Uncle Art sent an old original record of this song down and Pitts wrote the parts out to sound like the Doughboys," Montgomery recalled ("Doughboy recording sessions," 16).

In a testament to the Doughboys sense of brotherhood, Montgomery said the Doughboys who played on the session shared their earnings with the others. "The union musicians on these sessions were paid union scale," he wrote. "Ferguson, Brower and I put the money we got in the pot and it was divided equally between Pitts, Campbell, Parker, DeArman, Brower, Ferguson and yours truly" ("Doughboy recording sessions," 15–16).

After World War II, the new Doughboys were all to become union musicians themselves, and they would pay a high price for their allegiance to the union.

The death of original Light Crust Doughboy Milton Brown in 1936 had saddened the Doughboys, but the tragic death of their friend and bandmate Ramon DeArman in 1940 hit the group especially hard. DeArman had been playing bass and singing with the group since the O'Daniel days. "He was working on his car in a garage, and the gas tank was leaking," Joe Ferguson remembered. "It [the gasoline] ran down a crack, and a guy fired up a welding torch on that end [of the floor]. The fire came down and got him underneath the car. He came out from under there and started running down North Main Street with fire burning him up. . . . I got to see him to talk to him, but there wasn't a thing on his body that wasn't burned up" (40). DeArman survived a few days in the hospital, but then died from his burns.

Marvin Montgomery said Ramon's death came as a terrible shock to the Doughboys. "Parker [Willson] came in and said, 'Ramon died last night.' I said, 'Don't tell the guys till after the [transcribed] program,' which he didn't," Montgomery recalled. "Then at noon we didn't do our regular [live] program. We had an organ player go out and play the program. None of the guys were up to it. He was burned over about 70 percent of his body. I went over to see him the day before he died, and I thought, he's never going to make it. Sure enough, he died that night.

"He should have been dead a long time before he died," Montgomery fondly remembered. "He rode a motorcycle, always having wrecks. . . . We'd get off in the afternoon and ol' Ramon and I would go out to Eagle Mountain Lake, we had a boat out there. One evening, he was out in the middle of the lake, and I was sitting on the pier watching him, and he jumped out or fell out, and the boat just circled around and he grabbed on to it" (Interview, Jan. 3, 2001).

Ferguson said the Doughboys lost more than a musician and singer when Ramon DeArman died. "That was a good boy," he recalled. "That ol' Ramon, he was our fun man. He was a comic, and I mean a good one, too. He was always doing something funny and making faces or whatever. He always had something [funny] to do." J.B. Brinkley replaced DeArman in the Doughboys. Brinkley played guitar, but Ferguson added, "He [Brinkley] was a good singer, a real good singer" (40).

Another, far less tragic, loss also hit the Doughboys around that time. For Marvin Montgomery, it was not the same after Knocky Parker decided to leave the band. Ironically, Marvin had a hand in Parker's decision. "After Knocky left, I really lost interest. . . . Kenneth [Pitts] and I talked him into going out to TCU [Texas Christian University], to earn a college degree. . . . He finally did, and he quit the Doughboys so he could go full-time." Knocky played on least some of the Doughboys' radio shows into 1942, and also played on some "side dates" with some of the individual Doughboys, but apparently left the employ of Burrus Mill as a full-time Doughboy at the end of 1940 or early 1941. Ted Druer first replaced Knocky, and then Frank Reneau (Parker Oral history, 2, reel three; Montgomery,

"Doughboy recording sessions," 17). After earning his bachelor's degree in music from TCU in 1942, Parker later earned a master's degree at Columbia University in New York City and an Ed.D. at the University of Kentucky (Camp; Faig).

Marvin Montgomery and Kenneth Pitts already were studying music at TCU, and Knocky himself apparently was attending a few night classes, but was not making significant progress toward a degree. "They kept telling the teacher about the piano player they had out there [at Burrus Mill], and what he was doing and all," Parker remembered. "One time, they arranged for me to go out and meet [the instructor] Keith Mixson, and that was the turning point of my life" (Oral history, 8, reel one).

Knocky remembered: "The first day I went out there, I was scared to death. The teacher had me come out there, and play 'The Man I Love.' I was trying to play it like I imagined it was written. The teacher saw, at once, what was going on. He stopped me and had me play others things, and arranged to give me free lessons in the afternoons" (Oral history, 7, reel three).

Knocky was required to give a recital for one of his classes at TCU. Marvin Montgomery and Kenneth Pitts attended Knocky's performance. The irrepressible Parker pulled his music-reading fakery again. "For his recital he played [George Gershwin's] 'Rhapsody in Blue,'" Montgomery recalled. "He never learned to read the music, but he had the music there and had a boy standing there turning the music. Kenneth [Pitts] and I and our wives were sitting back there. We were just laughing because we knew he wasn't reading it. He learned the music off the records" (Oral history, 120–21).

Marvin took "all the music classes they had" at TCU, but did not complete a degree. Pitts did earn a music degree from TCU, and later taught music in the Fort Worth schools (Montgomery interview, March 21, 2001).

Knocky Parker said the desire to achieve "legitimacy" probably had a lot to do with his decision to complete his education. "Parker Willson had the idea that since we were the Doughboys, and since we sold flour, and traveled all over the country, we ought to have more prestige than just a hillbilly band. . . . We would go into the

Blackstone Hotel to play our program, and go through the salon where the violins were playing some kind of sweet music, and we would think we were not up to their standards, or *they* would think we weren't. This is, somehow, the reason I got my doctorate, I am sure. Because I was working there as an 'inferior' musician with this hillbilly band" (Oral history, 9, reel one).

But despite his educational achievements, Knocky Parker always took great pride in the Light Crust Doughboys. "There's no doubt about it. The Doughboys band, I think, undoubtedly was, from the standpoint of musicianship, the very best of them all in the '30s," Knocky said in 1963. "We were very proud of our group. We were very, very proud of it. I know that they were very much concerned when I left. They were happy for me to be going to school because they had made it possible. But, they were still concerned because it broke up the group. . . . We had our things worked out, and all, and it wasn't quite the same" (Oral history, 2–3, reel three).

Montgomery said that the Doughboys missed Knocky Parker's piano playing almost immediately. Writing about the February 27, 1941, Fort Worth recording session, he said: "On this session, we begin to lose our Doughboy rhythm style, due somewhat to the fact . . . we missed the 2/4 beat of Parker's piano," Montgomery wrote. "Reneau's piano, to me, seems overbalanced, I think because they ('they' being Parker Willson?) wanted to get the many, many, many bass runs Reneau added (and there goes the rhythm)" ("Doughboy recording sessions," 18).

In the 1970s, after Scott Joplin's ragtime tune "The Entertainer" became popular again from being heard in the movie *The Sting*, Marvin Montgomery and Knocky Parker recorded an album of 100 ragtime tunes from the years 1880 to 1950. Their last recording together was a four-volume album, *Texas Swing*, recorded in 1986, not long before Knocky's death (Schreyer).

The end of the Light Crust Doughboys' peak period of radio popularity, and the original program, came with World War II. "During the war, they [Burrus Mill] didn't have any need for advertising their flour, because they were selling all they could to the armed services anyway, so they fired us by remote control," Campbell recalled matter-of-factly. "We were on vacation in July of 1942, and they sent word not to come back. There we were, all out of a job" (12).

"Along about then, the Light Crust company gave us two-week checks and said, 'Don't come back,'" remembered Joe Ferguson. "That took care of the Light Crust Doughboys at that point" (10).

Marvin said it did not come as a shock when Burrus Mill dropped the program. "They couldn't get tires or anything for that big bus to send us around [because of war rationing]," Marvin recalled. "And several of the guys already had been drafted. . . . So we didn't have a band. We were having a hard time getting musicians. . . . We had to keep getting guys to come in who couldn't play." Montgomery said Burrus Mill continued to sponsor a 15-minute noon-hour program, but, instead of music, the program featured a college professor discussing the war (Interview, March 21, 2001; Oral history, 87–88).

As the war began, like many friends and partners, the Doughboys went their separate ways. Cecil Brower and Joe Ferguson joined the Coast Guard. Zeke Campbell took a job as a bookkeeper at the Vital Food Company. Knocky Parker, who had only recently left the group, and Frank Reneau joined the Army. J.B. Brinkley was declared 4-F. Kenneth Pitts became an inspector at a company that produced shells for the Army. Marvin Montgomery became a swing shift supervisor at the Crown Machine and Tool Co., producing six-inch shells for the Navy (Montgomery, "Doughboy recording sessions," 19).

Joe Frank Ferguson remembered that, years later, several of the pre-war Doughboys got together for a private reunion at Marvin Montgomery's home. "That was before these tape things [recorders] you've got now. You made a little disk. We had a little reunion there with a bunch of us—Cecil [Brower] and Knocky [Parker] and Kenneth Pitts and myself and Marvin. I remember that I was sitting in the middle of the floor. I sang 'Stardust' and Cecil Brower took one of the most beautiful fiddle choruses I have ever heard in my life. I've never been able to feel it [the emotion of the song] like I did with him backing me up. I took a pretty good chorus on it myself, sitting there in the middle of the floor. I've got a tape of it. Marvin [Montgomery] has sent it to me" (41).

Much later, the survivors of the pre-war group performed again in public. "A guy [Mickey Smith, a Doughboys fan and photographer] called me and wanted to know if I wanted to go over [to the Pocket Sandwich Theatre]," Joe Ferguson recalled. "I said, 'Well, somebody would have to come and get me, because I'm not going to drive through that Dallas traffic, and I couldn't find the danged Pocket Theatre if I went over there.' He said, 'I'll come over and get you.' About 30 or 45 minutes after I got there, here came Zeke [Campbell]. Nobody knew anything about Zeke showing up. That left Zeke and I and Marvin—the only three left of that bunch, if you get right down to it" (24–25).

When World War II commenced and the group was disbanded, any reasonable person, including, no doubt, the Doughboys themselves, surely believed that the Light Crust Doughboys were history. And, indeed, for a time, they were. But the name of "the Light Crust Doughboys" was so well-known and well-loved in Texas and the Southwest that the Doughboys would have yet another incarnation, one that has lasted until this day.

The original Light Crust Doughboys, 1931. Left to right: Bob Wills, announcer Truett Kimzey, Milton Brown, and Herman Arnspiger.

The Light Crust Doughboys. circa 1932. Left to right: Clifton "Sleepy" Johnson, Bob Wills, Milton Brown, and W. Lee O'Daniel.

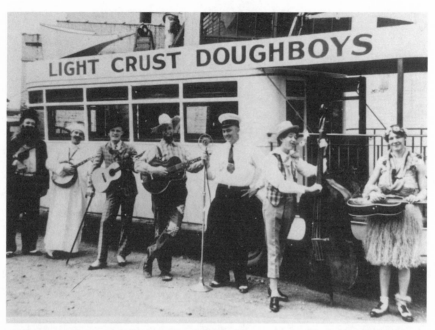

The Doughboys in comic regalia for a skit. Left to right: Clifford Gross, Sleepy Johnson, Leon Huff, Herman Arnspiger, W. Lee O'Daniel, Ramon DeArmon, and Leon McAuliffe.

Autographed photo from the Doughboys' former part-time announcer, Walter Cronkite.

The Wanderers. Dick Reinhart (first row, far left), Marvin Montgomery (first row, center), and Bert Dodson (second row, fourth
from left) would soon join the Light Crust Doughboys.

The famous custom tour bus. The photograph may have been taken
in California when the Doughboys went West to make the Gene Autry
movie. Left to right: Zeke Campbell (partially seen), Clifford Gross,
Dick Reinhart, Bert Dodson, Marvin Montgomery, Kenneth Pitts, and
announcer Eddie Dunn. The comic actor Smiley Burnette is at the far
right. The others are unidentified. The Texas Quality Network lineup
of stations can be seen on the bus: WBAP, Fort Worth; WFAA, Dallas;
KPRC, Houston; WOAI, San Antonio; WWL, New Orleans; KTHS,
Hot Springs, Ark.; KVOO, Tulsa, Okla.

The Light Crust Dough-boys in Hollywood to make *Oh Susanna* with Gene Autry. Left to right: Zeke Campbell, Dick Reinhart, Marvin Montgomery, Kenneth Pitts, Clifford Gross, and Bert Dodson.

Lobby card for *Oh Susanna*, the Doughboys' first movie with Gene Autry.

(left) Ad for Doughboys' recordings, 1936.

(below) The Doughboys' class clown, Ramon DeArmon, performing with a Gibson acoustic guitar (model L 10) that has been used on every Doughboys' recording session since the 1930s. Smokey Montgomery bought the guitar from DeArmon's widow after his fatal accident.

(below right) The Doughboys sampling the product, 1936, at KTHS in Hot Springs, Ark. Lower row, left to right: Marvin "Junior" Montgomery; Bert "Buddy" Dodson; Clifford "Doc" Gross. Back row, far left: Muryel "Zeke" Campbell; second from left: Dick "Bashful" Reinhart; third from left: announcer Eddie Dunn; fifth from left: Doughboys driver and radio engineer Jerry Stewart; second from right: Kenneth "Abner" Pitts; far right: Light Crust salesman James Pritchet. Others are unidentified.

The post-war Doughboys, performing at a rodeo in San Antonio, 1946. Left to right: Lefty Perkins, Carroll Hubbard, Charles "Knocky" Godwin, Hal Harris, Marvin Montgomery, Mel Cox, and Red Kidwell.

The Texo Hired Hands. Left to right: Paul Blunt, unidentified female singer, Carroll Hubbard, Smokey Montgomery, Lefty Perkins, Red Kidwell, and announcer Ted Gouldy.

(above) The Flying X Ranchboys, the first musical group to perform on television in Texas. First row, left to right: Bruce "Roscoe" Pierce, Smokey Montgomery, Lefty Perkins, Mel Cox, Carroll Hubbard, and Red Kidwell.

(right) Poster promoting Hank Thompson and the "Light Crust Doughboys," early '50s, care of Hank Thompson.

The '50s model Doughboys. Left to right: Paul Blunt, Johnny Strawn, Walter Hailey ("Jack Perry"), Jim Boyd, Ken Cobb, and Smokey Montgomery.

Smokey Montgomery in the early 1950s. Taken at Christopher Studio, Beaumont, Texas.

The Light Crust Doughboys performing in one of their many supermarket appearances, probably in the late '50s. Note the presence of drums, not a traditional Doughboys instrument.

The teenage rock 'n' roller Ronnie Dawson, surrounded by admirers, at a late '50s Doughboys show.

The Doughboys in the '70s. Left to right: Carroll Hubbard, Jim Boyd, Smokey Montgomery, Burney Annett, and Jerry Elliott.

The Doughboys are presented with Texas Senate Resolution #463, honoring the music and tradition of the band, at the state capitol, 1977. Left to right: Secretary of State Mark White, announcer Walter Hailey, Jim Boyd, Smokey Montgomery, Gov. Dolph Briscoe, Burney Annett, Jerry Elliott, Johnny Strawn, and State Sen. Peyton McKnight.

Smokey Montgomery's favorite piano player, Knocky Parker, in later years.

The 1980s Doughboys. Left to right: Johnny Strawn, Smokey Montgomery, Bill Simmons, Jerry Elliott, and Jim Boyd.

The 1990s Doughboys in rehearsal. Left to right: Bill Simmons, Art Greenhaw, Smokey Montgomery, Jim Baker, John Walden, and Jerry Elliot. Photograph by Randy Eli Grothe.

The Light Crust Doughboys on stage with the Southern Methodist University Mustang Band. Photograph by Barbara Montgomery.

The Doughboys with gospel singing legend James Blackwood (center, front). Clockwise from left: Smokey Montgomery, Jim Baker, John Walden, Art Greenhaw, Jerry Elliot, and Bill Simmons. The Doughboys recorded three Grammy-nominated CDs with Blackwood. Photograph by Jerry Crow.

Smokey Montgomery and Art Greenhaw with Hank Thompson (center), the Country Music Hall of Famer who performed with his band as "Hank Thompson and the Light Crust Doughboys" from 1952-54. Photograph by Barbara Montgomery.

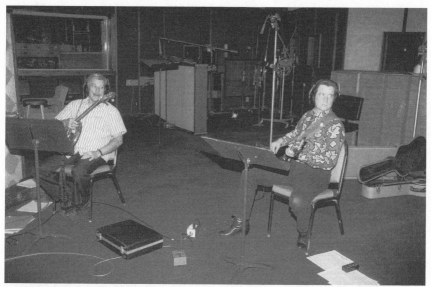

Smokey Montgomery and Art Greenhaw in the recording studio. Photograph by Jerry Crow.

Doughboy fiddlers John Walden and Jim Baker in the recording studio. Photograph by Jerry Crow.

The Doughboys with Nokie Edwards of the Ventures. Left to right: Jerry Elliott, John Walden, Edwards, and Smokey Montgomery. Photograph by Barbara Montgomery.

Displaying their Grammy nomination medallions, New York City, 1998. Left to right: Recording engineer Chuck Ebert, James Blackwood, Art Greenhaw, Smokey Montgomery, and Jim Baker.

Smokey Montgomery in the '90s. Photograph by Randy Eli Grothe.

Light Crust Doughboys, 1999. Front: Bill Simmons. Left to right: Jim Baker, John Walden, Jerry Elliott, Smokey Montgomery, and Art Greenhaw. Photograph copyright © J. Griffis Smith, used by permission *Texas Highways* magazine.

"I'm going back to work for the Doughboys"

♩. ♫ ♪

Texas after World War II was a rapidly changing place. The economy, jolted from the Depression by the demands of war production, continued to boom as thousands of young men returned home from the service. The massive migration from the farm to the cities, which began before the war, resumed, with country people being attracted by lots of good-paying jobs. Radio, dominated in the pre-war years by a handful of powerful regional stations, began to see an expansion into the smaller cities, as dozens of new stations went on the air (Head and Sterling, 40). Texans, flush with optimism, with money in their pockets, and more leisure time than ever before, were ready for life to return to normal, only better. All of these developments promoted the return of the Light Crust Doughboys.

The influx of people from the countryside influenced the programming on Dallas-area radio stations, and also paved the way for the return of the Doughboys. The Dallas-Fort Worth metropolitan area became a country music hotbed. WFAA and KRLD radio carried live country music programs that featured local, regional, and national performers. The Big D Jamboree, held in a large barn of a building called the Sportatorium on the edge of downtown Dallas, attracted some of the best-known names in country music and drew crowds of 4,000 people each Saturday night (Govenar and Brakefield, 161).

The war had brought a temporary end to the Light Crust Doughboys, but some members of the group continued to play together. Announcer Parker Willson got a job with the Duncan Coffee Company and hired several members of the Doughboys to play on a radio program as the "Coffee Grinders" from September 1942 to April 1946. Kenneth Pitts, Zeke Campbell, Cecil Brower, and J.B. Brinkley played with the Coffee Grinders at one time or another. Marvin Montgomery played sporadically on the program. Other members of the group included Red Woodward, Ted Graves, and Pappy McClough (Coffee Grinders).

Zeke managed to keep a job at the Swift Packing Company and play with the group on the side. "I went to play early in the morning, and then I would go to work out at Swift. Later, they changed the time of the program from about 8 A.M. to noon, and I couldn't get off, and had to quit playing with the 'Doughboys' [actually the Coffee Grinders]" (Oral history, 13).

Knocky Parker, who left the Doughboys just before World War II put an end to the existing group, entered the Army, and never returned to "hillbilly" music. "When I left to go into the Army, that was the end of all that," he said. "[After coming out of the Army in 1945] we took off right for Los Angeles, and left the [Western swing] scene entirely, forever, never to go back again. It couldn't have been the same." Although Knocky never returned to the Doughboys' style of music, he retained a great respect for Western music players. "The good hillbilly musicians fit easily into any good ensemble anywhere," he said. "Swing, jazz, either one, rag[time]. The same in reverse also." In LA, Knocky worked with drummer Zutty Single-ton, clarinetist Albert Nicholas and trombonist Vic Dickenson in a jazz group at the Cobra Club. "I was the only white musician in the band," he said. Knocky said the Los Angeles Board of Equalization asked him to leave the club because of a dispute that had arisen between Japanese citizens who had been detained during the war and the blacks who had moved into the neighborhood. But it turned out well because he ended up teaching at the University of Nevada in Reno and then moved on to Columbia University in New York where he earned his master's degree (Oral history, 6, reel three).

During the war, Montgomery worked full-time as a supervisor in a defense plant, leaving relatively little time for music. "I made shells for the Navy," Montgomery said. He was the supervisor of the swing shift at Crown Machine and Tool. Montgomery, who had attended what is now Iowa State University with the idea of becoming a high-school shop teacher, took a refresher course on machine shop work and badly injured one of his fingers, to the point where he had no feeling in it. "I've learned to play the banjo with no feeling in that finger," Montgomery said remorsefully (Oral history, 88).

Ironically, after World War II, the enduring popularity of the Light Crust Doughboys divided the musicians who had performed as the Doughboys in the pre-war era. "Burrus Mill made some overtures about wanting us to play [again] with them," Campbell recalled. "We told them it was going to cost more money or something like that. Anyway, they hired another group [to perform as the Doughboys]. They kind of hired Marvin out from under us to play banjo with them." Marvin replaced Walter Kirkes, the original banjo player in the reorganized Doughboys, on October 4, 1946 (Campbell, 15; "The New Light Crust Doughboys").

Bewley Mills had offered Marvin Montgomery a chance to play on a new program with Zeke Campbell and Kenneth Pitts. At first he accepted, but then he had a change of heart. "I had to go to the manager of the station and tell him, 'I can't play this Bewley Mills thing, because I'm going to go back to work for the Doughboys.' . . . He was really upset and kind of mad, but he was a pretty good friend," Marvin recalled (Oral history, 137).

Campbell and Pitts did play for the "Bewley Mills Gang" on KFJZ in Fort Worth. Montgomery occasionally played on the program. Campbell said the Bewley Mills program retained much of the Doughboys' musical excellence: "Because Ken Pitts believed in rehearsing. He got the music together for that [the Bewley Mills program], so it was pretty well-rehearsed, too," Campbell said (15, 80).

Zeke Campbell eventually left the full-time music business for an exciting new industry: television. In 1952, he went to work in the film library for WBAP-TV in Fort Worth, and stayed there in various capacities until 1976. After retiring from Channel 5, Campbell worked part-time at a music shop, "The Rhythm Band," until suffering a heart attack that forced him quit work in 1992 (19).

"My best memory [of the Doughboys] is that I learned a lot. When I came over here [Fort Worth], I was kind of raw. One thing is that I learned to play with other people. I'd been playing mostly by myself or with Jake Wright. I learned to play rhythm, to fit with a group. . . . I had the experience of working with some good musicians. I guess they were some of the best around here. We learned a little bit from everybody we were with. It kind of rubbed off on us" (52).

The chance to join the reorganized Light Crust Doughboys was too great for Marvin to resist, even if his old bandmates were not in the group. "When the war was over, Burrus Mill and the agency in charge [Tracy-Locke Advertising] wanted to come back into the country and western field. They hired a group off WFAA. It was a little trio [the Flying X Ranchboys]. . . The three guys were Mel Cox, Red Kidwell and Hal Harris. . . . They got a job on WFAA doing real pretty 'Sons of the Pioneers' types of things. The agency hired them [to be the new Doughboys] and added more guys to it. . . . They added Lefty Perkins on electric guitar and steel guitar, Charley Godwin, an accordion player and an ex-Marine, and Carroll Hubbard on fiddle." Cox also played fiddle and Kidwell played bass (Oral history, 131, 137). Hubbard had a reputation as a "hot fiddler," from his work with Roy Newman and his Boys, who performed on a popular WRR noontime show in Dallas (Govenar and Brakefield, 158).

"Of course, they [Tracy Locke] knew that I had been with the Doughboys for years and years. Burrus Mill asked them to see if they could get me back," Montgomery remembered. "Of course, I jumped at the chance to get back with them. . . . I went back with the Doughboys, and got the name 'Junior' again. I've been playing with them ever since. I guess if it wasn't for me, they'd have never lasted this long" (Oral history, 131, 137).

In late 1946, the new Doughboys were reaching 861,000 listeners per day on the live Texas Quality Network program, and the transcribed program reached another 2.285 million people, for a total of 3.146 million listeners, according to figures compiled by Burrus Mill. The new Doughboys program reached far beyond Texas and the Southwest, with stations in Alabama, Arkansas, California, Florida, Georgia, Louisiana, Mississippi, North Carolina, South Carolina, and Tennessee. The program was heard in such major cities as Atlanta, New Orleans, Memphis, and San Diego ("Burrus Mill and Elevator Company—Radio Stations"; "Network program").

The post-war Doughboys reached a new generation of fans. "I know a guy from Del Rio [Texas]," promoter Will Schotte related. "He knew when it was time to get up, because his mother would say, 'The Doughboys are on.' They came on from 6:45 to 7:00 in the morning." Schotte's friend was hearing one of the post-war Doughboy transcriptions, which the stations played at various times other than the Doughboys' traditional noon-hour time slot (Campbell, 73).

Texas music historian John Morthland believes the post-war Doughboys continued to have a major influence on the state's musicians. "When people talk about the Doughboys, they generally talk about the pre-war Doughboys," he said. "But obviously their power and their grip on the Texas public remained well after World War II. Bob Wills was out on the West Coast. They [the Doughboys] were sort of the standard bearers after Wills went West."

Morthland thinks the Doughboys may have had a more direct influence on the development of country music in Texas after World War II than Wills. "Being a little bit more of a string band [than Wills], when you get down to the smaller, honky-tonk type groups, maybe they were influenced a little bit more by the Doughboys than Bob Wills, because Wills had the big horn section," Morthland said. "After World War II, honky tonk really took over as the dominant form of country music. It was basically amplified string-band music. . . . The Doughboys were a little more traditional than Wills. Wills certainly was rooted in traditional fiddling in his own personal playing, but as far as the music in his bands went, he got pretty far away from that. The Doughboys swung like Wills did, they swung really hard, but they had a more traditional string-band lineup. Cliff Bruner's and Floyd Tillman's earliest records were really small-combo type records. I think they were influenced by the Doughboys as much as they were the Playboys" (Interview, May 4, 2001).

Marvin called the late '40s band the best musical aggregation to play under the Light Crust Doughboys name. "We had a good group when Knocky Parker was our piano player, that was a good musical group, too. But this other group was more modern," he said. "We did stuff that we shouldn't have done as the Doughboys, four-part harmony singing, stuff like that. We did a lot of popular songs" (Interview, January 3, 2001).

Recordings of the late-'40s Doughboys radio program reveal a band still rooted in the Western swing sound, but the vocal harmonies and Charley Godwin's accordion work brought a more polished pop quality to the group's music. As master of ceremonies, Mel Cox served as a jovial, professional announcer: "Here comes that Lefty [Perkins], big-foot Lefty, the boy with the thousand fingers, and his guitar all, well, wired up as usual. He's taking off on a special arrangement of 'Darling Nellie Gray.'" Perkins, in the tradition of Zeke Campbell, played a fluid, jazzy style of electric guitar. Cox and Carroll Hubbard played more-than-capable twin fiddles. Red Kidwell on bass and Marvin Montgomery on banjo gave the band its rhythm. The new Doughboys continued to perform comic novelty numbers, such as "I Wish I Was Single Again," which was interspersed with brief skits on marital "bliss:"

[Sound of a gavel, and courtroom chatter] Judge: Order in the court, order in the court. Why do you want a divorce, young man?
Young man: Well, sir, your honor, my wife said that all of my ancestors were monkeys, and that all monkeys had tails.

Judge: Mm-hmm. Well, I see nothing wrong with that.

Young man: But she said she wished I had a tail so she could cut it off as a neck piece!

Judge: Divorce granted!

. . . Wife [Montgomery, speaking in falsetto]: Hey, what do you mean staying out till 9 o' clock last night, you worm?

Husband: Now listen here, woman! Don't you call me a worm! That means "fight" in my country!

Wife: Well, why don't you fight?

Husband: Ain't my country! (Radio recordings)

Marvin did his best to keep the group together. Once, after Lefty Perkins had been "fired" by then-manager and group member Mel Cox in some kind of dispute over the radio program, the Doughboys were playing later in the day at Will Rogers Coliseum in Fort Worth. "Here came ol' Lefty with a hammer while we were up there playing. I saw him coming and I said, 'Mel, look!' There was a cop standing there, and Mel got the cop to stop him. They pulled him back off, and the next day I called Mel and said, 'Mel, don't can ol' Lefty.' We had a good thing going there" (Oral history, 77).

At various times, Perkins had played guitar with W. Lee O'Daniel's Hillbilly Boys, Bill Boyd's Cowboy Ramblers, the Universal Cowboys with Dick Reinhart and Cliff Gross, and the Musical Brownies after Milton Brown's death before joining the post-war Doughboys (Ginell, *Milton Brown*, 226; Montgomery, "Doughboy recording sessions," 8).

In the post-World War II incarnation of the Doughboys, the announcers, like the musicians, adopted a generic nickname: Jack Perry. "Since they were having new emcees every now and then, they decided to do the nickname thing with them," Marvin explained (Oral history, 138). The name belonged to the owner of Burrus Mill, Jack Perry Burrus. Mel Cox was the first Doughboy MC to go by the Jack Perry name (Montgomery, "Light Crust Doughboys announcers").

"Jack Perry" became the focus of the band in the post-war years. The band's letterhead stationery read, "Jack Perry and the Light Crust

Doughboys." When the Doughboys helped open a new tractor dealership in Shreveport, the news release read:

> They'll all be here—Jack Perry [Cox] who emcees the show, plays the violin and sings in the trio . . . Ezra [Carroll Hubbard], or "Ez" to the boys, the comedian and fiddle player, will delight lovers of old-time hoedowns with his varied accomplishments. You'll hear Junior, miracle-boy on the banjo, demonstrate his lightning speed on the strings. Knocky [Charley Godwin, not Knocky Parker], master of the squeeze box, accordion to you, will be featured in such difficult numbers as "Tico Tico" or "Accordiana." A highlight of each show will be the Doughboy trio—Sleepy, Curly and Jack [Red Kidwell, Hal Harris and Cox]—who excel on "My Adobe Hacienda." ("News release—Jack Perry)

Montgomery remembered that, as the comedian of the Doughboys, Hubbard would play the old fiddle favorite "Chicken Reel" [coincidentally, among the first tunes the Doughboys performed on the radio] and, to the audience's delight, "lay" an egg (Interview, March 21, 2001).

The Light Crust Doughboys' first return to radio lasted less than three years. The program on the Texas Quality Network began in late 1945 or early 1946 and concluded in mid-1948. The Doughboys' loyalty as members of the musicians' union put an end to the radio program.

As radio developed in the 1920s and 1930s, musicians weren't sure what to think of it. Clearly, it created new opportunities for musicians that had never existed before. A good example was the Light Crust Doughboys, who would never have existed without radio. On the other hand, to the extent that radio relied on recorded music, musicians had reason to fear that their occupations would be marginalized. Of course, musicians were needed to make recordings, but the recordings could then be played over and over again. At the same time, the labor unions were coming into their period of greatest power.

In this atmosphere arose a fierce leader of the American Federation of Musicians, James Caesar Petrillo. He called several strikes against radio, television, and recording companies to fight the increased use of recordings on the air ("Petrillo, James Caesar").

"Petrillo up in Chicago put a strike on union musicians making recordings," Montgomery said. "So we lost our jobs, as union musicians. And they [Burrus Mill] hired a scab outfit out of Dallas. They were on for about three months or so, with Jimmy Jeffries from the *Early Birds* show [on WFAA] as MC [under the name "Jack Perry"]. They just made transcriptions. They weren't on the air live. . . . The guys they [Burrus Mill] picked up were all union guys, but we had enough loyalty that we wouldn't do it [record the transcriptions] because we were union." The "real" Doughboys continued to perform live shows as the Light Crust Doughboys (Oral history, 138; Interview, January 3, 2001).

"Our main thing was making those transcriptions. Our live program was a minor thing at that time. We were going over to [Clifford] Herring's [recording studio] every afternoon and making a master transcription, from which they made thirty or forty more, with different commercials, the local commercials, for different stations in different parts of the country. We couldn't do any more of that recording," Montgomery lamented (Oral history, 138). Thus the Doughboys began a period of performing under a kaleidoscopic assortment of identities.

Fortunately for the "real" Doughboys, the union dispute came just as television was getting its start. The Doughboys, including Marvin Montgomery, Lefty Perkins, Red Kidwell, Carroll Hubbard, and master of ceremonies and vocalist Mel Cox, revived the Flying X Ranchboys. Bruce "Roscoe" Pierce, who had been a member of the Doughboys for a brief time just before Montgomery joined the group, replaced Hal Harris in the group. "After the union put a ban on recording, we went back on the air at WBAP [TV] as the Flying X Ranchboys," Marvin recalled. "This was in '48 and WBAP was just fixing to go on the air with television. We weren't on the radio station, but they'd send us out to the Lions Club and stuff demonstrating the television sets before they went on the air" (Interview, March 21, 2001).

The Ranchboys became the first musical group to perform on television in Texas, when WBAP-TV, the first television station making regular broadcasts in Texas, made its first test transmission on June 20, 1948 (Schroeder, 139; Ginell, *Milton Brown*, 226, 268). Former Doughboy Zeke Campbell played with the Ranchboys on that historic broadcast (Campbell, 17).

Frank Mills, for many years an announcer at WBAP radio and WBAP-TV, said the historic broadcast was something less than a polished gem. Mills was the master of ceremonies. He and the Ranchboys were waiting for a signal that they were on the air. In the meantime, they were entertaining the powerful WBAP and *Fort Worth Star-Telegram* owner Amon Carter and various dignitaries. The Ranchboys spent as much time cutting up as they did rehearsing their songs. "We had one clown who was always coming out with something; he'd walk up there in front of the camera with the microphone standing there; and he'd get off some corny joke and 'haw, haw, haw,'" Mills remembered. What Mills and the Ranchboys didn't know was that their clowning performance was indeed going out over the air. "All of sudden Johnny Smith [a broadcast engineer] burst through the door, and his face was red," Mills recalled. "He had run up the stairs; we were on about the second or third floor, and he hadn't stopped. 'You're on the air! You're on the air.' I said, 'Come on, Johnny.' 'The two [Tally] lights [on the cameras] are out; the phone's out!' he exclaimed." Mills quickly apologized to Carter and casually directed the Ranchboys to take it from the top. "I thought, this is the beginning and end of me in television," Mills said ruefully (Schroeder, 140).

The gaffe didn't hurt the careers of Mills or the Flying X Ranchboys. Beginning in September 1948, the Ranchboys performed for about a year on a WBAP (now KXAS, Channel 5) program sponsored by Philco (Remick; Flying X Ranchboys promotional card).

Marvin Montgomery acquired his nickname of "Smokey" while performing on television as a member of the Flying X Ranchboys.

> I lost my nickname [Junior] in September of 1948, when I went on Channel 5, which was WBAP at that time, the first TV sta-

tion in the area. It was black and white. . . . When I played my banjo, a solo, my hand would blur. That old black-and-white television couldn't keep up with my hand. Ol' Mel Cox, our MC, would say, "Junior will now smoke up the banjo." One night, he said, "Smokey will now smoke up the banjo." That's how I got a new nickname. I said, "Give me the name Smokey from now on, and get rid of 'Junior.'" (Oral history, 59)

"Roscoe" Pierce played the clown with the Flying X Ranchboys. Smokey remembered a near X-rated moment in a Ranchboys television performance when Roscoe, wearing long johns as "the man on the flying trapeze," accidentally became exposed. Fortunately, Smokey said, the camera at the time was on his upper body, but the studio audience roared with laughter.

"Here's what ended that group on television: Somebody talked Roscoe into running for the House of Representatives against [WBAP owner] Amon Carter's man. Roscoe said, 'When I get elected, I'll give all you guys jobs up in Washington, D.C.' And the next day we didn't have a job," Smokey said, laughing. "So about that time, that's when [WBAP radio farm-and-ranch announcer] Ted Gouldy called me to organize the Texo Hired Hands, and get back on the radio for Burrus Mill" (Interview, March 21, 2001).

Texo Livestock Feed was manufactured by Burrus Mill. As the Texo Hired Hands, they performed on WBAP at 12:30 P.M. daily from the Fort Worth Livestock Exchange. "We'd go out and make these trips around the state, down to Louisiana and Arkansas. In one town we'd be the Texo Hired Hands with Ted Gouldy as our MC, and the next town we'd be the Light Crust Doughboys. We'd just put on a Doughboys shirt, and Paul Blunt, our steel guitar player, would MC. He took the place of Mel Cox" (Interview, Jan. 3, 2001).

H.C. "Light Crust" Kelly, a top salesman for Light Crust, said Blunt was a natural as a master of ceremonies. "Paul was probably one of the funniest people I've ever known," Kelly said. "Real dry [sense of humor]. I don't think I ever heard him laugh. But he was real dry-witted, and he would get you tickled, and then he would *stomp* you, just keep goin'. [He was] one tremendous musician, he played the steel guitar and piano" (Interview, May 9, 2001).

Following the sound of WBAP's famous cowbell station identification, the Texo Hired Hands program began with the sound of a judge's gavel. Gouldy intoned, "We're going to try Texo!" One of the Hired Hands then responded, "Your honor, when you try Burrus Texo Feeds, you'll never use any other kind!" The band then played the energetic theme, sung to the tune of "Camptown Races," beginning "Texo Feed is in the bag . . . Burrus! Texo!" and ending: "Burrus' finest Texo Feed will get results for you!" As master of ceremonies, Gouldy employed a relatively staid style in comparison to the breezy approach of Eddie Dunn, Parker Willson, and Mel Cox.

On one program, the Hired Hands presented a show very reminiscent of the Doughboys' programs under W. Lee O'Daniel. It was an Armistice Day tribute to the U.S. armed forces. It featured a medley of the anthems representing each branch of the services, with Smokey Montgomery's lively banjo leading the way. A female vocalist, Shirley Davis, sang on a regular basis with the Hired Hands, and she delivered the popular World War II song, "Praise the Lord and Pass the Ammunition." In a polished, tenor voice, Paul Blunt (billed as "Paul Parker") sang the old tear-jerker, "My Buddy," which the Doughboys had recorded in the '30s. Gouldy solemnly recited the lyrics to "America the Beautiful," and the Hired Hands sang the melody as the program came to an end (Radio recordings).

Smokey Montgomery said although the Texo Hired Hands bore a striking similarity to the Light Crust Doughboys, some fans didn't realize they were one and the same. "We had a different theme song, one I fixed up," Montgomery remembered. "We went to the regular ol' Light Crust Doughboys-type music. We would go make personal appearances out at these little fairs and things. . . . We built up a pretty good following as the Hired Hands. A lot of the oldtimers would come up to us and say, 'Didn't you used to be with the Doughboys?'" (Oral history, 142; Remick).

In 1950, during the Texo Hired Hands/Light Crust Doughboys dual-identity days, Walter Hailey took over the "Jack Perry" persona for the Doughboys' live shows (Montgomery, "Light Crust Doughboys announcers").

Hailey did not play or sing with the group, unlike some MCs, such as Parker Willson and Mel Cox. But he was quite an entertainer, just the same. "I didn't carry a tune very well, and the boys used to reach over and kick my ankles and say, 'You're singing.'" In college at the University of Texas, Hailey had worked as a salesman for a future governor of Texas, John Connally, when Connally served as general manager of KVET in Austin, which was owned by the future president, Lyndon Johnson. He sold advertising and did a little announcing in college.

The job as the Doughboys MC came to Hailey in very routine fashion. "I went down and applied for a job after I got out of college. I went to the employment agency in Dallas. The job showed up and I just went in and applied for it."

As the new "Jack Perry," Hailey read commercial continuity and told jokes. "Told about how good the biscuits were, with the syrup dripping on your tie, you know. I was just selling flour," he wryly recalled. Hailey said the "Jack Perry" idea went all the way back to O'Daniel. "W. Lee O'Daniel mentioned his [own] name about 15 times on a program and mentioned Light Crust two or three times," Hailey said. Eventually, Burrus hit on the idea of a standard name for the masters of ceremonies, Hailey said.

"We started doing performances at [grocery store] openings and things like that, and the [local] radio stations would come out and broadcast those. So we got the radio for free. . . . We did some TV, you know. We'd go to places and perform, and if there was a TV camera there, they'd put us on."

Hailey gives the Light Crust Doughboys credit for launching his spectacular business career. He found that he relished performing before crowds. "I loved that. It helped me build a bunch of companies, by being able to get up and speak in front of people and being comfortable with groups. I was able to MC big banquets, got elected president of civic organizations and things, and I give the Doughboys credit for that."

Hailey always was aware of the Doughboys' mythic status. "W. Lee O'Daniel had been elected governor, the 'aha!' from Bob Wills. We were kind of a legend."

Eventually, Hailey was named sales manager of Burrus Mill. He continued as the master of ceremonies for the Doughboys' live shows until 1960. After that, he served as the band's MC on special occasions such as in 1989 when the Doughboys were inducted into the Texas Western Swing Hall of Fame (Montgomery, "Light Crust Doughboys announcers"). When he left Burrus Mill in 1955, he started Lone Star Life Insurance, primarily selling insurance to grocers, with whom he had established great contacts after his years with Burrus Mill and the Doughboys. "I sold a billion dollars worth of insurance in eight years, and sold the company to K-Mart for $78 million," he proudly recounts (Interview, Feb. 16, 2001).

In 1951, the Doughboys returned to the air, for what would be the final time on a regular basis. The membership remained Montgomery, Blunt, Hubbard, Kidwell, and Perkins. "They [Burrus] got on this Mutual Network, or the Dixie Network [a part of Mutual], and we did some of that," Montgomery said. "This was in 1951 and 1952." During that time, the group recorded transcriptions at the WFAA studios in Dallas. A WFAA announcer, Dan Valentine, took the "Jack Perry" role ("Light Crust Doughboys: Picture Chart"; Oral history, 145).

Smokey Montgomery remembered that, for the Dixie Network show, the Light Crust Doughboys played on Monday, Wednesday, and Friday programs. On Tuesday and Thursday, Smokey (on guitar) and Paul Blunt (on steel guitar) played with an organist and a singer, while a woman broadcaster delivered Light Crust recipes. "They [Burrus Mill] didn't want to pay enough to have the Doughboys five days," Smokey said wryly (Interview, May 28, 2001).

The early '50s radio incarnation of the Doughboys was heard on a far-flung network. "When we went off the air on a regular basis . . . we were on about 170 stations," Smokey said. "The Dixie Network just covered all of the stations south of the Mason-Dixon line, clear over to the coast. We didn't go out West, past New Mexico, but we went clear to the East Coast, Florida. We traveled down there, doing personal appearances and TV shows and everything else. . . . Every town that had a TV or radio station, we played programs on it, just to tell them that we were in town. Most of them [the programs] were, like, six o' clock in the morning. Most of the things we did were in little towns in Mississippi, or [for example] at the TV station in Wichita Falls" (Oral history, 115, 167).

But television was rapidly emerging and radio, in its original incarnation, was declining. The top 40 and middle-of-the-road (MOR) formats, both oriented toward the repetitive playing of hit records, would be radio's response. As the biographer of Top 40 radio pioneer Gordon McLendon, Ronald Garay, noted: "The power brokers on Madison Avenue had declared that 'television was king and radio was dead'"(Garay, 43). Radio wit Fred Allen commented that advertisers and network executives were abandoning radio "like the bones at a barbecue" (Whetmore, 102). The Light Crust Doughboys would be among the casualties.

For a time in the late 1940s and early 1950s, the "Light Crust Doughboys" imprimatur was placed on several transcribed radio programs, but the programs featured the Doughboys in name only. The popular Parker Willson served as the announcer for these programs.

For a brief period in 1949, after the regular Doughboys left radio in the union dispute over the recording of transcriptions, yodeling country singer Slim Whitman performed as the lead singer with a group of ersatz Light Crust Doughboys. On August 20, 1949, Slim made his premiere national radio appearance on the Mutual Network's "Smokey Mountain Hayride." He was hailed as "the new sensation of the folk music world." Within two weeks, he was the star attraction in a new show called "Slim Whitman and the Light Crust Doughboys." Years later, when asked if he sang with the Light Crust Doughboys, Whitman shot back, laughing, "What do you mean, did I ever sing with the Light Crust Doughboys? I *was* the Light Crust Doughboys." The show aired on Monday, Wednesday, and Friday evenings at about dinnertime and was sponsored by Chevrolet, which pulled out after about six months. In May 1950, Slim Whitman became a member of the "Louisiana Hayride," the Shreveport radio show best known for giving Elvis Presley wide exposure . Whitman went on to have major hits with "Indian Love Call," "China Doll," "Rose Marie," and others (Gibble, 60; Knapp).

Tennessee Ernie Ford, who had a huge hit with "Sixteen Tons" and became one of the most popular television stars of the 1950s and 1960s, made transcriptions in California under the Light Crust name for a brief time in 1951. "I had a transcription [of Ford], I don't know what happened to it," Smokey said. "He used the old theme song and the whole bit. He must have just started [his career], because it sounded like his voice hadn't changed yet. They'd send them [the transcriptions] into Fort Worth and Parker would put the commercials on, some way. Parker Willson was always on those. He had some good musicians on there, too good for the Doughboys. He [Ford] had people on that program from Hollywood" (Interview, Jan. 3, 2001).

A Light Crust Doughboys collector in Oklahoma City, Glenn White, has two of the Tennessee Ernie Ford/Doughboys 15-minute programs. White said the Doughboys connection to the program is tenuous, even though the programs opened with Parker Willson announcing, "The Light Crust Doughboys are on the air!" followed by a recording of the Light Crust Doughboys performing their famous theme. After the theme, Willson introduced "The Light Crust/ Tennessee Ernie Show." Ernie Ford then introduced keyboardist Billy Liebert and his band, along with Helen Forrest, who was well known as a vocalist with the Harry James, Artie Shaw, and Benny Goodman big bands. "The program consists of three or four songs, a few jokes, commercials, etc. Definitely, in my opinion, the Ernie Ford portion is spliced in," White said. White said he believes pioneering West Coast steel guitarist Speedy West also played on the programs (White, March 24, 2001).

From 1952 to 1954, Country Music Hall of Fame member Hank Thompson led a group that recorded transcriptions in Oklahoma City as the "Light Crust Doughboys" (Thompson interview, March 8, 2001). Thompson had already sold five million records with hits such as "Wild Side of Life" and "Waiting in the Lobby of Your Heart" ("Announcing the Light Crust Doughboys"). Meanwhile, a touring group of Doughboys led by Montgomery hit the road. "We were doing the traveling. We were doing the hard work. He [Thompson] was doing the easy work," Montgomery said (Oral history, 167).

Thompson said his group, the Brazos Valley Boys, doubled on the radio as the Light Crust Doughboys. "It was Hank Thompson as the 'Light Crust Doughboys.' It was my band, the Brazos Valley Boys. We were the 'Light Crust Doughboys.' Now, we were only the Light Crust Doughboys when we were on the radio." Thompson and his continued to make personal appearances as the Brazos Valley Boys.

The transcribed shows were recorded at WKY radio in Oklahoma City, where Thompson then lived. "Parker Willson would come up there every couple of weeks and we'd spend a couple of days recording. They were five days a week, 15 minutes. So we would record the shows about two or three weeks ahead of time. And then they'd come back later and we'd do them again." By that time, magnetic tape had been introduced, replacing the old transcriptions.

"I made out the programs. I selected the songs that we were going to do. Whatever songs we were doing on our appearances anyhow, we would do. We never went into the studio there and learned songs, everybody knew what we were going to do. We all got in the studio and had fun. After each song we'd clap our hands and whoop and holler like there was studio audience, and we'd laugh if something was funny. Of course, it was taped but it was still a live performance. If we really made a really bad blunder, then we'd go back and correct it, but otherwise, if there was some little mistake in there, we'd go on like it was a live show. Now once in awhile, Parker Willson might stumble on something, and we'd start over, because the commercials were keeping it on the radio. But if somebody hit a bad note or something, we'd let it slide." Thompson said it would take three or four hours to record a week's worth of programs, and they'd take a couple of days to record two weeks of performances.

Thompson said Burrus Mill asked him to do the Light Crust Doughboys radio show because of his already established reputation. "I was very popular at that time with a song called 'The Wild Side of Life,' a number-one record, and we were recognized as the number-one country-and-western band in America. We had a good following and it was actually a good vehicle for them to advertise with."

Thompson said the program more or less followed the traditional Doughboys format, with the addition of some of his own hits. "We did the popular songs of the day, the tunes that were in the top 10 in the music charts, and then I did songs that I had made famous, my repertoire. Then we'd do some old standards, things that people always enjoyed, and then we did some gospel numbers." And, of course, they always opened with the Light Crust Doughboys theme. "'Listen everybody from near and far'—I've picked it many a time," he said with a laugh.

But Thompson said there was clear difference in his music and the music of the "real" Doughboys. "Mine was more like what Milton Brown was doing when he left the Doughboys. He got drums and twin fiddles and actually started what we know as Western swing, where the Doughboys were using the banjo and [mostly] no electric instruments, other than a steel. They were more traditional."

"We were on throughout the entire South. We were on big stations like WSB in Atlanta, WWL in New Orleans, KWKH in Shreveport, and, of course, WBAP in Fort Worth. Of course, the South was where Light Crust Flour was distributed, and, oddly enough, it was not [distributed] in Oklahoma, and that's where we recorded the shows, but the show was not broadcast in Oklahoma" (Interview). A promotional poster from the time showed the program on 24 stations. Most of the stations broadcast the show at its traditional noon hour time, but some aired it as early as 7:30 A.M. and others as late as 5:30 P.M. ("Announcing the Light Crust Doughboys").

The Doughboys radio program with Hank Thompson as the star of the show came in the last days of the early radio era, the era of sponsored, regularly scheduled, entertainment programs that were distinct from one another. Radio's future would be tight playlists of hit records, commercial "spot sets," and brief news, weather, and traffic reports. "'Live' radio was fading," Thompson said. "Some of your network shows, like *Gunsmoke*, went into the '50s. But television was really taking hold about that time. We were kind of in the waning days of live radio. If I had had that show five or 10 years before, it would have been a great success. Radio became a secondary thing." Thompson said, finally, Burrus Mill did not renew the contract for the show. The final listing of the Light Crust Doughboys' radio program in the *Dallas Morning News* appeared on May 31, 1954 ("Radio Timetable").

During the same period, Thompson and his band performed on a three-times-weekly evening radio show for Falstaff beer on the Mutual network under the "Brazos Valley Boys" name, also recorded at WKY. "It was kind of ironic that here we were on radio as the Light Crust Doughboys, and we were also advertising Falstaff beer, and here was Smokey Montgomery and the Light Crust Doughboys [performing] over at another deal. I guess it was kind of confusing," Thompson said, chuckling. In fact, Thompson said he doubts many listeners realized the difference at the time between the radio Doughboys and the performing Doughboys.

Thompson said he was a fan of the Light Crust Doughboys as a boy in Waco. Like many Texans who grew up in the '30s and '40s, he related the story about hearing the Doughboys' radio program coming from open windows in the summer. "Oh, I grew up listening to the Light Crust Doughboys. Back there in the early '30s, they were probably the most popular band in the Southwest. Gosh, they were just a household word. . . . Then, later when Milton Brown pulled away from the Doughboys, and formed his own group, he [and his band] became probably the most popular musical group in the Southwest, but his very promising career was cut short by an automobile accident."

Thompson already was successful when he agreed to do the Doughboys radio program, but he was still thrilled by the opportunity to perform under the famous name.

> Sure, it was exciting. At that time, I didn't have the wildest dream that we [he and his band] would become the Light Crust Doughboys. "Someday, you'll be the Light Crust Doughboys!" That would have been the farthest thing from my mind as a young boy. So when I did get the chance [to do the radio show], I got to thinking, "Boy, I remember when I was kid listening, I never thought there would come a day when I would become the Light Crust Doughboys." I remember the first time I stepped on the stage of the Grand Ole

Opry, I thought, "How many times at home when I was a kid listening to this show, and I never dreamed that one day I'd be stepping on the stage here and be a part of it." I've never lost that. Even today, I'm always a little awed by it. (Interview)

Keeping up with the numerous incarnations of the Doughboys and Doughboys-related ensembles is a challenging task. At one time during Smokey's 11-year tenure as music director of the Big D Jamboree, an every-Saturday-night music show in downtown Dallas, the Doughboys performed on the regular Saturday-night show as the "Country Gentlemen."

"Same guys playing the same style," Smokey said. "At the Big D Jamboree, we were backing other acts. We always did one or two instrumentals. Paul [Blunt] would sing a song, maybe. Weekends, one way or another, we were playing someplace" (Interview, Jan. 3, 2001).

It was during one of these performances that Smokey encountered the fury of Jerry Lee Lewis, the untamed rock 'n' roller from Louisiana. "He was a wild man, and probably still is. I'm surprised he's still alive," Montgomery reflected. "I had this little piano there, and we finished up our part. I had a little mike of mine down at the piano. Paul Blunt had been playing that little piano. The mike wasn't working, so when Jerry came up, I reached in to get that mike out. He said, 'What are you doing?' I said, 'I'm taking this mike.' He said, 'Leave that mike in there.' I said, 'No, it's my mike.' He said, 'No,' and he was going to whip me right there on the stage, so I left the mike in there and walked off. He was ready to cold cock me, one of the many times that I've been cold-cocked" (Oral history, 187).

Smokey remembered another rough-and-tumble story involving Blunt. "The first day he came to work, he'd been doing a recording session the night before with Lefty Frizzell. That was back when everybody got drunk on these recording sessions," Smokey said with a rueful laugh. "Lefty was an old prize fighter, and cold-cocked him and broke his jaw. Paul came in with his mouth wired shut. He could just open it up enough to eat soup. That was his first day with the

Texo Hired Hands, alias, Light Crust Doughboys." Somehow, Blunt sang on the program (Interview, January 3, 2001).

The Doughboys were touring Texas as the Country Gentlemen when they crossed paths with an up and coming young singer named Elvis Presley. This would have been in late 1954 or early 1955 when Elvis was frequently performing in East Texas while appearing every Saturday night on the "Louisiana Hayride" radio program in Shreveport, Louisiana (Guralnick). "We played a show down in Beaumont with him. This was just before he became a big deal. Johnny Hicks was the MC, and Presley was telling these little risqué jokes and doing his shaking, which was all right," Montgomery remembered.

> All the time these little 16-year-old girls were just lining up at the theater to see him. After every show, Johnny would say, "Elvis, you don't need to tell those jokes, just sing." Presley would say, "Yes sir, Mr. Hicks," but he'd still tell the jokes on the next show. . . . We did three shows a day in this theater. We had to go get him; he'd go back to the room and go to sleep. He was a sleepy kid; he was lazy or something. He was tired, I guess. We'd go wake him up: "Time to do a show, Elvis! Come on!" (Oral history, 70)

Montgomery also got a revealing look at the way Elvis' famous (or infamous) manager, Colonel Tom Parker, operated. "The first time that ol' Colonel Parker heard Elvis in person, he [Parker] had just broken up with Eddy Arnold. . . . He was looking for somebody, and he came to the Big D Jamboree to see Presley. We had Presley on that night. . . . Mr. [Ed] McLemore, the owner of the Big D Jamboree and the Sportatorium was lining up shows to go down to Houston to play a series of shows down there. I was supposed the get the guys [in the Country Gentlemen] to take off from their jobs to go down. 'Marvin,' he said, 'how much money are the guys going to need to go to Houston.' I said, 'Thirty dollars a day.' Ol' Colonel said, 'Oh, you don't have to pay them $30 a day. Union scale is only eighteen.' It wasn't any of his business. . . . He thought he was doing

Mr. McLemore a good deed, I guess. But he was a scrounger." McLemore paid the $30 a day, Montgomery said (Montgomery oral history, 71–72).

For many years after their regular radio program ended, the Doughboys continued to appear on behalf of Light Crust Flour. Their days as network radio stars were over, but, as dedicated musicians, they carried on. And their fans still came out to hear them. By the mid-'50s, Carroll Hubbard, Red Kidwell, and Lefty Perkins had been replaced by Johnny Strawn on fiddle, Ken Cobb on bass, and the pre-war Doughboy, Jim Boyd, on guitar and vocals, although Perkins continued to play occasional gigs with the group ("Light Crust Doughboys: Picture Chart"). Burrus Mill salesman H.C. Kelly arranged performances for the Doughboys during the mid- and late-1950s in West Texas and New Mexico.

"We used the Doughboys for sales promotion," Kelly said. "We would get them [grocery stores] to run a promotion and advertise a lot, and for that we would schedule a Doughboys show for maybe two or three days during the week. We would schedule the Doughboys to appear at the schools, the radio stations and TV stations, and we'd promote the devil out of the Doughboys at the same time promoting the merchant we were in town for. We would try to develop good will and good PR." Kelley said he and the Doughboys brought Light Crust to the number-one position in flour sales in his market, which centered around Midland-Odessa. "Within about a year and a half, we not only were number one, but we were outselling all of our competitors combined. And that was through the use of the Light Crust Doughboys. They were really terrific" (Interview, May 7, 2001).

Jerry Elliott, who would join the Doughboys in 1960, explained, "My understanding was they had to buy a boxcar load of Light Crust Flour products to get the Doughboys to come and perform. And they had these sales people in different areas, and we would go and report to those guys. They'd get us up early the next morning. We'd start off with a radio program. We'd run out to a school and do a school program. Then we'd go to a grocery store and we'd play two or three hours at one, and we'd load up right quick and eat lunch and run to another one, and play a couple hours. It was nothing to play three or four grocery stores a day. And, boy, it was not an easy thing.

"They [Burrus Mill] were running us all down into Mississippi, and from Mississippi we'd go way down into South Texas. They had us on the road all the time," Elliott recalled. "They'd send us out at the first of the week and we'd go down into Louisiana and be there a couple of days. We'd stay gone four or five days, sometimes even longer before we'd come back in. . . . Another guitarist, Billy Hudson [who joined the group in the early '60s], and I drove that station wagon hundreds of miles every week, touring grocery store shows for the Burrus Mill from one end of Texas to the other. The best ride was to be propped in the middle of the back seat where you could sleep." If Smokey Montgomery was on the trip, the middle seat belonged to him. "I held that middle seat for so long that, for years, I couldn't sleep unless I sat straight up and held a banjo in my lap," Smokey said wryly (Elliott interview, March 8, 2001; Smith, 18).

Montgomery readily agreed that playing the supermarkets was hard work. "At one time HEB had 15 stores in San Antone. We played 'em all in one day, 30 minutes each. We started at six o' clock in the morning and got through at eight o' clock at night without eating. And then they wanted us to go out and play an insane asylum, which we did. We were making 30 bucks a day [each], which in those days was pretty good money. They were paying all our meals, but, boy, they got their money's worth" (Interview, Jan. 3, 2001).

The Doughboys were in enough demand during this period that sometimes they were literally in several places at once. "Sometimes they'd have two or three different groups of Light Crust Doughboys playing at the same time," Elliott said. "They'd have the regular group going, and they'd get another group going and send 'em out to West Texas. The main group would be down in South Texas someplace. Smokey would handle the whole thing" (Interview, March 8, 2001).

The appearances at the grocery stores were a long way from glamorous gigs. "Sometimes we'd be outside on a flatbed truck. Sometimes we'd be inside the store and have a stage set up. Sometimes we did it on the flat ground. We just made do," Kelly said (Interview, May 9, 2001). Elliott said while the crowds for the supermarket openings might not have been as large as the throngs that the Doughboys enjoyed for their appearances in the '30s and '40s, the fans' warmhearted feelings for the group remained strong. "Mostly it was drop-in people, but they did some advertising in the local papers, and we had quite a few grocery shoppers who would gather round for 30 or 40 minutes, and kept going and coming. Somebody would always call up and say, 'Hey, we just heard your broadcast on radio. And we'd love for the Doughboys to come out and eat supper with us.' And we never had to worry about food. We always had plenty to eat" (Interview, March 8, 2001).

The promotional visits gave the Doughboys continued exposure on local radio and television. "We would book them for free appearances on many TV stations. Every one that was in the area we played in, we'd book 'em," Kelly said. "We booked 'em at all of the radio stations. . . . Sometimes we'd be booked on a radio program at six o'clock in the morning, and sometimes late at night. Some of the Doughboys sort of got mad at me because I booked 'em just about as many places as I could, and I worked the hell out of them. But I figured if they were out there [West Texas], we might as well spend our time working. And it really paid off. I was friends with all of them. I don't think any of them got real mad at me" (Interview, May 7, 2001).

Kelly received a thank-you letter from John Vacca, the station manager of KOSA-TV in Odessa:

> Just thought I'd drop a note of appreciation to you in the regard to the many appearances of the Light Crust Doughboys on Channel 7. Wish that you would make it a point to express our pleasure to the group for their excellent on-the-air presentations and the high quality of their musical abilities. It is always a pleasure to know that the Doughboys are in our area and we are pleased with the opportunity to present them on Channel 7. Needless to say, we are looking forward to the group's next appearance in May. We know that our audience feels the same way about the Doughboys. (Vacca, April 18, 1958)

The programs were easy-going, loose affairs. Kelly sometimes would sing with the Doughboys. In a fine Irish tenor, Kelly would sing such traditional numbers as "When Irish Eyes are Smiling" and "McNamara's Band." On one such occasion, for a broadcast on Odessa radio station KOYL, announcer Walter Hailey gave the young salesman a jocular introduction:

> Speaking of gold mines, we have a young man who's a gold mine right here in the Light Crust organization, young man name of "Light Crust" Kelly. [Off-mike, one of the Doughboys, "Oh, he's a go-getter!"] He's a go-getter! He's the type fella, he got his wife a job and he takes her to work every morning, and about 5:30 he gets up and goes and gets her. Ha! Ha! Ha! Get that? A real "go get her!" And here comes "Light Crust" Kelly, now, the pride of Burrus Mill, with "Tura Lura Lura!" (KOYL recording)

"When Walter Hailey couldn't come and do the part of 'Jack Perry,' Jim Boyd would take over and MC," Kelly said. "And he was a good MC."

On occasion, Kelly would sing an ode to Light Crust Flour on the local broadcasts:

> Light Crust baking, so tender and light,
> Use Light Crust Flour, do your baking right,
> Buy a sack or a carton, and then you will see,
> Exactly how wonderful Light Crust can be. (KOYL recording)

Kelly said the Doughboys were always a fun-loving, lighthearted bunch. "I tell you what, if you were a stick in the mud, they'd absolutely bury you. . . . They were all such great friends. They just loved each other," Kelly said affectionately. "We didn't have anything but fun. There weren't any downers at all" (Interview, May 9, 2001).

♪ ♫ ♪

Ever adventurous, the Doughboys flirted with rock 'n' roll in the late 1950s and early 1960s when Smokey discovered a young singer and musician named Ronnie Dawson.

Dawson was a recent Waxachachie High School graduate whose father's band, Pinky Dawson and the Manhattan Merry Makers, had its own radio shows on KRLD and WRR in Dallas. Dawson and his rock 'n' roll band, Ronnie Dee and the D Men, had won the Big D Jamboree talent show ten weeks in row. He had some regional hits with "Action Packed" and "Rockin' Bones," and later signed with Dick Clark's Swan Records and appeared on *American Bandstand*.

"I looked like I was about 12 at the time, which always helped," Dawson recalled. "I did a pretty hot act. . . . They just kind of adopted me. I really didn't know the Doughboys. My father had been a Western-swing musician during that era, and I had certainly heard of them, but I didn't realize till long after I had left them that they probably were the first Western-swing band. . . . And I really didn't care at the time. Man, I wanted to do rock 'n' roll. It was my music, it was . the music of my time" (Dawson interview, March 14, 2001).

"He was playing with the Big D Jamboree with a little band," Smokey said. "And I was taking the Doughboys out [on the road], and we'd come home and do the Big D Jamboree. And I started taking Ronnie along as one of the members [of the Doughboys]. Ronnie played pretty good rhythm guitar. This was when rock 'n' roll was just starting." The Doughboys continued to play their usual repertoire of Western swing music, but added Dawson's raw rock 'n' roll numbers to their show.

"First time I took him down to Lake Charles, Louisiana, we were doing a bunch of shows. A [Burrus Mill] salesman said, 'What'd you bring that blond-haired kid for?' Ronnie looked like he was about 16; he probably was about 18, maybe 17. He had that burr haircut, blond hair. We went out to play at a high school, and he was singing Elvis Presley songs, 'Heartbreak Hotel' and those things, and these high-school kids would just go crazy. They didn't want us to quit. So when we left, the [salesman] guy said, 'Be sure and bring that blond-haired kid again next time'" (Interview, January 3, 2001).

Dawson said Smokey Montgomery recognized at the time that the Doughboys could use an infusion of young blood. "That was probably the most uncool time of all for fiddle bands like the Doughboys," he explained. "So that's one of the reasons they took me with them, because they had to play a lot of school programs. I've even heard Smokey say that. He wanted me to do what I did at the Big D Jamboree, which was 'Johnny B. Goode' and stuff like that." Supposedly with-it teenagers held fiddle bands in such low regard at the time that Dawson tried to keep his membership in the Doughboys from his friends. "I didn't want anybody to know that I was playing with them. They'd have made fun of me. Completely uncool."

But Ronnie said he and the Light Crust Doughboys were good for each other. "I think I gave them a burst of energy, and they did me, too. It was a good exchange. They really needed it [a boost]. They'd been playing and traveling, and God a'mighty, they were jaded, and talked negative. And they stopped doing that. They actually started having fun on the gigs.

"I certainly benefited from them and I liked them. But I was a source of entertainment for them, because I could tell them stories about my love life, and they loved it. It was just a good meeting. We had a lot of fun."

Of course, introducing a hot-shot rock 'n' roller into a group of old pros like the Doughboys did not go down without some conflict. In particular, Dawson clashed with Jim Boyd. "He just treated me like a kid for a long time. Finally, we were eating and something happened and he kind of threw his napkin at me. And I just got him off [alone] later on, and had an adult conversation with him, and that's all it took. After that, he respected me, and we were very cordial. Jim was like that, he would test you. But I'm glad he did. You just have to tell them, 'Hey, get off my ass, man. I'm just as serious [about music] as you are.'"

Playing rock 'n' roll with a Western-swing band like the Doughboys presented some definite challenges. "I played my own lead [guitar], which really did help," Dawson said. "But they didn't have a drummer. Sometimes Johnny [Strawn], the fiddle player, would play his mandolin. He hated to take his fiddle out of the case at schools because they'd hoot. You know, kids would make fun it. That's how divided it was [between rock 'n' roll and country-style music] at the time. He would say, 'God, I hate to take this old fiddle out of the case. I wish I had me a guitar.'"

Dawson, sporting a then-stylish flattop and known as "the Blonde Bomber," would be featured on two or three rock 'n' roll numbers and, especially for the school assemblies, the rest of the Doughboys again showed their remarkable ability to adapt other styles of music to their own.

"We got into doing things like 'Red River Rock,' that was an instrumental that was popular," Dawson recalled. "It had a rockin' beat. I could do the Chuck Berry kind-of-thing on the guitar, and the steel guitar player and Johnny on the fiddle could do the lead that the organ did on the record. And then they'd do, 'Sugartime,' that was kind of a pop song at the time [by the McGuire Sisters]. . . . They [the Doughboys] would have done all right [at the school assemblies] anyway. They would have gone in there and altered the show a little bit. But I could connect with the kids. They'd look up and see me, and I was one of them. 'Cool. They've got one of our guys.' I'm telling you, man, these kids would go crazy. We'd announce, 'After school, you kids come down and see us, we'll be down at the HEB food store at four o' clock,' and, man, we'd have 300 or 400 kids show up.

"We played black schools. They loved it. I'd do 'Rock Me Baby,' or something like that, and they'd go crazy. [Laughing] I can see us going in there now, these guys with string ties on. . . . There would be a little stiffness at first, but before the end of it, they'd be into it. It was great. We were one of the few bands that could get into schools and do shows, because the show was clean and they [the Doughboys] were part of Texas history."

Ronnie sometimes felt stretched between two eras, playing grocery-store parking lots with the Light Crust Doughboys while preparing for a network television appearance on *American Bandstand*. "We were playing in Melvin, Alabama. This was a place that had dirt streets. We'd played all day long around the Meridian [Mississippi] area, and Melvin wasn't very far from there. So we went down there. And we pulled up in front of this grocery store and it was a dirt street, had one gas pump out there. Something you'd see in *Deliverance*. And we were on this flatbed truck playing, and the bass player, Kenneth Cobb, turned around and said, 'If Dick Clark could only see you now.'"

"We worked our asses off, man. I'm telling you. . . . Sometimes we'd drive all night long and start in playing as soon as we'd get there, seven or eight o' clock in the morning, and play all day long. We did that a lot of times. . . . If we went to San Antonio and this [Burrus Mill] salesman booked H.E. Butt [HEB] food stores, we'd play every damn one of them in a day. I'm telling you, it was work" (Interview).

Smokey said Ronnie Dawson also spent some time in the recording studio with the Light Crust Doughboys. They recorded a couple of Montgomery-composed songs, "Poor Little Johnny Smith" and "Pauline." The records were sold at the Doughboys' performances, but never distributed until they were included on a recent CD of Dawson's songs. Smokey said the CD sold about 20,000 copies. "That's pretty good for a local CD," he said (Interview, January 3, 2001).

Dawson played with the Doughboys until 1961, when he started playing at the Levee Club, a popular Dallas nightspot owned by Smokey's friend Ed Bernet (a former pro football player with the Dallas Texans of the American Football League), where Smokey himself also became a regular. In fact, Montgomery, Dawson, Bernet, and Bob Christopher formed a very popular singing group called "The Levee Singers."

The Levee Singers started off performing folk music. "You know, the Kingston Trio was popular at the time, so I jumped on that and did several of their things. Later on, we did a lot of country," Dawson recalled. Dawson said the Levee Singers made some recordings, mainly to sell in the club. But he is still quite proud of one of them. "We had one album [called *Take Me Home*] that we did original material on. And now it really sounds good. I'm really proud of that. It was the best musical statement that we ever made" (Interview).

Five nights a week, Sunday through Thursday, the Levee Singers packed 'em in at 5616 Mockingbird Lane in Dallas. "We had folks we'd see nearly every night," Dawson said. "Sometimes there'd be so many people that it'd take us 15 minutes to get to the stage." Dawson met his wife Christi at the club. "It was such a small place, with these long tables that were so narrow that you were rubbing knees with the people across from you. Everybody knew everybody else," Christi recalled.

Bob Christopher mused, "I sat down and did the numbers once. We played five nights a week for 10 years. A million people saw us at The Levee, and probably six million saw us live across the country"(Weitz).

Smokey Montgomery said the Levee Singers went big time when they got a Hollywood manager, David Sonntag, who booked them in Las Vegas.

> He booked us at the Sands and the Mapes [Hotel]. We opened the Joey Bishop show [at the Sands]. That's when the Rat Pack [Bishop, Frank Sinatra, Dean Martin, Sammy Davis, Jr., and Peter Lawford] was there. The Bishop show followed Sammy Davis, Jr. Sammy stayed and watched us rehearse, came and shook our hands and wished us all good luck. Guys like that were really good to us. Milton Berle was the same way. We played the Mapes and got to know Milton there. When we opened at the Sands that first night, we were all kind of scared. And in the front row was Milton Berle. He jumped up and yelled, "There's my boys, there's my boys!" And we weren't scared anymore. He got the crowd with us. Really, the big guys will help you all they can if they like you. (Interview, March 21, 2001)

The Levee Singers performed on many network television shows in the '60s, including *The Danny Kaye Show, The Hollywood Palace, Hootenanny,* and *The Jimmy Dean Show.* Dean, the lanky country singer best known for "Big Bad John," had loved the Light Crust Doughboys when he was growing up in West Texas, and Smokey found again that his Doughboys connection always followed him. "He [Dean] had us sing the [Light Crust Doughboys] theme song on the dress rehearsal, just as a gag," Smokey remembered. "So the director of the show said, 'Be ready to do that theme song because he'll probably have you do it on the live show.' And sure enough he did.

"That's the show that Minnie Pearl was on, and Lefty Frizzell, and Roger Miller. Roger played with the Doughboys for awhile, just [occasional] jobs, he played fiddle with us. He said, 'Marvin, I just came from making a hit record.' They flew in from Nashville, him and Lefty Frizzell. And it was 'King of the Road.' It sure was a hit record, biggest one he ever wrote" (Interview, January 3, 2001).

In recent years, Ronnie Dawson and Bernet performed with Doughboys at the Pocket Sandwich Theatre. "The crowd didn't want 'em to quit," Smokey remembered (Interview, January 3, 2001). Then, in early 2001, all four Levee Singers reunited to play a benefit in Dallas for breast cancer research (Weitz).

Dawson has become a cult favorite, especially in Great Britain. Compilations of his early recordings have been successful there. Recent recordings by Dawson have been included in the movies *Primary Colors* with John Travolta and *Simpatico* with Jeff Bridges and Sharon Stone, and Dawson has performed in recent years on *Late Night with Conan O'Brien* and on Willie Nelson's Fourth of July picnic.

♩ ♪ ♪

While the Doughboys scuffled along the back roads of Texas, Smokey Montgomery was forging a remarkable career in music separate from the Doughboys and even the Levee Singers. In 1959, Smokey released an album of banjo instrumentals called *Banjo Capers*. WBAP declared "Marvin Montgomery Day" and the station played selections from the recording throughout the day. Even then, the banjo seemed to suffer from a lack of respect. An article by Jack Gordon appeared in the *Fort Worth Press* with a headline that delivered a barbed compliment: "Banjo? Oh, NO! But Yes, if Marvin Montgomery Plays It." Gordon wrote admiringly, "When Marvin

Montgomery, the world's greatest banjoist, puts that banjo on his knee, the world's most reviled musical instrument sounds like the Philharmonic" (Gordon).

After Artie Glenn wrote "Crying in the Chapel" in 1954 (see Chapter 1), he joined the Light Crust Doughboys and played bass and sang with the group for several years. During that time, he and Smokey Montgomery started a music publishing company, Glendell Music Company, which still exists today. Although it didn't publish "Crying in the Chapel," the publishing company had a number of profitable songs. Glendell published "Percolator," which was the B-side of the Boots Randolph hit "Yakety Sax" and was a big hit in Europe (Montgomery interview, May 28, 2001).

Improbably, Smokey became a renowned Top 40 record producer in the pre-Beatles era. He produced Bruce Channel's "Hey Baby" in 1962. The smash hit was recorded in Fort Worth. Smokey played piano on the record and the versatile Ronnie Dawson played drums.

Smokey also became Channel's manager. "Bruce was traveling, so I would take off from the Levee and fly with him. One time we flew up to Minneapolis and rented a car, and drove way over to South Dakota someplace, played a show, got back to the airport about 12 midnight, got on a plane, went to New York, and the next night we were up in Canada someplace. I had to do all the driving, get him there and get him back. He'd go off and leave his clothes hanging in the hotel if I wasn't there to get 'em" (Interview, Jan. 3, 2001).

"Hey Baby" featured the bluesy harmonica playing of Delbert McClinton, the white rhythm 'n' blues singer known in later years for "Givin' It Up for Your Love" and other hits. McClinton's harp blowing on the record caught the ear of a young Englishman named John Lennon, who produced similar sounds on the Beatles' first three British hits, "Love Me Do," "Please Please Me," and "From Me to You." The Beatles even performed "Hey Baby" in their early stage act (*Beatles Anthology*, 101).

Smokey took Channel, along with McClinton, to England for a four-month tour. While there, they unwittingly witnessed a musical revolution in the making. They met the Beatles at The Cavern, the dank Liverpool club where they got their start. "They knew about

Delbert's mouth-organ playing," Montgomery remembered. "Delbert, of course, had his mouth organ with him, and he sat there and played with them. And the Beatles just went nuts. They didn't have their regular drummer with them then [this would have been shortly before Ringo Starr replaced Pete Best]. It was just a little club downstairs. I wish I had remembered more about that, but later on, I realized what we were watching" (Interview, March 21, 2001).

"I just stayed over there two weeks and came back. We had other acts on the shows, too, five or six different acts. Well, we get over there and the back-up band were young kids, and they didn't know the song, but they read music. So I immediately had to sit down and write out the music to 'Hey, Baby' for them.

"We went down to London on a Saturday to do a radio show on the BBC [British Broadcasting Corporation], and Delbert went and left his mouth organs in the taxi cab. Bruce had to do his show on Saturday night without Delbert because Delbert couldn't find his mouth organ." For some reason, they could not find replacement mouth organs in London. "Sunday morning, Major Bill [Smith, a former Air Force officer who owned a regional label that initially released "Hey, Baby" and the local studio where the tune was recorded] called some guy in New York and told him to meet my plane with a set of mouth organs. So we flew seven hours on an old prop plane, and landed there, and the guy brought the mouth organs. We went back to London, got back there late Sunday night. And the guy with the taxi cab had turned these mouth organs in, and Delbert had his own mouth organs back. That was an exciting day." While in London, Smokey produced a recording session with McClinton for Decca. In the session, McClinton recorded a Smokey Montgomery song, "Angel Eyes" (Interview, Jan. 3, 2001).

In 1963, Smokey produced an even bigger hit, "Hey, Paula" by Paul and Paula, and played guitar and vibes on the recording. Again, Ronnie Dawson played drums, and latter-day Doughboy Bill Simmons played piano. Like "Hey Baby," "Hey, Paula" was recorded in Fort Worth. "Paula" was actually Jill Jackson. "A mama called me from Brownwood. The kids were going to school at that little church college [Howard Payne]," Smokey remembered. "She said, 'My daughter's a singer, can you listen to her sing?' I said, 'Yeah, I'm doing a session tomorrow, and I'll get through at four o' clock, come see me.' I'd listen to everything, because you never did know when you're going to find a good one. She [the mother] had Ray Hildebrand, 'Paul,' with 'em. We named 'em 'Paul and Paula.'

"So she [Jill] sang a song, the one that's on the back of 'Hey, Paula,' and I didn't think much of it. And she [the mother] said, 'Sing that song that Ray wrote for you last night.' And they sang it together, and it was 'Hey, Paula.' And what struck me was that they sang together, there was no harmony part. I'd heard duets before, between a boy and girl, but there was always a harmony part. So I said while we're waiting [another singer was supposed to be there, but he hadn't shown up], why don't we record this 'Hey, Paula.' We did it with just four pieces.

"About that time, Major Bill came in, and he said, 'Make me an acetate and I'll take it over to KFJZ tonight and see what they think of it.' Well, about midnight, the phone rang and it was Major Bill. 'Hey, Marv, we've got a cotton pickin' hit!' He said, 'Get Bill Simmons, and come down tomorrow and we'll add the vibes and the electric organ'" (Interview, January 3, 2001). Released in late 1962, "Hey Paula" earned a gold record, sold 1,030,000 copies, and became the second-biggest selling single of 1963 ("2 Singles," 3).

"I'll die with them, if they'll keep me that long."

♪. ♫ ♪

That the Light Crust Doughboys survived the period from the mid-'50s to the
'90s is not so much a miracle as a testament to the love that the members—in
particular Smokey Montgomery—had
for their music. Through all of the social
and musical changes of the '60s, '70s,
'80s, and '90s—a time extending from the
days of black-and-white TV to the arrival
of the Internet—the Light Crust
Doughboys never quit playing their
music. Grocery store openings, county
fairs, conventions, private parties—the
venues were not glamorous, but they
played them just the same.

During the time Smokey was performing with the Levee Singers, he became a
part-time Light Crust Doughboy. "I was
playing The Levee and I wasn't going on

many of the trips then, but I was doing the payroll and turning the bills into the mill," Smokey remembered. "Jerry Elliott did a lot of those [trips]. And Bill Hudson, who played the guitar, and Paul Blunt. Lefty Perkins made a lot of those trips" (Montgomery oral history, 168; Elliott interview, March 8, 2001).

The arrival of Jerry Elliott signals the beginning of the modern period of the Doughboys. Jerry joined the Doughboys as a substitute for Smokey during Smokey's Levee Club days. Elliott is a distant second in seniority with the Doughboys, at a considerable 40-plus years of service. "In any other group, that would sound like a very long time," he said with a smile (Smith, 19).

Elliott was working as the manager of a Fort Worth music store. Doughboy Johnny Strawn, a fiddler modern-day Doughboy Art Greenhaw calls "a great artist," actually invited Elliott to join the group. "Johnny came by out at the store one time, and said, 'Hey, Smokey is going into the Levee Club, and we need somebody to go on the road with us and play banjo.' And I said, 'I don't play banjo very much. I play a few chords well enough to sell 'em across the counter.' And he said, 'Well, that'll do. You sing and sing parts, so come to work with us on the road with the Doughboys.' And I said, 'Well, I said I don't even know how to play banjo very well.' And he said, 'Well, tune it like a guitar.' Well, I tried that a time or two, but that just didn't work for me. So I learned to play the darn thing right, but I never could play solos like Smokey. But I knew all the chords and did all the vocals, so I started traveling with the Doughboys."

Elliott met Johnny Strawn when Jerry joined Ted Daffan and his Texans. Daffan, a member of the Nashville Song Writers Hall of Fame, wrote "Born to Lose" and had a million-selling hit with the song in 1942 before Ray Charles covered it with enormous success in 1962. Daffan also had a big hit with his song "I'm a Fool to Care," which also was a hit in 1954 for Les Paul and Mary Ford. Strawn was a member of Daffan's band. At one time, Strawn played in Country Music Hall of Famer Red Foley's band (Interview, March 8, 2001; "Ted Daffan").

Jerry had started his musical career at the age of 11 playing and singing on a Lufkin, Texas, radio station with his brother D.L. After graduating from high school, he played with groups in Galveston, in Hawaii while in the Navy, and in Fort Worth, where he played with Daffan.

Incidentally, Elliott's stint with Ted Daffan is not Daffan's only connection to the Light Crust Doughboys. In his extensive discography of the Doughboys recordings, Smokey Montgomery related a story from a February 27, 1941, session at WBAP in Fort Worth. "Ted Daffan had just finished a session or was waiting to do a session or was hoping Uncle Art would let him do a session. Daffan kept pestering Uncle Art to let him play on a Doughboy record, and so, with Parker Willson's approval, Daffan played on two songs with us on this session: 'Too Late' and 'Five Long Years.' This is the only time Daffan ever played with the Doughboys" ("Doughboy recording sessions," 17).

Elliott led a Western-swing dance band at Rosa's club, formerly Stella's, in Fort Worth for five years before joining the Doughboys. "I had some of the best fiddle men to ever play Western swing in that band. [Former Doughboy] Buck Buchanan, of course, and Johnny [Strawn] started off with me out there. A boy by the name of Buddy Wallis, who doesn't play anymore. A real fine trumpet player named Jim Oliver [who plays today with the Doughboys on occasion; see Chapter 1]. Some of the greatest five years of my life were running that band."

Jerry said his family, like many in rural Texas, was so poor that they had no radio, and so he didn't hear much of the Light Crust Doughboys. "Finally my dad had a little Chevrolet car that he traded for an old radio, one of those old church steeple-looking radios. It had an 'A' battery, and a 'B' battery, and a 'C' battery, and you had to have an antenna way up in the air. I started listening to the Grand Ole Opry on Saturday night. That was about the only time we played the old radio."

It was a time when people did for themselves, out of necessity. "My dad built an old homemade guitar. He played a little bit of guitar. And he took a trunk of a tree and sawed it out into a block, and started carving a guitar out of it. He showed me three chords on a guitar." When the farm belonging to Jerry's family began to decline, Jerry's father went to find work at a manufacturing plant in the East Texas town of Diboll. "From there, things got better and better" (Interview, March 8, 2001).

While the personnel has changed frequently over the years, the Light Crust Doughboys have continued to perform unabated in some fashion since their rebirth after World War II. After Ed Bernet sold the Levee in 1971, Smokey returned to performing with the Doughboys on a regular basis (Remick). "We'll go out and play now and the older folks will come up to us and say, 'We didn't know you were still going,'" Montgomery said. "But we never stopped." In the mid-1980s, the Doughboys were making 50–60 appearances a year, and selling 250 recordings per week to fans who mailed in coupons from the back of Light Crust Flour packages. "We appeared in Mt. Pleasant [Texas] recently and drew the biggest crowd I've ever had," Smokey commented in the '80s. "We're a name to the older people" (Remick).

Smokey said Burrus Mill sponsored the Doughboys until Cargill, the giant food-manufacturing corporation, bought the company in 1972 (Bruemmer), which continued to sponsor the group on tours around Texas. "They sent a guy [Gary Murray] down there [to Fort Worth] who didn't know anything about country music, but he liked us. He sent us out for the mill, to San Antonio and around," Smokey said. "They [the Doughboys' shows] were along the same lines as what we do now," Smokey said. "Personal appearances. We'd just get out and do a 30- or 40-minute show, singing country-and-western songs. Store openings mostly. Big supermarkets."

"Murray said, 'You guys keep booking the Doughboys, but don't play any honky tonks, just play the [radio] program stuff. We don't want to get a reputation as a honky-tonk band.' So we've kept doing it. The store had to buy so much flour to get us. Then they'd get us for nothing" (Oral history, 148).

The grocery-store shows continued for most of the '70s and '80s. In the mid-1980s, a *Cargill News* story evocatively described a

Doughboys performance at a supermarket in Corsicana. Playing plenty of Western swing standards, many, like "San Antonio Rose" or "Milk Cow Blues" associated with Bob Wills, the Doughboys would, as much as possible, re-create the sights and sounds of the old radio show:

> Shifting from ballads to country blues and Western swing with a few hymns thrown in for good measure, the Doughboys prove with every performance that their appeal is ageless. The combination is a guaranteed crowd-pleaser, skillfully nudging the memories of the older folks, making a colorful chapter of Texas history come alive for a slightly younger set and enchanting a new generation with the Doughboys' special brand of Texas-style music. (Johnson, 15)

The shows would provide the audience with an entertaining history lesson on Western swing and country-and-western music, with plenty of anecdotes about the Doughboys' radio days and W. Lee O'Daniel. During that period, Jim Boyd took a prominent role in the Doughboys' performances:

> Of course, no performance would be complete without bass player and vocalist Jim Boyd's irrepressible "commercials" for Light Crust Flour. In one of them, Boyd urges customers to rush right in to Mr. Fullerton's store after the concert to "pick up some of that good Light Crust Cornbread mix—the mix that's guaranteed to please, guaranteed to be the best cornbread you ever flopped a lip over."

Between sets of the casual performances, fans would come forward to exchange handshakes, collect autographs, and ask Boyd and the other Doughboys to play their old favorites (Johnson, 15).

Art Greenhaw admired Boyd's way of dealing with the public. "He was a mixer, visiting with fans and making them feel good about the music. He was a Texan in his personality, embodying many cool qualities, such as self-confidence, a certain rugged individualism, and a look, walk, and talk filled with showmanship and style" (Personal communication, Dec. 30, 2001).

A friend of Boyd's, Jay Streetman of Denton, said Boyd's stage presence and personality was an important part of the Doughboys' show during those days. "Maybe it's just because he was a friend, but I got the impression that he was the favorite of the people," Streetman said. "Just standing back and watching people talking to him during breaks, he was by far the person that they all wanted to talk to. . . . Smokey did a lot of the announcing in those days, but most of it, Jim did. He was very quick-witted. The jokes were corny, but people liked those kinds of jokes. We hunted all over Texas, and everywhere we went in Texas, we'd run into people who knew him and remembered him. Seems like he never met a stranger" (Interview, May 7, 2001).

Through the years, Jerry Elliott continued to hold regular jobs with employers who allowed him to take time off with the Doughboys. He worked for T.H. Conn Music Company before joining the Doughboys, and later worked in the music department with Leonard Brothers Department Store. "They didn't care too much," Elliott said. "I said, 'Hey, I play music with Light Crust and I'm out two or three days at time.' I never had a vacation. Always used it to go out on those jobs." Elliott also worked as an administrative assistant with Tarrant County Commissioner B.D. Griffin (a musician himself who would later earn a unique place in Doughboy history), and as a pilot with the Tarrant County Water District, "flying pipelines."

"It was kind of rough for me to hold down my day job and still play up until I retired, it really was. . . . We would go out on a job, and I wouldn't get back home till one, two or three o' clock in the morning. I'd try to catch a nap on the way home, and I'd get up the next morning and be on the job at nine o'clock and work all day. Sometimes, I would get back in here just in time to shave and shower, change clothes and head to work. . . . But I don't regret it, and I made a lot of friends and sold a lot of instruments when I worked for those music companies," Elliott reflects.

Jerry Elliott's job as administrative assistant to Tarrant County Commissioner B.D. Griffin led to the only appearance by the "Light

Crust Doughboys" on the Grand Ole Opry. Griffin had a country music band in which Elliott played part-time. "I got a group together to take out there [to Nashville]. There weren't any others of the regular [Doughboys] group except me. Billy Walker [a Texan who had country music hits such as "Charlie's Shoes," "Cross the Brazos at Waco," and "A Million To One"] had a segment of the Grand Ole Opry, and we appeared on the Billy Walker show one Saturday night on the Grand Ole Opry. We had twin fiddles. I can't even remember all the guys who went. We went in there and did it as the Light Crust Doughboys" (Interview, March 8, 2001).

Smokey Montgomery gave the group his blessing, with some later regrets. "They were going up to Washington, D.C., to play a Texas party," Smokey remembered. "Griffin called me and asked it was all right if they stopped by the Grand Ole Opry on the way back and played as the Light Crust Doughboys. I loaned 'em some shirts. They played 'San Antonio Rose,' and the singer sang it in the wrong key. Jerry [Elliott] said it was the worst thing he ever put up with" (Interview, May 3, 2001).

In the late '80s, years after the sale of Burrus Mill to Cargill, the Doughboys survived yet another sale. At least they received some warning. "They [Cargill] sent another guy down here who kept using us," Smokey said. "He didn't especially like us like Gary did, but he kept using us. The last time I saw him, he said, 'You guys need new uniforms. Get them right now, because Cargill is selling out Light Crust.' That was when we bought those last blazers. I went and bought those as quick as I could, and, of course, they paid for them."

Cargill sold the Light Crust brand to Martha White, the cake mix company. "Martha White has never used us but twice," Smokey said. "They paid us twice, and that was not because they knew who we were and wanted to do it. But every year, Saginaw, where the [Burrus] mill is, has a Wheat and Train Celebration. They paid for the Doughboys to go over there and play for two years in a row for the big celebration. . . . Martha White has their own thing on the Grand Ole Opry. They just bought the food products name [Light Crust Flour]. They didn't buy the mill. Cargill still owns the mill out there" (Oral history, 149–150). The sale to Martha White ended the

Doughboys' days of touring the state on a regular basis until 1996, when the Texas Commission on the Arts began supporting a wide variety of venues.

It is inevitable in a group more than 70 years old that some members will be lost to death. "We've lost some good ones," Elliott said sadly. "Burney Annett [pianist, who joined the band in the 1970s] was a real good friend of mine, and especially [fiddler] Johnny Strawn. He [Annett] really played a good, driving, real nice piano" (Interview, March 8, 2001).

After Burney Annett's death, Bill Simmons joined the Doughboys as keyboardist in 1981. Bill's career began in 1939 in Florida when he began playing on the radio with Toby Dowdy and the Jubilee Hillbillies, later the Florida Playboys. For a time, the Dowdy band played for the barnstorming "Johnny J. Jones Exposition, featuring Clyde Beatty's Wild Animal Circus." While playing on a radio program in Memphis with the Eddie Hill Band, Simmons met James Blackwood and the Blackwood Brothers. About 50 years later, as a member of the Light Crust Doughboys, Simmons would record with Blackwood. Later he played with Curly Williams and his Georgia Peach Pickers, during which time he wrote "M-I-S-S-I-S-I-P-P-I" with Williams (as described in Chapter 1). He later played with country star Sonny James, of "Young Love" fame, and orchestra leader Ted Weems.

He came to Dallas-Fort Worth in 1954 to play on a short-lived WFAA radio show, *Friday Night Shindig*. And then, in 1955, he played on a daily WBAP-TV, Channel 5, show, *[Neal] Jones' Place* and on a WBAP radio show with Bob Crawford and the Southwesterners, also known as the Cedar Ridge Boys. "[It was an] early morning show, like eight o' clock, and then we'd transcribe the thing to be played in the afternoon, and then we'd do the noon show, and we were off for the rest of the day to go and do whatever." In Dallas, Bill began playing on recording sessions at Beck's Recording Studio. There he recorded with Lefty Frizzell and Marty Robbins, among many others.

Not long after coming to Texas, Bill met Smokey Montgomery, who invited him to become a part-time Doughboy. Bill played sporadically with the Doughboys starting in 1955. "The Doughboys were booking two or three things a night. And so, they'd have different groups [representing the Doughboys]. The first time I played as a Doughboy was in Crowley, Louisiana, at the Rice Festival. That was a two or three-day thing." He played "a gig here and there" with the Doughboys for two or three years.

Simmons also played with some of Smokey's many side groups, including the "Hot Five" Dixieland group and the "Islanders," a Hawaiian-music group. Finally, Montgomery invited Simmons to become a full-fledged Doughboy. "He just approached me one night and wanted to know if I'd be interested [in joining Doughboys] and I said, 'Yeah, why not?' Because I was just freelancing then, I didn't have anything regular. Of course this is not what you'd call 'regular,' but it's been steady. It's not like a full-time thing. Nobody wants to work every night anymore, as old as we are."

Growing up in Florida, Bill had been only vaguely aware of the Light Crust Doughboys. "I heard some of their records. I didn't even know who they were. I heard Milton Brown also, they were playing his records down there on the radio. I didn't know who they were, but later when I found out, I knew I'd been listening to them since I was seven or eight years old."

For a member of a group as musically diversified as the Light Crust Doughboys, it's not surprising that when Bill Simmons is asked what music most influenced him growing up, he said "all of it. . . . The first thing I remember hearing were some old records that my grandmother had up in Georgia. I started banging around on a keyboard when I was about four years old. I didn't know what I was doing but I liked it, so I picked out little tunes here and there. About in the first grade, I remember hearing this 'cat' yodeling, man, on the radio, and I thought that was different, you know. But what I really dug all the time was big bands and the classics [classical] and straight-ahead jazz." Bill plays sax, clarinet, trumpet, standup bass, electric guitar, and fiddle in addition to the keyboards. Simmons said, at his age, the only reason to keep going is for the love of music. "If it stops being fun, I'm out" (Interview, March 16, 2001).

♩ ♪ ♪

After playing on occasion with the Doughboys as far back as the '50s, John Walden, whom Smokey Montgomery refers to as "the wild man of the fiddle," succeeded Johnny Strawn as the featured fiddler of the Doughboys in 1993.

Strawn played his last show with the Doughboys at a festival in downtown Fort Worth. "We were doing the last tune on the show," Jerry Elliott recalled. "He was playing the classical tune 'Czardas' and on the very end of that, it [the tune] went haywire. Just completely haywire. And I looked at him and he had the oddest look on his face. He said, 'Something has happened.' He had a light stroke and that was the last show he ever played with us. It was not too many months after that till he died" (Interview, May 8, 2001).

"He was one of the greatest fiddle players that Light Crust has ever had," Elliott said. "Johnny had a jazz touch, and he played his choruses like a clarinet player would. His mind ran a little different the way he formulated his choruses. He wasn't just a sawing fiddle player. He played real good take-off choruses like a horn man would play. He was really a one-of-a-kind Western swing fiddle player. He had his own style. And a nice guy to go along with it, too" (Interview, May 8, 2001).

Smokey Montgomery also admired Strawn. "Johnny Strawn was one of the truest violin players we ever had. He played real jazz, not just a bunch of wild notes," Smokey said. Strawn, like Jim Boyd, later became a very successful homebuilder. "I remember going down the road to Corpus Christi or somewhere and Johnny reading a book on how to become a millionaire. He bought an old apartment house in Fort Worth and fixed it up, and he went on from there" (Interview, May 28, 2001).

Art Greenhaw remembered Johnny Strawn with great respect and affection. "Johnny Strawn had some of the best ears and technique in the world on violin," Greenhaw said. "Always playing beautiful melodies and counter melodies with a great sense of space. He had a fabulous sense of pitch and remarkable bowing techniques. He was a wonderfully, laid-back personality. A consummate professional, yet never one to make much of a fuss over equipment and he was always adapting to the situation. An interesting testimony to his personality is the fact that he never carried his own amplifier on gigs. Too much of a hassle, too much unnecessary stress! He always simply plugged into the extra input on Jerry's amp!" Yet, Greenhaw said that Strawn, like Smokey Montgomery, kept up with the latest technology. He owned his own computer for music writing and was experimenting with new electronic violin models (Dec. 30, 2001).

Joining the Doughboys gave John Walden the opportunity to make music his occupation. "I couldn't travel because I had a business, but I sold my place, and I've been able to travel with 'em and go anyplace they need to go," he said. Walden's connection to the group extends all the way back to Kenneth Pitts. After serving in the U.S. Navy in World War II and the Korean War, and starting his own welding shop, Walden began studying the violin under Pitts' tutelage. "He was just one of the finest people I've ever met," Walden remembered fondly. "I had studied music as a child, and then I had to begin making a living for my family. I began studying with Kenneth. I was told that he taught music and he was an ex-Light Crust Doughboy."

John had already developed his classic Western swing-style fiddle playing before meeting Pitts. He began playing under his father's guidance at the age of five. "Dad would begin teaching us just as soon as we could reach our fingers around [the neck] and make a 'D' chord on the guitar. . . . I accumulated that [the Western-swing style] down through the years, listening to the Light Crust Doughboys and Bob Wills and Leon McAuliffe. Those guys were the pioneers. I just came along later." But Walden said Pitts taught him classical violin. "I learned a lot of things from Kenneth Pitts. [He taught me] vibrato: I had a nervous tremble instead of vibrato. He taught me to play pretty instead of having a nervous tremble and shake. I'd had classical training when I was young but I wasn't able to continue with it." Walden said Pitts also taught him to read music properly, although he could read and write music in a limited way before studying under Pitts.

Walden's first professional experience as a musician was with his father and two older brothers. "We played as a band," he recalled. "We played for fairs in Iowa Park [Texas], we played for the Women's

Forum in Wichita Falls, we played at the country clubs, and dance studios." John later played with the Miller Brothers Band in Wichita Falls. "I couldn't work with 'em all the time. I was making a living for my family as a welder." Later, he came to Dallas to work for Lone Star Gas, and joined Dewey Groom's band. Groom was a country singer who later owned and operated the legendary Longhorn Ballroom in Dallas (Young). "Of course, I had the job of a welder in the daytime, and played with him [Groom] at night."

John has vivid memories of seeing and hearing the Light Crust Doughboys as a child. "My father took my two brothers and myself to hear 'em," he remembered. "We were playing together at the time. But we were very much influenced by the Light Crust Doughboys. We'd run to the radio everyday at noon when they came on, and hear the 'plink, plonk – The Light Crust Doughboys are on the air!' We had a battery radio, you know, didn't have electricity. We'd have three heads up crammed up to the speaker of the old radio trying to hear, the old battery would be low sometimes. They were somebody to us, I guarantee you. We liked to hear them play, they had some great players. . . . They came to the fair at Iowa Park every year." It probably wasn't very long after Bob Wills left the Doughboys that John and his brothers saw the group in person. "I remember this guitar player [possibly Sleepy Johnson] saying to the fiddle player [probably Clifford Gross], 'Play it, Bob!' and they had a big laugh."

In recent years, the Light Crust Doughboys have performed with the Dallas Wind Symphony, the Texas Wind Symphony, the Abilene, Texas, Philharmonic, and the Midland-Odessa Symphony. John Walden said that playing the symphony concerts has been the most satisfying of the recent projects. "For my own satisfaction, being able to be on the stage with one of the finest orchestras in the country [the Dallas Wind Symphony], that's about as high as you can go, for a musician," he said. "It's like buying a new instrument, or buying a new car, or doing anything that you would have liked to do, but never could" (Interview, March 29, 2001).

Bill Simmons agreed that the symphony shows have been the most enjoyable performances in his 20-plus years with the Doughboys.

"I'd always dug that stuff since I was a kid, the long-haired [classical] music. I never got into real deeply myself, because I was on that jazz kick when I was kid. It was so dadgummed much fun to be playing with the whole symphony, man, and hearing them right there with us." The arranger with the Abilene Philharmonic, Ed George, scored one of Simmons' "boogie-woogie" numbers for the symphony. "I thought that was pretty good," Bill said with considerable understatement (Interview).

Even after more than 65 years of playing with the Light Crust Doughboys, Smokey Montgomery could still be thrilled by an experience such as playing with a symphony orchestra. "We played in Abilene a couple of years ago, and their arranger made some arrangements of some things like 'Tumblin' Tumbleweeds.' We had a big rehearsal, and they had all these violins playing behind us on 'Tumblin' Tumbleweeds,' and it gave me goose pimples," Smokey said, laughing at his own exhilaration (Interview, March 21, 2001).

"With the talent that these guys have, they're not your typical honky-tonk musicians," Art Greenhaw said. "They play with finesse, they have classical backgrounds. Bill Simmons is the finest jazz pianist you could find anywhere. I made a tremendous effort to get the Doughboys plugged into the classical realm with ballet, dance and symphonies. And we've been successful in that field" (Interview, March 26, 2001).

When the Doughboys play with a symphony, they essentially play numbers from their regular repertoire and the symphonies add their instrumentation to the arrangements. But Smokey said the melding of the Doughboys' Western swing and country with the formal style of the symphonies is not always perfect. "We played with the Dallas Wind Symphony down at the Meyerson Symphony Center [April 1998]. They have drums, and they put their drummer down in front. He was always about a half-beat off from us all the time. They're not used to playing Western music. You know, Bob Wills always played ahead of the beat. That's what makes it swing. These symphony guys, they don't know how to do that," Smokey said good-naturedly. "We just battled on through it." But, Smokey said, whatever small imperfections might exist in the Meyerson show and other symphony performances, they are always exciting. "Down at the Meyerson, we had a full house, and the people came to hear us. Everything we did that night, they just loved" (Interview, March 21, 2001).

Throughout the past four decades, Marvin Montgomery has kept a busy music career going apart from the Doughboys. Besides the Hot Five and the Islanders, he had a Dixieland band called "Smokey and the Bearkats." Montgomery's virtuosity on the banjo led him, in a flight of fancy, to create the Dallas Banjo Band in 1989. The band has played at musical conventions in New Orleans, Kansas City, St. Louis, and Sacramento, California. It plays regularly at the Texas State Fair.

As *Dallas Morning News* columnist Jacquielynn Floyd observed, "Until you hear them play, the notion of 30 or so banjos and a lone tuba sounds like a novelty skit from a 'Hee Haw' rerun." But the group tackles such unlikely banjo numbers as Beethoven's Fifth Symphony and George Gershwin's "Rhapsody in Blue." Smokey gleefully acknowledged, "We do lots of things you're not supposed to do on the banjo." In fact, the Banjo Band's repertoire also included Smokey Montgomery arrangements of "Gonna Fly Now" (the theme from *Rocky*) and of John Philip Sousa tunes. Floyd enthused, "Every tune that played when I sat in on a practice last weekend made me think idly about picnics and summer swims and somebody's great-grandfather throwing down his crutches and dancing at a tent revival" ("For a joyful").

In one of most improbable recording projects ever, the Dallas Banjo Band helped record the soundtrack for a 1997 documentary about actor Bela Lugosi, *Lugosi: Hollywood's Dracula*. Art Greenhaw took the lead in composing and arranging the music for *Lugosi*. He worked on the project with University of Oklahoma instructor Gary Rhodes, who has also produced a documentary film on the Light Crust Doughboys. The project received a rave review in *Filmfax* magazine. "*Lugosi: Hollywood's Dracula* is a novel, quirkily satisfying audio trip through things Lugosi. From the start, dedicated Lugosi scholar Garydon [sic] Rhodes and musical collaborator Art Greenhaw (a Texas-based composer, arranger, and musician) were apparently undeterred by their limited budget," the anonymous reviewer enthused.

The reviewer found the use of the Dallas Banjo Band to interpret the classical music in the soundtrack especially creative:

> For instance, take Greenhaw's treatment of the overture to Tchaikovsky's "Swan Lake," the Dracula signature melody, interpreted here three times—first by piano, baritone saxophone, and (hold on) banjos, playing the melody as a lively fox trot. I know this seems peculiar, but Greenhaw and the Dallas Banjo Band make it work. I don't believe I've ever heard as effective a mix of 19th-century European classicism and 20th-century Americana.

The reviewer also praised Greenhaw's use of electric guitar in the style of the '60s surf-rock group the Ventures on "Swan Lake Rock." "The cut is simultaneously rockin' and traditionally melodic. I loved it," the review said ("Lugosi").

Yet, despite the success of the Dallas Banjo Band and his many other enterprises, Smokey's first priority was always the Doughboys. "The Doughboys have always been the primary thing in my life," he said. "Where people got to know me was as a Doughboy" (Interview, January 3, 2001).

Modern-day Doughboy fiddler Jim Baker came to the Doughboys in 1993 through the Dallas Banjo Band. "I'd heard about Smokey all my life," he said. "I think they claim there are 11 founding members. If that's so, I must have been number 12, because I was in on the beginning. I'd always liked tenor banjo. I got acquainted with him [Smokey] there." Smokey learned that Baker also played fiddle, and asked him to join the Doughboys in the early 1990s.

"People don't realize what a great arranger Smokey is," Baker said. "He can just do stuff on the fly. The first [recording] session I got to do with the Doughboys, we had three fiddles, Johnny Strawn, John Walden, and me. He had some stuff written out and we weren't quite getting it, so he just grabbed it up, rearranged it, and slapped it back down, and we went on. He's a whiz."

Baker's mentor was the late Dallas-area fiddler Jimmy Belken, who played with Bob Wills, Mel Tillis, Ray Price, Willie Nelson, and

Merle Haggard, among others. They played together at a Mesquite dance hall called The Texas Stroll. Baker names Western-swing fiddler Johnny Gimble of Austin, who has played with Bob Wills and Willie Nelson, as his major musical influence. "Gimble's the swingingest guy around, a great player from the heart," he said. And, of course, Bob Wills himself has been an inspiration to Baker.

Baker, a full-time telecommunications professional, has played for many years in the band at the Grapevine Opry, a very popular Saturday-night country music venue. "I feel like a trailer hitch on a Rolls Royce [playing with the Doughboys]," Baker said. "To me, the Doughboys were the band that was in the laboratory when Western swing was invented." But, of course, he's much too young to have memories of the Doughboys in their radio days. "I didn't come in from pickin' cotton and listen to the radio on the car battery," he laughs. "But I certainly knew who they were and highly respected them."

Baker got a late start in music. "I didn't really start early like most great players do, who play when they're three years old, or whatever. I didn't pick up a violin until I was in my last year of high school. I had piddled around with a guitar." But like many of the Doughboys throughout the history of the group, Baker is a serious student of music. He has formalized his music education by taking courses in classical music at Dallas-area colleges. "Jazz is my main interest now, except you can't make a living playing that. You have to be really talented to play it anyway. If you're ever going to improve, you have to go to theory in jazz. . . . I'm just highly frustrated now, because the more you learn the more you realize you don't know. Boy, I just feel like I'm really beginning. On the bandstand I stand in between Bill Simmons and Smokey, and to me, those guys are just geniuses musically, so I can't hardly concentrate because I'm knocked out by their playing" (Interview, April 17, 2001).

The symphony performances and the other remarkable enterprises of the Light Crust Doughboys in the 1990s and in the new millennium are largely the products of Art Greenhaw's imagination and promotional skill. "Art booked us off and on way back when he was going to college at Eastfield [College, Mesquite] and SMU," Smokey recalled.

"He booked us for a big show there [SMU] and for some things down in Mesquite. And when Jim Boyd died, he just naturally fell in. He had never played bass before, and he picked it up real quick, and he gets better on it all the time. He's always had a good sense of rhythm, but he plays better notes now than when he started.

"He got us going again. He kind of revived us. I was just booking us at conventions and stuff as they came along. But he went out looking for work. . . . It's all him. Otherwise, we'd be kaput, we'd have been through a long time ago" (Interview, March 21, 2001).

Like most of the other Doughboys down through the years, Greenhaw started in music at an early age. "I was blessed to have a dad who was a professional musician, and he started me playing the piano by ear when I was about three years old," Greenhaw said. His father Frank, who plays brass instruments for the Doughboys and assists with the management of the group, was a music graduate of Southern Methodist University in Dallas. Frank served for several years as the director of music for the Mesquite Independent School District in suburban Dallas and for 38 years served as the music director of the First United Methodist Church in Mesquite. At eight, Art picked up the guitar, and by the fourth grade, he had his own band, "The Doodlebugs." Later, during the psychedelic era, came a rock band named "The Inner Soul."

"We did Temple Emmanuel events and all types of Dallas society party events. A lot of the Dallasites were excited about having real young kids playing rock 'n' roll music," Greenhaw said. With the Inner Soul, Greenhaw met physician George Miller, the father of rock musician Steve Miller. The elder Miller hired Greenhaw's group to play at various parties. "And so, because of that connection I started listening to Steve Miller's music when he first started doing the underground San Francisco scene in the '60s with songs like 'Living in the USA' and 'My Dark Hour,' and always used Steve Miller as a heroic musical figure in my life. . . . In college, I started doing completely my own thing with my own band. I guess, kind of in keeping with my rock 'n' roll hero Steve Miller [whose group is named 'The Steve Miller Band'], I dubbed my band the real creative name of 'The Art Greenhaw Band.'

"I've always done real character building things, which took a little bit of musical guts. For instance, I opened up Sanger-Harris' Town East [shopping mall] store as a strolling singing musician. That takes a little bit of courage for a 17-year-old, especially when they assigned me the lingerie department, strolling through the brassieres and panties." As inspiration, Greenhaw used Elvis Presley's performance as a strolling, guitar-strumming singer in the movie *King Creole*. "That's one of the songs that I did, 'Lover Doll,'" Greenhaw remembered with a laugh. "I may be one of the few guys who knows every obscure Elvis and Jordanaires song from every soundtrack, from 'Song of the Shrimp' to 'Who Needs Money' to all the *Clambake* songs. . . . So I can do hours of lingerie strolling."

Greenhaw's interest in guitar led him to country music at an early age. "Even though the guitar work that first so inspired me was in rock 'n' roll, you easily learn when you're a kid that the guitar is a real important part of country music, too. I would seek out the Porter Wagoner Show and the Willburn Brothers Show [on television] to see the guitarists, and I would bring my mom in and say, 'Look at this.' She had a hard time relating to the Willburn Brothers and Loretta Lynn, but I've just always gravitated toward that. Not too many kids that I knew of who were eight, nine, and 10 avidly watched the Willburn Brothers and Porter Wagoner. I always sought out the gospel music, Tennessee Ernie Ford, Elvis, the Jordanaires. When the other kids were listening to Jimi Hendrix, I was listening to Tennessee Ernie Ford and the Blackwood Brothers. I was listening to Hendrix, too, but I always appreciated that rural music that had a synthesis of the black blues and rhythm 'n' blues. I've always liked low-brow music." At the same time, Greenhaw studied classical music as a child at the SMU Piano Preparatory Department. Years later, Greenhaw received his college degree from SMU.

Starting in 1983, Greenhaw served as the musical director and band leader of a weekly country music revue, the Mesquite Opry. "I remember I ran into one of my heroes, Mike Love [of the Beach Boys] in the airport in the 1980s, and I told him how influential he had been, and he said, 'What are you doing, Art?' And I told him, 'Well, I'm musical director of the Mesquite Opry in which we perform every Saturday night.' And he said, 'Oh, man, a steady gig!' We grew it into the second largest and most successful show of its type in Texas, I would say. The only thing that was more successful, in terms of attendance, was the Johnny High Revue in Arlington." Traditional country performers such as Charlie Louvin of the Louvin Brothers, Patsy Montana, and one of Art's favorite female singers, Norma Jean, performed at the Mesquite Opry.

"I played for years accompanying LeAnn Rimes on stage at the Mesquite Opry. Her dad would even call me and I would accompany her at church things. This was when she was seven or eight. I'd be in the back seat and she'd be in the front, asleep."

Art first worked with the Light Crust Doughboys when he booked them to play at the Mesquite Folk Festival in 1983, which Greenhaw had founded. "I brought the Doughboys in and that was real successful and I dealt with Smokey on that, and, thereafter, I just hit it off with them and I would call them up for something nice and big, like a convention. The Light Crust Doughboys were always my first choice."

In January 1993, Greenhaw became more closely involved with the Doughboys. "Along about that time, we had a joint offer to do a convention. It was for the Southwest Hardware and Implement Association. The convention was at the Marriott in Arlington, next to the Arlington Convention Center. That was the first performance that we did together. I did some numbers as a guest soloist, and the Doughboys and I got standing ovations all that evening, so we felt like, 'Well, this is working pretty well.'" Soon, Greenhaw stepped in as a full-fledged group member and business manager.

The hardware-convention show in Arlington proved almost providential for the Light Crust Doughboys. "The last performance they did with Jim Boyd was the first one I did with them," Greenhaw said. "Jim was in good shape, but after that, his health declined real rapidly, and he passed away just a couple of months after that performance. And so that left the bass guitar position open. The door closed on that era and the door opened on a new era, and it was like it was meant to be."

Greenhaw had played very little bass guitar up to that point, but as a veteran guitarist, picked up the instrument very quickly. "For a chance to play with the Light Crust Doughboys, I had to get real, real good, real, real fast. The bass guitar now has become my primary instrument, and I really love it."

Greenhaw became excited about the prospects for the venerable band, which had been working only sporadically for several years. He brought his marketing talents to bear. "I started trying to think of ideas we could try to promote the great name of the Light Crust Doughboys even more. Smokey and I came up with the addition of the horns on select performances, thinking we could get a lot more society balls and major events interested in a slightly different sound. And we started doing the Pocket Sandwich Theatre events [in September 1993] to have a home base that we could, on a real regular basis, tell our fans, 'You can come see us here so many times a year.' It's kind of our lab for new sounds."

Walter Hailey, the Doughboys' master of ceremonies as "Jack Perry" in the 1950s, was born in Mesquite and is a close friend of Art's family, so Art had been steeped in Light Crust Doughboys lore growing up. "I've always been real interested in history, and I've always really loved the Texas roots and Texas heritage, and I like the Texas approach to things. I like the flamboyance of Texans and the aggressiveness of the music. And the Doughboys have always been the personification of that, the aggressive approach to country music, the jazz-oriented approach, the swing, the hot fiddle playing, the real hot guitar playing. You know, they were never a part of that real easy-listening, Nashville-type sound. They've always been folk, rockabilly, aggressive musicians, and I've always really loved that.

"Walter Hailey was a real famous son of Mesquite, he's always been an idol [of Art's] in business, as well as in music. I always thought that part of the reason he was so successful was his association with the Light Crust Doughboys. I've just always had it in my mind that anything the Light Crust Doughboys rubbed off on, like Walter, is successful.

"I always had a real, real high opinion of the Light Crust Doughboys. I always thought they were the best in the West, and then the older I got, I felt they were really unsung heroes. I felt that they hadn't been given near the recognition they deserved, particularly in the Dallas area. As Jesus said, 'A prophet is without honor in his own country.' And that's certainly true of the Light Crust Doughboys. The further out from Dallas we get, the more popular we are. I not only wanted to be a part of that music, but I wanted to use as part of my ministry and my calling to get these guys recognized as the seminal musicians that they are.

"I don't really care a flip about the commercial appeal of somebody [in music] or the financial status of somebody, I care about how the music relates to me. And that's why I've chosen to do everything I can to support and be the number-one promoter of the Light Crust Doughboys."

Art said he and Smokey Montgomery always worked very well together. "He and I have a tremendous amount of the same ideas that flow together, which is real neat even though he could be my grandfather agewise. We have real similar business goals and music goals" (Interview). Art and Smokey acquired the rights to the group's famous name. "Art and I have control of the name, we have 'The Light Crust Doughboys' registered in our name, copyrighted and trademarked, the whole bit," Smokey said (Interview, January 3, 2001).

The Doughboys have been involved in a dozen or more separate recording projects since Greenhaw came into the band. Before Art joined, they had not recorded since about 1985, when they made *150 Years of Texas Country Music*. The group has racked up a string of Grammy nominations for its latter-day CD recordings. The first came in 1998 for *Keep Lookin' Up: The Texas Swing Sessions*, which was nominated for "Best Southern Gospel, Country Gospel or Bluegrass Gospel Album of the Year." The Doughboys made the recording with gospel music legend James Blackwood, the last surviving member of the original Blackwood Brothers. The first sessions took place in November 1996 and the CD was released in the summer of 1997.

"We worked for many months forging a new sound in folk music with a gospel message," Art said. He and Smokey also employed a gospel group, the Eastgate Mass Choir from Dallas. "It's a real unique sound, plus we've got an African-American gospel choir on there. It's a very interesting project, very different" (Morrison).

The next year, the Doughboys did it again. In 1999, they earned a Grammy nomination for "The Best Southern, Country or Bluegrass Gospel Album of the Year" for *They Gave the World a Smile: The Stamps Quartet Tribute Album*. This time, they worked with the James Blackwood Quartet. The album also received a nomination as best Southern gospel album of the year for the Dove Awards, presented by the Gospel Music Association, in addition to a nomination for best Southern gospel album by the Inspirational TV Network ("Press release: A Grammy Nomination").

In 2001, yet another Grammy nomination came for *The Great Gospel Hit Parade*. On this CD, the Doughboys recorded with Elvis Presley's old vocal backing group, the Jordanaires, and again with Blackwood. "It's amazing to be in the top five [nominated records]," Greenhaw said. "You have to consider we are a small, independent record label [Art Greenhaw Records] with virtually no budget for promotion and such. . . . Some of these releases have a million-dollar budget, and we're a mustard seed in comparison to that.

"Winning the Grammy would be the greatest gift I could give to the people who have been my musical heroes over the years. . . . People like Smokey Montgomery who has kept the Doughboys going since the '30s through the hard times and good times. He's never won a Grammy and it's about time" (Watkins; Greenhaw interview).

Greenhaw said, for him, working with the Jordanaires and James Blackwood was the realization of a dream. "The Jordanaires were my first gospel-music idols, actually even before James Blackwood. Ray Walker, the great bass singer of the Jordanaires, was my earliest bass singing idol. I first discovered them in 1960, when I was six years old, and I followed their career real, real closely. And in 1966, I discovered James Blackwood and, to me, he's been the greatest lead singer ever in gospel music" (Interview).

Grammy nominations were nothing new for James Blackwood. Blackwood, as a member of the Blackwood Brothers, and later the Masters V and the James Blackwood Quartet, received Grammy nominations 28 consecutive years in the gospel field, and won nine Grammys. The Gospel Music Association named Blackwood its top male vocalist seven consecutive years. He was the third living person to be voted into the Gospel Music Hall of Fame ("James Blackwood Sr."). Still, Blackwood was eager to work with the Light Crust Doughboys.

"I found out Art Greenhaw had been a fan since childhood," Blackwood said. "His father was a minister of music at a church in Mesquite, and he [Art] got me to sing at the morning service." Later, Greenhaw approached Blackwood with the idea of recording with the Doughboys. "It was a neat idea, an innovative idea for me and my group to record with the Light Crust Doughboys. A gospel group and a Western swing group had never recorded before."

Blackwood, however, was concerned how the combination of the two styles of music would be publicly received. He was relieved when the reaction was almost entirely positive. "Several trade papers said it was a wonderful idea to combine gospel with Western swing music. It was well-accepted in gospel circles and Western swing circles."

Actually, the melding of the two musical styles was not that difficult, Blackwood said. "Gospel music has always had a beat. It wasn't like the old hymns of the church. It wasn't much of a problem," Blackwood said. Of course, the Doughboys' style covers a lot of territory, ranging beyond Western swing. Blackwood said it helped that they recorded some gospel tunes that had also been pop hits, such as "Crying in the Chapel," composed by one-time Doughboy Artie Glenn, "Just a Closer Walk with Thee," and "He's Got the Whole World in His Hands."

"It's been a wonderful association," Blackwood said. "Smokey Montgomery and I hit it off from the very beginning. We knew a lot of the same old people in music and a lot of mutual friends. They welcomed me with outstretched arms. . . . We all went to Hollywood together for the Grammy Awards. It's great to have such a wonderful, warm friendship" (Interview, April 5, 2001).

The Grammy nominations have been gratifying to the Doughboys because the recordings are not widely distributed, and so are not big sellers. Greenhaw said while the recordings have been critically well-received, they have not been money makers. "I just move from one project to the next, hoping that on some of them we do a little more than break even. It's real tough to break even on these recordings because they're so expensive. It takes a lot more sales than we generate to even break even on these things. That's why you have to look at years out, and you have to keep trying different things hoping that you get a hit" (Interview).

The Doughboys Fan Club president, Sharon Dickerson, went to Los Angeles with the group for the 2001 Grammy ceremonies. Smokey Montgomery, she said, was not content with simply being nominated. "Smokey and [his wife] Barbara sat to the right of me at the presentation ceremony. And to see the disappointment in his little face just crushed me. I told him, 'Smokey, you're all winners or you wouldn't be in the top five in the world.' . . . He is an absolute perfectionist to the 'nth' degree" (Interview, May 2, 2001).

Greenhaw said the Grammy Award nominations provide the Doughboys with a hard-earned spotlight. "The neat thing about the Grammys is they're just exactly down my alley, in that they don't have anything to do with sales volume or mass appeal as per their mission statement. They only exist to recognize quality, innovation, excellence in recording. So looking around at how limited our sales were, I figured out early on that the Grammys would be our arena for recognition. The Grammys are the most important, highest honor in the whole music industry, so I'd rather be associated with them than anything. And we've had Grammy nominations three of the past four years which I've been told puts us among the most elite Grammy-recognized artists in the gospel field."

Greenhaw sends the Doughboys' recordings to people in the gospel-music industry who vote on Grammy nominations. "Of course, that has to be done subtly, because we don't really politic. We never say, 'Vote for me,' or anything like that. But there's a certain amount of recording exchange that goes on between musicians anyway. And then there's a little booklet that comes out every month that goes out to all of the Grammy voters, and it makes all of the releases that are available all over the world available at review prices way less than retail to encourage Grammy voters to pick the recordings up and listen to them. So that's the main way the music gets out. Now with the Internet, you can key on to 'Grammy.com' when we have a nomination and go directly to our recording and hear clips from at least five or six tunes off of our Grammy-nominated album, which is very, very helpful" (Interview).

The Grammy-nominated records represent only some of the Doughboys' modern recordings. Almost always, they have collaborated with a veteran musician who has been a musical inspiration for Greenhaw. One of them is Nokie Edwards, the lead guitarist of the 1960s surf-rock band the Ventures, known for their instrumental hits such as "Walk Don't Run" and "Hawaii-Five-O." Another is steel guitarist Tom Brumley, best known for his work as a member of Buck Owens' group the Buckaroos in the 1960s and Rick Nelson's Stone Canyon Band in the 1970s. Both Edwards and Brumley contributed to the Doughboys' 2000 album, *Adventure in Country Swing*.

"Nokie has been my biggest inspiration on the guitar, and I started becoming real familiar with his music when I was eight years old," Greenhaw said. "I like his tone, I like his persona, I like his approach to playing the guitar. He's just always played with so much melody and space.... I felt like he would be just perfect for working with us because I was so familiar with his work. He comes from strong country roots."

In 2000, the Doughboys traveled to Nokie's current home near Eugene, Oregon, to play at a concert Edwards had organized. After the concert, the Doughboys and Edwards went into a local studio with digital audio tapes of the rhythm tracks for dozens of songs the Doughboys had only begun to record. Edwards spent the next 13 hours putting his signature lead-guitar work on many of the tracks. The Doughboys went back to Texas with material for two CDs, which came out as *Adventure in Country Swing* and *A Surf 'n' Swing/Fret 'n' String Christmas*.

"I came up with about 60 songs, and I presented them to Nokie and he picked them," Art said. "I wanted to put together songs that would be the best of his style and the Light Crust Doughboys' Western-swing style, and I knew he wanted to do a whole lot with the melody, so I picked songs that had a real strong melodic line."

Edwards said he did it all by feel. "Well, I can't read music, so I listened and I arranged it in my head.... I don't know if being able to read would improve my picking. I think if you could read music and had studied it and were just a reader and you played something, I think it would be musically right but sound mechanical. There are great musicians who read, and I don't have anything against them. I would rather put my own feelings into it."

Greenhaw recalled, "We had all of the Doughboys with us, but I was the only one in the recording booth. I was sending him hand signals. I wouldn't presume to tell him how to play anything. He's the king of guitar. Like a fine violinist, he's just gotten better and better with age. Nokie's dexterity is still first-rate." The sessions yielded unique versions of songs ranging from Fats Domino's "I'm Walkin'" to Hank Williams' "Your Cheatin' Heart."

For the '60s-style album cover for *Adventure in Country Swing*, Melinda Hoeye, a producer with Equus Productions, the studio where the tracks were recorded, said, "They were trying to make it look like an old Ventures album cover with the pretty girl out front and the guys falling down around her. The guys didn't want to fall down. They just sat. They said they were too old to be falling down" (Taylor).

Of the album with Nokie Edwards, Greenhaw said, "It's a melting pot of so many things I love. What we've tried to do is combine the good times of Americana sounds of guitars, girls, a little bit of surf music, a little bit of swing music, dancing, Hawaiian steel guitar. We wrapped it all up in a country package" (Barber, "Doughboys put jingle").

Besides *Adventure in Country Swing*, Tom Brumley collaborated with the Doughboys on their recent album *Steel Away*, with James Blackwood, the Jordanaires, Smokey Montgomery's Dallas Banjo Band and the Preston Hollow Presbyterian Church choir. Brumley is the son of Albert E. Brumley, the composer of more than 800 gospel songs including "I'll Fly Away" and "Turn Your Radio On" and one of the original members of the Nashville Songwriters Hall of Fame. "Art called and asked if I'd be interested in the project and I said I certainly would," Brumley said. "I grew up with gospel. It was an honor to play with James Blackwood. Of course, he had known my Dad for years." Under Greenhaw and Montgomery's direction, Brumley recorded with Blackwood in the Ozark resort city of Branson, Missouri, where Brumley and his band play year-round at the 76 Music Hall. Brumley came to Dallas for further sessions. While he has met Nokie Edwards, the two were never in the studio at the same time for the *Adventure in Country Swing* sessions. "Art was fantastic to work with," Brumley enthused. "The guy has so much imagination to put such things together. He's amazing to me. I have a couple more ideas that I want to talk with him about."

Besides playing with Buck Owens and Rick Nelson, Brumley has played his distinctive pedal steel on country star Dwight Yoakum's records. But he received inspiration from playing with the venerable Smokey. "He's amazing. He joined the Doughboys, when? 1935? That's when I was born. To be his age and sit there and play with perfect tempo, perfect pitch. I hope I'm doing the same thing when I'm his age. I plan to be" (Interview).

Greenhaw said he had always dreamed of working with Brumley before calling him and proposing the collaboration with the Doughboys. "He [Brumley] exceeded every expectation," Greenhaw said. "He plays in a fabulous style all of his own. To have the chance to make music with him is really phenomenal. I hope it's the first of many, many more projects" (Guest).

While the Doughboys have spent a lot of time in the recording studio in recent years, they remain primarily a live performance band. And not only for concerts: In recent years the Light Crust Doughboys have crossed over into the performing-arts arena.

The Doughboys' 1998 collaboration with the Lone Star Ballet in Amarillo, *God Bless Amarillo (and All the Cowboys, Too)*, resulted in a highly acclaimed stage show with the ballet troupe, and a CD containing the music that Smokey Montgomery, his wife Barbara Cohen (whom he married following the death in 1992 of his wife of 55 years, Kathleen) and Art Greenhaw composed for the event. Greenhaw called it a "Western swing pocket symphony." It includes the title song, plus "Amarillo, Where the Winds Blow Free," "Amarillo,

You're My Town," and "Amarillo Quick Step." Smokey and Barbara wrote the words and music for "Amarillo, Amarillo (You're Home Sweet Home to Me)":

> Lonely Sunday morning, brush the cobwebs from my mind.
> Open up the curtain, but today the sun won't shine.
> Raindrops keep on falling, can't wash my dreams away.
> Miss you, Amarillo, and I'll be back someday.

"That was the hardest show we ever played," Smokey remembered. "They [the ballet troupe] learned the songs off the recordings. When we got out there, we had to play exactly like we did on the recordings. We're not used to doing that" (Interview, May 28, 2001).

The collaboration with the Lone Star Ballet was initiated by the artistic director and founder of the ballet group, Neil Hess. The project started when the Texas Commission on the Arts selected both the Light Crust Doughboys and the Lone Star Ballet as official touring acts for the state. "I noticed that the Doughboys were on the touring roster for the commission," Hess said. "I thought it would be neat thing for a country swing band to join with classical ballet dancers, and maybe reach a new audience. I talked to Art, and he decided it would be a lot of fun, too. It was very successful. We made a lot of new friends for the ballet. Some of them were surprised that ballet dancers would let their hair down and do a country & western production." It was by no means the first time Hess had been involved in combining artistic dance with country music. He staged the famous outdoor spectacular *Texas* at Palo Duro Canyon from its inception in the 1960s until recent years. Hess' daughter, Lisa Hess-Jones, choreographed the 15-minute Doughboys suite.

Hess was only vaguely familiar with the Doughboys' history before becoming involved with the group, but quickly learned about them. "As I talked to people in the community, they remembered the Doughboys [from their radio era]. They said, 'Oh, yes, They're an important part of the musical history of the state'" (Interview, April 24, 2001). One of the sponsors of the event commented, "There have been 26 years of programs here in the Amarillo Civic Center, and the best one ever was the one we saw tonight" (Bryant).

In Fall 2000, the Doughboys teamed up with the Lone Star Ballet again for a program called "Gospel, Strauss and Patsy Cline," which combined religious, classical and country music. James Blackwood and the Doughboys sang the gospel numbers. Irish singer Ciaran Sheehan, who has sung in the Broadway production of *Les Miserables* and performed as the Phantom in a New York production of *Phantom of the Opera*, stepped out of character to sing Western songs. Burgundi Rose, a country singer from the Panhandle town Dumas, sang the Patsy Cline numbers.

Hess, the director of the dance department at West Texas A&M University, said the Doughboys handled the classical Strauss and Beethoven numbers without a hitch. Of course, several of the current Doughboys, like some of their predecessors, are formally trained musicians. "With classically trained artists, their skill comes through in everything they do," Hess said. "It was a beautiful evening." Besides the Strauss medley, the selections included "Music of the Night," "Crazy," Beethoven's "Ode to Joy," "Walkin' After Midnight," "Peace in the Valley," "Sweet Dreams" and a full-cast rendition of "I'll Fly Away."

The reviewer for the *Amarillo Globe-News* found the concept a little too broad to his liking, but still had much praise for the Doughboys:

> "Gospel, Strauss and Patsy Cline," Lone Star Ballet's season opener performed Saturday in the Amarillo Civic Center auditorium, had a surfeit of concepts. Witness the title alone—three incredibly different styles of music on one bill. . . .The classic pickin' and fiddlin' of the Light Crust Doughboys proved why they're regarded so highly. . . . The Doughboys were a pleasure. . . . Eagerness was evident all night, from the madly grinning dancers to the clap-happy audience. But next time, a single, simple concept might be nice. (Chandler)

Even so, the performance earned the Lone Star Ballet a "Golden Touch" award for its creativity from the Amarillo Chamber of Commerce Arts Committee (Hess interview).

"It was a thrill to work with those distinguished gentlemen and artists," Hess said. "It gave us a new perspective on our world, enriched us, and gave us a little glimpse back in history. As the same time, I value the importance of their presence today. I think they make a very significant contribution to the music and art worlds" (Interview).

In 1998, the Doughboys played for the Retro Dance Fest at Texas Christian University's Landreth Auditorium in Fort Worth. Their music accompanied the dancing of the Contemporary Dance/Fort Worth troupe. "The Doughboys standing at the side and playing vigorously were much the more entertaining part of the deal," wrote one reviewer (Putnam).

In 1997, the Light Crust Doughboys made a recording, *The High Road on the Hilltop*, with the Southern Methodist University band. "When we collaborated with the SMU band, I knew younger people would like the Doughboys if they only knew about them," Art Greenhaw said. "The review in SMU's publication *The Daily Campus* said, 'Maybe Grandpa was right all along with his musical taste.'"

Wherever the Light Crust Doughboys perform, they impress audiences with their musicianship and showmanship, notwithstanding their advanced years. A reviewer for the *Wichita Falls Times-Record News* wrote of a Doughboys performance in Fall 2000:

> One thing that can be said about the Doughboys—with 70 years behind them, these guys know how to play. And it was the solos that got the audience's blood pumping. Banjo player Smokey Montgomery, at 87, impressed with his lightning-speed strumming. He was challenged by quick-fingered fiddle player John Walden, who got so riled up he threw himself off balance. Bill Simmons, with his pounding style of chord playing, also excited the crowd with his coverage of the keyboard, while guitar player Jerry Elliott added the finesse of the evening.

The reviewer took note of the Doughboys' showmanship, and their penchant for not using a set play list, as Smokey called out numbers that seemed to fit the mood of the moment from their repertoire of more than a thousand songs ("Press release," October 7, 2000).

The Doughboys performances in recent years have not been limited to concert stages in Texas. Just as they had been named the official representatives of the Texas Centennial Celebration in 1936, the state legislature in 1995 named the Light Crust Doughboys "Official Music Ambassadors for the State of Texas." That same year, they performed a series of concerts called the Country Christmas Festival in Austria.

"Art arranged it with a promoter from over there who came to Texas," Smokey said. "He promoted us over there for three shows. It was like a paid vacation. We made some money and got to see a lot of the country." One of the shows was in a theater where Smokey's boyhood hero Charlie Chaplin used to perform.

"The bad thing about it was, everybody still smokes over there. And when we got through at night, we'd just be almost blind and, 'cough, cough, cough' [imitates sound of coughing] from breathing other people's smoke." Smokey said the shows were in large halls. "And we had a lot of young people, in their teens and twenties. They would speak enough English to say 'hello' and 'goodbye.' The first show, I tried to tell a joke or two, and they didn't know what I was talking about. I didn't tell any more jokes, but if I'd say, 'Bob Wills' or 'San Antonio Rose,' they'd applaud before we'd ever start playing. They knew the songs. And they danced. Some of them would come and stand around the bandstand, but, in the back, they'd be dancing" (Interview, March 21, 2001).

Another achievement for the Light Crust Doughboys has been the publishing of two songbooks, *The Light Crust Doughboys Songbook* and *The Ultimate All-Day Singing Songbook*, by Mel Bay Publications, one of the world's top publishers of sheet music. "Your work in songbook form is a tremendous legacy for the future," Greenhaw said. "Fewer and fewer songbooks are being published so it's really an honor for Mel Bay to do the two for the Light Crust Doughboys. The Ventures, the biggest selling instrumental band in the world, hadn't had a songbook since the 1960s and they've just recently had a new songbook. So it took them 36 years to have a songbook done. It's just a very small percentage, maybe the top one percent of all artists, who have songbooks. There's still a real small market for that [songbooks], with limited sales, but it's one of those things that get the Light Crust Doughboys name out worldwide, and that's so important."

Art said the Light Crust Doughboys will continue as a band for many years to come:

> We'll always keep doing these wonderful historical shows like the Doughboys have done since the 1930s, which is the essence of what we do, the five or six-man string-band swing. No gimmicks, no synthesizers, just the pure music of the Light Crust Doughboys. We'll continue to be even more innovative, if that's possible, with our recordings and try to collaborate with people who can bring added dimensions to the Doughboys sound. We'll keep doing our gospel music. Hopefully, we'll keep having many, many more Grammy nominations, and even Grammy Award wins. That's one of my top priorities in life, to continue the Light Crust Doughboys, to have it bigger and better, every year, and make sure it continues to be the longest running country band in the world. (Interview)

In 2001, the Doughboys added a new member when Dale Cook became the group's first drummer. Cook had played special dates with the group since the 1970s (Greenhaw, Dec. 30, 2001).

At the time of this writing, Greenhaw's fertile imagination had led him into a project with a dance instructor at the University of Texas to combine the Doughboys' Western swing with the Far Eastern sounds of Indian classical music. "We call it 'Lone Star Sitar,'" Greenhaw said. "We'll be moving in those real avant garde, world-music directions" (Interview).

Jerry Elliott does not foresee a day when he will quit the Light Crust Doughboys. "I've just been with them too long," he said with a laugh. "I guess I'll be like the rest, I'll die with them, if they'll keep me that long. . . . I love the Light Crust group, I loved all the guys or I wouldn't have stayed with them" (Interview, March 8, 2001).

Smokey reckoned himself one lucky fellow. His more-than-five-decade marriage to Kathleen gave him two sons, Gary and Steve, four grandchildren and two great-grandchildren. And he modestly attributed his extraordinary music career to good fortune. "I was lucky being in the right place at the right time," he said:

> When J. Doug [Morgan, the tent show manager] sent me the wire, and I did the amateur show. I got to Texas, and then I got to Dallas. I met the guy and went to the stag show and got the job with the Wanderers. Then when they went to the Doughboys, I got to go. When I met Ed [Bernet, his partner in Sumet Studios and in the Levee Singers], that was another lucky time. Then when I met you [referring to Greenhaw], that was another lucky time. Those are the things that I say are being in the right place at the right time. It's always happened to me. Like I also say, I should be dead, but the Good Lord is keeping me alive for some reason. (Oral history, 197)

In 1997, Smokey told an interviewer that he had already planned his own funeral. A hymn he wrote with Barbara, "Lord, Take All of Me," would be sung. He had recorded a banjo performance of a favorite song, the Bing Crosby classic "Bells of Saint Mary's" (also a latter-day Doughboys standard) and a brief farewell speech. He was a member of the Masons, and they were to be represented. The Bearkats and the Dallas Banjo Band were to play. But the greatest performance was to take place beyond the sight and hearing of the mourners: A reunion of the departed Light Crust Doughboys. "When I get there, we'll have the biggest jam session ever" (Tarrant).

Postscript

An account of key members of the Light Crust Doughboys and those closely associated with the group whose later years and deaths are not covered in the main text:

Herman Arnspiger, one of the original Light Crust Doughboys, also played with Bob Wills and the Texas Playboys from 1934–1940. Arnspiger had a second career in Tulsa as a pilot. He worked as the chief pilot and instructor at the Spartan School of Aeronautics, and later became a test pilot for Douglas Aircraft. Arnspiger established the Sunray Oil Company's aviation department. He retired in 1964, and died in a Tulsa nursing home at the age of 79 in 1984 ("Last original member").

Cecil Brower played for Leon McAuliffe and on Red Foley's television program following his service in the Coast Guard during World War II. Brower followed Foley to Nashville, and became a much sought-after session musician. In the 1960s, he joined Jimmy Dean's band. On November 21, 1965, Dean performed at Carnegie Hall in New York. At a party held at the Waldorf Hotel following the show, Brower suddenly died from a perforated ulcer at the age of 51 (Ginell, *Milton Brown*, 223).

William Muryel "Zeke" Campbell died March 5, 1997, at his home in the Dallas-Fort Worth suburb of Hurst. He was 82. After retiring from WBAP-TV (later KXAS), Campbell played guitar and taught Sunday school at the First United Methodist Church in Bedford. "He was teaching Sunday school up to the time he died," Smokey Montgomery said. Will Schotte, a booking agent for the Light Crust Doughboys, said, "Zeke and Smokey were roommates [when the band traveled] because they weren't into chasing wild women, partying and drinking. His love was for Christ. He spent a lot of time at the church and at the Sunday school. Making a movie [with Gene Autry in 1936] wasn't that big a deal. It was just an event. The most important things were his church, his family, his kids and his wife" (Halsey).

Tommy Duncan was the first member of Bob Wills' band to join the armed forces at the beginning of America's involvement in World War II. He rejoined Wills in 1944, left to form his own band, Tommy Duncan and His Western All-Stars in 1948, and then rejoined Wills in 1959. After several years of touring and recording, Duncan and Wills parted company again. Following a performance in Imperial Beach, California, on July 24, 1967, Duncan was found dead of a heart attack in a San Diego hotel room at the age of 55 (Townsend, "Thomas"; Death certificate).

Joe Frank Ferguson III died February 14, 2001, in Fort Worth. He was 86. After leaving the Coast Guard following World War II, he worked as a rancher and welder, but continued to play music part-time. After retiring, he played with the latter-day version of the Texas Playboys from 1977 to 1989. Occasionally, Joe Frank performed as a guest artist at the Light Crust Doughboys' Dallas Pocket Sandwich Theatre series. Two months before his death, he played his final show, a Christmas concert at the Johnny High Music Review in Arlington (Murillo).

Truett Kimzey, the radio engineer who was the Doughboys' original announcer at KFJZ, went on to build the first experimental television station in Texas. Other experiments had transmitted pictures over telephone lines, but Kimzey was the first in Texas to transmit over the airwaves. Kimzey demonstrated the station, Station W5AGO, at the 1934 Southwestern Exposition and Fat Stock Show in Fort Worth. "I thought television was just around the corner," Kimzey said, "and sunk all my savings—$1,500—in the equipment." He served for many years as the chief engineer of the Texas State Network (not to be confused with the Texas Quality Network), and died in January 1968 (Schroeder, 131–132; Kimzey).

John "Knocky" Parker earned a master's degree in English from Columbia University and an Ed.D. from the University of Kentucky. He became a professor at the University of South Florida in Tampa. In 1964, USF named him its "professor of Ragtime." Ron Faig, the media coordinator for USF, wrote: "I actually had the pleasure of meeting him shortly after I began working at USF 16 years ago. What a character! He was one of those few people who, even though there was only brief contact, leaves such a lasting impression and pleasant memories. He did enjoy talking and entertaining. In the early years of USF (the '60s), he was part of a group known as 'The Red Hot Profs.' They played around campus for the faculty, staff and students. . . . Back then, everyone knew and loved him." In addition to his English classes, Parker taught a film classics course that became legendary among the university's students. In the class, Knocky played piano for silent films. Parker continued to play occasionally in Dixieland bands with Smokey Montgomery. In 1983, Knocky recorded an album with Big Joe Turner and his Houserockers that was nominated for a Grammy Award. He once said, "My life is my music. That's who I am. That's what I am, and that's all I am." Knocky retired to Los Angeles where he died on September 4, 1986, at the age of 68 (Faig; Camp; Ginell, *Milton Brown*, 268).

Kenneth Pitts served as a high-school and junior-high teacher, and then directed middle-school band and orchestra for many years. He played viola in the Fort Worth Symphony and the Fort Worth Opera orchestra. He died in June 1992 (Stout, personal communication).

Dick Reinhart formed his own band called the Lone Star Boys, recording on the Okeh label under the guidance of Uncle Art Satherley. Reinhart then joined with Jimmy Wakely and Johnny Bond in a group named the Bell Boys, promoting an Oklahoma City department store on WKY. Later, they successfully auditioned for Gene Autry, and performed with him as the Rough Riders on his *Melody Ranch* radio show. The group later adopted the name of the Jimmy Wakely Trio and enjoyed continued success. Reinhart died December 3, 1948, from a sudden heart attack at the age of 40. He had returned to Fort Worth and was working in a furniture factory at the time. "I didn't know he was back in Fort Worth until his niece called me and asked me to be a pallbearer," Smokey Montgomery recalled ("The Cowboys"; "Johnny Bond Publications"; Ginell, *Milton Brown*, 260; Montgomery interview, May 3, 2001).

Parker Willson, the Doughboys' popular announcer, operated his own advertising agency after the group's radio program left the air. He served as the master of ceremonies for the Cowtown Jamboree and the Big D Jamboree. He died in March 1962 (Montgomery interview, May 3, 2001; Willson).

W. Lee O'Daniel made two unsuccessful comeback attempts to regain the Texas governor's mansion in 1956 and 1958. He remained active in business, and died in 1969 at the age of 79 ("'Pappy' O'Daniel").

Bob Wills continued to perform and record through the 1960s. But Wills' health began to fail in the early 1970s. He found himself confined to a wheelchair after a series of strokes and heart attacks. Finally in December 1973, country superstar Merle Haggard gathered some of the surviving Playboys in Dallas for one last recording with their mentor and friend. The 24 tracks resulting from the session were released as *Bob Wills and His Texas Playboys: For The Last Time.*

The sessions also represented a final link between Wills and the Light Crust Doughboys. Smokey Montgomery was at the sessions.

> They brought Bob Wills over in a wheelchair. He'd give the guys the right tempo, then we put a mike in front of him so he could do some of his "ah-hahs." He was so weak we couldn't use them. Hoyle Nix was there, who could imitate Bob to a tee. We got Hoyle Nix to do a bunch of "ah-hahhs." Those "ah-hahhs" you hear [on the record] are Hoyle. That night, [Bob] had one of those massive strokes. I don't think he ever got out of bed after that.

Smokey said the musicians continued recording the next day without Wills, unsuccessfully fighting back the tears as they played "(New) San Antonio Rose," feeling certain that the stroke would be the one that ended Wills' life. "And of course it was," Smokey said.

Wills never recovered from the stroke before he died on May 13, 1975, at 70. The epitaph on his gravestone in Tulsa is the opening line from "(New) San Antonio Rose": "Deep within my heart lies a melody" ("Famous Texans: Bob Wills"; "Bob Wills and the Texas Playboys").

Appendix 1
Light Crust Doughboys Recording Sessions
1936–1948

Compiled 1989 by Marvin "Junior" Montgomery, known since 1948 as "Smokey" Montgomery. [Substantially unedited]

[Abbreviations used:
acd   accordian
b   bass
bj   banjo
elg   electric guitar
gtr   guitar
md   mandolin
pno piano
rhy   rhythm
tbj   tenor banjo
tgtr   tenor guitar
vcl   vocal]

Over the years I have seen many miscues on record jackets, magazine articles, etc., regarding the Doughboy Recording sessions—who played what, sang what, yelled what, or just plain old what—I decided (with a lot of prodding from Bob Pinson and some back-up from Muryel "Zeke" Campbell, Kenneth "Abner" Pitts, Jim "Bashful" Boyd, Joe Frank "Bashful" Ferguson, Frank Reneau and Leroy Millican) to put the record straight. As Zeke, Abner and Junior (yours truly) are the only living members who played on all of these sessions it stands to reason that this is as correct as the record will ever get.

April 4, 1936, Fort Worth, Texas
A & R (producer): "Uncle" Art Satherley. Musicians: Dick "Bashful" Reinhart, rhythm gtr, vcl; Bert "Buddy" Dodson, b, vcl; Clifford "Doctor" Gross, fid and b vcl on quartets; Kenneth "Abner" Pitts, fid, acd, baritone vcl on trios and quartets; Muryel "Zeke" Campbell, acoustic lead gtr; Marvin "Junior" Montgomery, tbj, tgtr and a vcl now and then. (My first recording session with the Doughboys along with Reinhart, Dodson and Campbell.)
Eddie Dunn was our radio announcer and boss; he was not a musician.

On all twin fid work, Gross played the lead part and Pitts the harmony part. Each song discographed in order of performance.

FW-1250. I'm a Ding Dong Daddy from Dumas
1. Twin fids, Gross-Pitts
2. Vcl, Reinhart
3. Acoustic gtr solo, Campbell
4. Tbj solo, Montgomery
5. Vcl
6. Acoustic gtr solo, Reinhart
7. Vcl
8. Hot fid solo, Pitts
FW-1251. My Buddy. Unissued.

FW-1252. I Like Bananas (Because They Have No Bones)
1. Twin fids
2. Vcl unison, Dodson, Reinhart, Pitts, Montgomery, Gross
3. Verse: lead vcl, Dodson; background vcl, Pitts, Reinhart, Montgomery, Gross
4. Chorus trio: Dodson, lead; Reinhart, tenor; Pitts, baritone
5. Twin fids
6. Vcls: Dodson, group; Pitts group; Montgomery (one line); Reinhart (one line); group
7. Gtr solo, Campbell; fid solo, Pitts; tag-group

FW-1253. The Wheel of the Wagon Is Broken. Unissued.

April 5, 1936 (same place, same musicians)
FW-254. Little Hillbilly Heart Throb. Unissued.

FW-1255. Did You Ever Hear a String Band Swing? (Composer Marvin Montgomery)
1. Intro-fid, Pitts
2. Vcl lead, Montgomery group, Pitts, Reinhart, Dodson, Gross
3. Fid, Pitts
4. Talk, Montgomery; Pitts, fid; talk, Montgomery; Dodson, acoustic b solo
4. Gtr solo, Campbell
5. Bj solo, Montgomery
6. Fid, Pitts

FW- 256. Tonight I Have a Date (Composer, Marvin Montgomery). Unissued.

FW-1257. Saddle Your Blues to a Wild Mustang
1. Intro twin fids, Gross, Pitts
2. Vcl, Dodson
3. Twin fids
4. Vcl

FW-1258. Gloomy Monday. Unissued.

FW-1259. Memories. Unissued.
Notice: As you read on you'll find that on a lot of the songs Gross did not play, due to the fact that he couldn't read music and was a slow learner. On the recording sessions we didn't like to waste time waiting for him to learn a song, and so Pitts (who acted as leader on the sessions) and I would leave him out. Gross would go to the corner and sulk.

May 26 & 29, 1936. Los Angeles.
We were in Hollywood at Republic Studios to make the movie *Oh, Susanna* with Gene Autry. Pitts remembers that "Uncle" Art Satherley was *not* at those sessions, but thinks the producer's name was Gray.

Musicians: Reinhart, Vcl, rhythm gtr and md (the one I have and intend to send to The Country Music Foundation in Nashville soon). You'll hear it on "My Buddy." Dodson, vcl, b; Pitts, fid; Gross, fid; Campbell, lead acoustic gtr; Montomgery, tbj & tgtr.

May 26, 1936
LA-1121. Little Hill-Billy Heart Throb
1. Twin fids, Gross, Pitts
2. Vcl, Reinhart (Dick had a sore throat and sang this in a key almost too low for him)
3. Twin fids
4. Vcl 5. Gtr solo, Campbell
6. Vcl.

LA-1122. My Buddy.
1. Twin fids, Gross, Pitts—Fills; Montgomery, tgtr
2. Vcl trio: Dodson, lead; Reinhart, tenor; Pitts, baritone.
3. Md solo, Reinhart
4. Vcl trio.

LA-1123. The Wheel of the Wagon Is Broken
1. Intro, tgtr, Montgomery
2. Vcl, Reinhart; tgtr fills, Montgomery
3. Twin fids, Gross, Pitts
4. Vcl, tgtr ending.

LA-1124. Tonight I Have a Date. Unissued. (Uncle Art still didn't like my song, and I don't blame him.)

LA-1125. Lost
1. Twin fids, vcl, Dodson; fills on tgtr, Montgomery; fid fills, Pitts; twin fid, gtr solo, Campbell; vcl. Pitts remembers he played both 2nd and 3rd harmony notes part of the time.

May 29, 1936 Los Angeles.
LA-1126. Sweet Uncle Zeke. This song was composed by Freddy Casares, fid player with the old Wanderers fid band which Dodson, Reinhart and I played with before we joined the Doughboys. This song was also used as background music in the movie *Oh, Susanna.*
1. Gtr solo, Reinhart
2. Fid solo, Pitts
3. Gtr solo, Campbell
4. Bj solo, Montgomery
5. Gtr and fid duet, Reinhart and Pitts.

LA-1127. All My Life
1. Twin fids, Gross, Pitts
2. Vcl, Dodson, tgtr fills, Montgomery
3. Twin fids
4. Vcl

LA-1128. Jig in "G." Unissued.

LA-1129. When the Moon Shines on the Mississippi Valley
1. Twin fids
2. Vcl, Reinhart
3. Fiddle, Pitts
4. Vcl.

LA-1131. It's Been So Long
1. Fid, Pitts
2. Vcl, Dodson
3. Gtr solo, Campbell
4. Vcl.

LA-1132. Cross-Eyed Cowboy from Abilene (Composer, Marvin Montgomery)
Notice: I wrote these terrible songs and I couldn't get anybody to sing them so I had to sing them myself.
1. Fid, Pitts
2. Vcl, Montgomery
3. Gtr solo, Campbell
4. Vcl

September 10, 1936, Fort Worth, Texas
Producer (A & R) "Uncle" Art Satherley, Don Law. Musicians: Reinhart, rhythm gtr, vcl; Dodson, b, vcl; Pitts, fid, acd; Gross, fid; Campbell, solo acoustic gtr; Montgomery, tbj. Notice: Along about this time Uncle Art asked me to play 4/4 time on the bj. Up until then I played mostly 2/4. You'll hear me doing 4/4 from now on.

FW-1262. I'd Love to Live in Loveland (With a Girl Like You). Unissued.

FW-1263. Happy Cowboy. (Notice: We met the Sons of the Pioneers and played on their radio show while we were in Hollywood. When we got back to Texas we started doing a lot of their songs.)
1. Twin fids
2. Vcl, Dodson. Trio: Dodson, lead; Reinhart, tenor; Pitts, baritone
3. Twin gtrs, Reinhart, Campbell; Twin fids; Trio.

FW-1264. Blue Guitar. Unissued.

FW-1265. A Mug of Ale. Unissued.

FW-1266. Sweet Georgia Brown. Unissued.

FW 1267 Oh, Susanna
1. Bj, Montgomery
2. Vcl, Dodson. Quartet: Dodson, lead; Reinhart, tenor; Pitts, baritone; Gross, b. Solo gtr, Campbell; fid, Gross; Bj, Quartet. Rhythm acd played by Pitts.

FW-1268. The Strawberry Roan. Unissued.

FW-1269. The Big Corral. Unissued.

FW-1270. I Want a Girl (Just Like the Girl That Married Dear Old Dad). Unissued.

FW-1271. When You Wore a Tulip (and I Wore A Big Red Rose). Unissued.

June 12, 1937 Dallas, Texas
A & R Producer, Art Satherley, Don Law. Musicians: John "Knocky" Parker, pno, acd, first recording session with the Doughboys. Raymond "Snub" DeArman, slap b, rhythm gtr, vcl (his second time as a Doughboy—he left the first time to join Cecil Brower in Columbus, Ohio to make transcriptions, shortly before Reinhart, Dodson and I joined the Doughboys. He replaced Dodson in the band playing slap b.) Pitts, Gross, Campbell, Reinhart, Montgomery. From now on most of the yells, etc., on the records will be DeArman. Campbell plays electric gtr for first time.

DAL-268. Emaline
1. Pno intro, Parker
2. Fid, Pitts
3. Vcl, Reinhart
4. elg, Campbell; bridge & fid to end of chorus, Pitts
5. Pno, full chorus to end, Parker.

DAL-269. Let Me Ride By Your Side in the Saddle. Unissued.

DAL-270. Tom Cat Rag. Unissued.

DAL-271. Blue Guitars
1. Pno intro, Parker
2. Elg, Campbell
3. Pno
4. Gtr
5. Fid, Pitts
6. Gtr

DAL-272. Dusky Stevedore
1. Twin fids, Gross, Pitts
2. Vcl duet: DeArman, lead, Reinhart, tenor
3. Bj solo, Montgomery
4. Acd, Parker; Pitts plays pno rhythm
5. Vcl duet

DAL-273. If I Don't Love You (There Ain't a Cow in Texas)
1. Twin fids, Gross, Pitts
2. Vcl, Reinhart
3. Elg, Campbell
4. Acd, Parker; Pitts to pno
DAL-274. Roll Along, Jordan
1. Twin fids, Gross, Pitts
2. Vcl verse, DeArman
3. Quartet: DeArman, lead; Reinhart, tenor; Pitts, baritone; Gross, bass
3. Gtr, Campbell
4. Twin acds, Parker, Pitts
5. Vcl verse, Quartet chorus.

DAL-275. One Sweet Letter from You. Unissued.

DAL-276. Song of the Saddle. Unissued.

DAL-277. Anna Lou. Unissued.

DAL-278. Avalon
1. Twin fids
2. Pno: four hands, Pitts on bass end and Parker on high end
3. Bj
4. Gtr
5. Acd, Parker; Pitts stays on pno rhythm

June 20, 1937 Dallas.
Same musicians. Notice: The jump in record numbers means that between our recording sessions Uncle Art and Don Law recorded several other groups.

DAL-385. Gig-a-Wig Blues (Composer, Marvin Montgomery)
1. Fid, Pitts
2. Bj, Montgomery
3. Pno, Parker
4. Gtr, Campbell
5. Acd, Parker; Pitts to pno

DAL-386. In a Little Red Barn
1. Twin fids, Gross, Pitts
2. Vcl, DeArman
3. Pno, Parker
4. Gtr, Campbell
5. Fid, Pitts

DAL-387. Beaumont Rag
1. Fid, Gross
2. Bj, Montgomery
3. Fid, Gross
4. Gtr, Campbell
5. Fid, Gross
(Rhy gtr, Reinhart; rhy acd, Pitts; yells and slap bass, DeArman—he yelled a lot didn't he? More than Bob Wills?)

DAL-388. The Eyes of Texas
1. Twin fids, Gross, Pitts
2. Vcl quartet: DeArman, lead; Reinhart, tenor; Pitts, baritone; Gross, bass
3. Gtr, Campbell
4. Pno, Parker
5. Quartet

DAL-389. Washington and Lee Swing
1. Twin fids, Gross, Pitts
2. Bj, Montgomery
3. Acd, Pitts
4. Gtr, Campbell
5. Pno, Parker
6. Twin fids

DAL-390. Stay on the Right Side Sister. Unissued.

DAL-391. Just Once Too Often
1. Gtr intro, Reinhart
2. Fid, Pitts
3. Vcl, Reinhart
4. Gtr, Campbell.

DAL-392. Stay Out of the South. Unissued.

May 14, 1938, Dallas, Texas
Parker Willson is now our M.C. and boss-man. He sang b with the quartet and now and then sang a solo. The Doughboys also have a mascot, Charles Burton, eleven or twelve years of age, who sang on the radio show several times a week and went on some of our personal appearance shows. His real name was Willson. Parker Willson had Charles use Burton as a last name because Parker Willson didn't want the public to think that Charles was his son. Musicians: Same as last session. Fids, Gross, Pitts; gtrs, Reinhart, Campbell; pno, Parker; Bj, Montgomery; b, DeArman. Producer: A & R, Uncle Art Satherley, Don Law.

DAL-529. Sitting on Top of the World
1. Elg, Dick "Bashful" Reinhart
2. Vcl, Reinhart
3. Fid, Pitts
4. Vcl, Reinhart
5. Elg, Reinhart. Campbell played rhy gtr.

DAL-530. Weary Blues
Fid, Pitts; elg, Campbell; pno, Parker; Bj, Montgomery; Rhy gtr, Reinhart; Slap b and yells, DeArman. Notice: All harmony parts played on elg, fid and pno. Gross went to his corner on this one.

DAL-531. Gulf Coast Blues
1. Pno Intro, Parker
2. Fid, Pitts
3. Vcl, Reinhart

4. Pno, Parker
5. Gtr, Campbell
6. Vcl

DAL-532. The Budded Rose
1. Twin fids, Gross, Pitts
2. Vcl, DeArman
3. Gtr, Campbell
4. Vcl

DAL-533. I'll Get Mine
1. Twin fids, Gross, Pitts
2. Vcl verse, Reinhart; quartet, DeArman takes lead, Reinhart goes to tenor, Pitts, baritone, Gross, b
3. Gtr, Campbell
4. Pno, Parker 5. Fid solo, Pitts
6. Vcl verse, quartet

DAL-534. Blue Hours
1. Twin fids, Gross, Pitts; steel gtr, Reinhart; Parker on pno to bridge then puts on acd
2. Acd, Parker with steel background
3. Steel played in harmony (Bridge) steel plays single string lead
4. Tag, fids and steel; bowed B, DeArman; tgtr, Montgomery; Rhy gtr, Campbell.

DAL-535. Three Shif-less Skonks.
1. Twin fids, Gross, Pitts
2. Vcl solo, DeArman; quartet, DeArman, lead; Reinhart, tenor; Pitts, baritone; Gross, b
3. Fid Solo, Pitts
4. Pno, Parker
5. Vcl solo, quartet
6. Elg, Campbell
7. Vcl solo, quartet

DAL-536. Kalua Loha. Unissued.

DAL-537. Slow Down, Mr. Brown
1. Fid, Pitts
2. Vcl, Reinhart
3. Gtr, Campbell
4. Pno, Parker
5. Vcl out

DAL-538. Beautiful Ohio
1. Twin fids, Gross, Pitts
2. Vcl, Charles Burton (Doughboy Mascot)
3. Elg lead, Campbell, twin fid background
4. Vcl.

DAL-539. Waiting for the Robert E. Lee
1. Twin fids, Gross, Pitts
2. Vcl, Reinhart
3. Acd, Parker, Pitts to pno
4. Gtr, Campbell
5. Vcl

DAL-540. Hills of Old Wyomin'
1. Fid, Pitts
2. Vcl, Charles Burton
3. Unison hum, Parker Willson (MC), DeArman, Pitts, Reinhart
4. Vcl, hum
5. Vcl quartet, Reinhart, tenor; DeArman, lead; Pitts, baritone; Wilson, b
6. Vcl with hum

DAL-541. Tom Cat Rag (Composer, Marvin Montgomery)
1. Fid, Pitts
2. Vcl, DeArman; lead, Reinhart; tenor, Pitts, baritone
3. Gtr, Campbell
4. Pno, Parker
5. Bj, Montgomery
6. Vcl

DAL-542. Gig-a-Wig Blues (Composer, Marvin Montgomery)
Notice: Gig-a-Wig Blues is also number 385. I do not know which version they
released but I would think that it would be the last one we cut (542).

DAL-543. Knocky-Knocky (Composer, Knocky Parker)
1. Pno
2. Fid, Pitts
3. Pno
4. Gtr, Campbell
5. Pno

DAL-544. The Birth of the Blues
1. Gtr intro, Reinhart
2. Twin fids, bridge, pno, twin fids
3. Vcl, Reinhart
4. Gtr, Campbell; pno, Parker
5. Fid solo, Pitts; vcl out

DAL-545. Rockin' Alone (In an Old Rockin' Chair). Unissued.

DAL-546. Pretty Little Dear
1. Twin fids
2. Vcl, DeArman
3. Gtr, Campbell
4. Vcl
5. Twin fades, Pitts solo at bridge; twin fids
6. Vcl.

DAL-547. Sweeter Than an Angel
1. Fid, Pitts
2. Vcl. Reinhart
3. Gtr
4. Pno
5. Fid solo, Pitts
6. Vcl

DAL-548. Stumbling
1. Tgtr lead, Montgomery; 2nd gtr (acoustic), Campbell; 3rd gtr (acoustic), Pitts
2. Acoustic gtr solo, Campbell
3. Pno, Parker
4. Fid, Pitts

DAL-549. Clarinet Marmalade
1. Fid, Pitts
2. Elg, pno & fid in harmony (Campbell, Pitts, Parker)
3. Fid, Pitts
4. Gtr, Campbell
5. Pno, Parker
6. Harmony parts
7. Fid, Pitts

We recorded twenty-one songs on this session all in one day. The longest session we ever had in one day.

November 30, 1938, Dallas, Texas
Producer (A & R) Art Satherley, Don Law. Musicians: "Buck" Buchanan, fid replacing "Doctor" Gross (who left before getting fired after pulling a knife on Parker Willson, our boss-man). Jim "Bashful" Boyd replacing Dick "Bashful" Reinhart who left because Burrus Mill hired Parker Willson as MC and boss instead of him. Reinhart joined Gross and they formed the Universal Cowboys for Universal Flour Mills. Boyd states that he joined the Doughboys in August of 1938. Buchanan joined about one month earlier. Ken "Abner" Pitts, fid; "Zeke" Campbell, elg; "Junior" Montgomery, bj and kazoo; "Knocky" Parker, pno, acd; "Snub" DeArman, slap b.

DeArman and Boyd changed off between b and rhythm gtr. You can identify DeArman's b playing because he slapped it more than Boyd, also he was inclined to play a lot of backward b. Example: to play a C chord in 2/4 time you should play C then G. DeArman would reverse the rule and play G then C: Hence the term "Backward B." This was very upsetting to some of the musicians in the band, most especially "Knocky" Parker. Notice on this session that Boyd did all the solo vcl. For some reason DeArman was left out. Also Uncle Art (or Parker Willson) calmed him down on the yells.

DAL-641. It Makes No Difference Now (Boyd's first record as a Doughboy. On the following recordings I also have input coming from Boyd. He believes it is his younger brother, John Boyd, who is playing steel on this song. Pitts and I both agree with this. John recorded several songs under his own name for Uncle Art during this session. Not long after these sessions, John was killed in a motorcycle accident.)
1. Elg, Campbell, steel fills (John Boyd)
2. Vcl, Boyd
3. Campbell & steel
4. Vcl, Boyd
5. Twin fids, Pitts, lead; Buchanan, harmony
6. Vcl, Boyd; tgtr, Montgomery; B, DeArman; rhy gtr, Boyd
Notice: While Buchanan was on the band Pitts played lead and Buchanan played the harmony parts.

DAL-642. Blue-Eyed Sally
1. Twin fids, Pitts, Buchanan
2. Vcl, Boyd
3. Elg, Campbell
4. Pno, Parker
5. Twin fids
6. Vcl, Boyd, rhythm; DeArman, b; bj, Montgomery.

DAL-643. You're the Only Star (In My Blue Heaven). The Columbia release has DeArman listed as the vclist, NOT TRUE. It was Jim Boyd.

1. Twin fids, Pitts, Buchanan
2. Vcl, Boyd
3. Two gtrs: tgtr lead, Montgomery; Acoustic standard gtr, Campbell; harmony twin fids (Bridge) twin gtrs
4. Vcl, Boyd; DeArman, b

DAL-644. Baby, Give Me Some of That (Composer, Marvin Montgomery)
1. Twin fids, Pitts, Buchanan
2. Vcl, Boyd
3. Pno, Parker; Elg, Campbell
4. Twin fids, hot solo fid, Buchanan; vcl, DeArman, b

DAL-645. Dirty Dishrag Blues (Composer, Zeke Campbell)
1. Acoustic gtr intro, Boyd
2. Elg, Campbell
3. Vcl, Boyd
4. Pno, Parker
5. Fid solo, Pitts
6. Vcl
7. Elg
8. Vcl, DeArman b; Montgomery, bj

DAL-646. (New) Jeep's Blues
1. Pno intro, Parker
2. Twin fids, Pitts, Buchanan
3. Elg, Campbell
4. Pno
5. Elg
6. Twin fids

DAL-647. Zenda Waltz
1. Twin fids, Pitts, Buchanan
2. Elg, Campbell
3. Twin fids, tgtr, Montgomery; Bowed b, DeArman; rhy gtr, Boyd

DAL-648. Grey Skies. Unissued.

DAL-649. Thousand Mile Blues
1. Twin fids
2. Fid solo, Buchanan
3. Vcl, Boyd
4. Elg, Campbell
5. Pno, Parker; Kazoo, Montgomery
6. Vcl; slap b by DeArman

DAL-650. Gin Mill Blues
1. Pno, Parker
2. Elg, Campbell; twin fid, background, Pitts, Buchanan
3. Pno, Parker
4. Pno, twin fid, BG
5. Fids and pno, bowed b, Boyd; tgtr, Montgomery; rhy gtr, DeArman

DAL-651. Yancy Special. Unissued.

DAL-652. The Farmer's Not in the Dell
1. Elg, Campbell
2. Vcl, Boyd
3. Pno, Parker; hot fid, Buchanan, pno
4. Twin fids, Pitts, Buchanan; DeArman, B; Boyd, rhy gtr

DAL-653. Foot Warmer
1. Twin fids, Pitts, Buchanan
2. Elg (Campbell) in harmony with fids
3. Pno, Parker
4. Elg
5. Fid solo, Buchanan
6. Elg
7. B, Boyd; rhy gtr, DeArman; bj, Montgomery

DAL-654. Troubles
1. Twin fids, Pitts, Buchanan
2. Vcl, Boyd
3. Humming trio: Boyd, tenor; DeArman, lead; Pitts, baritone
4. Elg, Campbell
5. Vcl
6. Hum trio. (Boyd thinks Willson sang baritone on this one; Pitts thinks it was he; take your pick.)

DAL-655. Pussy, Pussy, Pussy (Composer, Marvin Montgomery)
1. Vamp-Girl Voice, Montgomery
2. Group Voices, Pitts, Boyd, DeArman, Montgomery
3. Elg, Campbell
4. Fid, Buchanan
5. Pno, Parker
6. Cat, DeArman; Girl, Montgomery; male voice, DeArman
7. Group voices
8. Elg, fid background. Boyd on b. (This record got on more juke-boxes than any other song I ever wrote.)

Dallas, June 14, 1939
Producer (A & R) Art Satherley, Don Law. Musicians: Cecil Brower, fid, replacing Buchanan. Pitts, Campbell, Parker, DeArman, Boyd, Montgomery. Charles Burton, our mascot, did some vcl as well as Parker Willson, our MC and boss-man. Musically, this is probably the best session we ever did. We recorded in the old Brunswick Warehouse with no air conditioning, and it was hot. We played with our shirts off and I suspect the bottle was passed around a few times among some of the band members as well as the boss-man—why hide it—Willson, Brower, DeArman and Don Law and maybe a swig or two by Boyd.

DAL-803. Let's Make Believe We're Sweethearts
1. Elg, Campbell
2. Vcl, Boyd
3. Twin fids: Brower lead, Pitts Harmony
4. Elg, fids in unison, vcl. Boyd on b; DeArman, rhythm gtr; Parker on pno; Montgomery, bj.
Notice: After Brower joined the Doughboys he played lead fid and Pitts played the harmony fid.

DAL-804. Thinking of You
1. Twin fids, Brower, Pitts
2. Vcl, DeArman
3. Elg, Campbell
4. Accordian, Parker (Pitts switched to rhythm pno)
5. Vcl. Boyd, b; DeArman, rhythm

DAL-805. If I Didn't Care
1. Intro, unison fids
2. Vcl, Charles Burton
3. unison fids, tgtr fills, Montgomery; Boyd on b

DAL-806. Mary Lou
1. Elg, Campbell
2. Vcl, Charles Burton
3. Twin fids, Brower, Pitts
4. Elg, vcl. tgtr, Montgomery; b, Boyd; rhy, DeArman

DAL-807. In Ole' Oklahoma
1. Twin fids, Brower, Pitts
2. Vcl, Parker Willson
3. Twin fids, vcl. Boyd, b; Montgomery, tgtr; DeArman, rhythm
I might mention the Parker Willson, Charles Burton vcl recordings did not sell very well—Uncle Art recorded and released them as a favor to Parker Willson.

DAL-808. She Gave Me the Bird (Composer, Marvin Montgomery)
1. Twin fids, Pitts, Brower
2. Vcl, Boyd
3. Elg, Campbell
4. Fid solo, Brower
5. Girl Voice, Montgomery (sound effects, Boyd & DeArman)
6. All Sing (Voices), Pitts, Montgomery, DeArman, Boyd, Willson, the Bird, Willson.

DAL-809. Three Naughty Kittens (Composer, Marvin Montgomery)
1. All sound effects, Parker Willson. Voices: Willson, Boyd, DeArman, Pitts, Montgomery
2. Little girl, Parker Willson
3. Pno, Parker
4. Little Girl, Willson
5. Low voice, Willson: Vcl Group
6. Gtr, Campbell
7. Little Girl, Willson

DAL-810. We Must Have Beer (Marvin Montgomery)
1. Twin fids, Pitts, Brower
2. Vcl Group, Pitts, Boyd, DeArman, Willson
3. Acd, Parker; Twin fids
4. Acd, Twin fids
5. Interlude
6. Acd
7. Twin fids
8. Interlude, Twin fids
9. Gtr Solo
10. Vcl Group
11. Pno, Parker
12. Twin fids & gtr

DAL-811. Tea for Two
1. Twin fids, Pitts, Brower
2. Pno, Parker
3. fids & pno
4. Gtr, Campbell; pno; twin fids (rhy gtr, DeArman; b, Boyd; tgtr, Montgomery)

DAL-812. Little Rock Get-a-Way
1. Pno, Parker
2. Pno, twin fids, Pitts, Brower, pno
3. Elg, Campbell
4. Harmony, gtr, fids, pno; harmony, pno, fids (b, Boyd; tgtr, Montgomery; rhy gtr, DeArman)

DAL-813. We Found Her Little Pussy Cat (Marvin Montgomery)
1. Vamp, Cats, DeArman, Willson; Girl Voice, Montgomery
2. Voices: DeArman, Pitts, Willson, Boyd, Montgomery
3. Elg, Campbell
4. Pno, Parker
5. Fid, Brower
6. Vamp, Cats, Male Voice, DeArman; Girl, Montgomery
7. Vcl Group
8. Gtr & fids; tag, voices, cat, Willson (b, Boyd, Rhy. Gtr, DeArman, tgtr, Montgomery)

DAL-814. Old November Moon (Marvin Montgomery). Unissued.

DAL-815. The Cattle Call
1. Twin fids, Pitts, Brower
2. Vcl, Boyd; Trio: Boyd, high; DeArman, middle; Willson, low voice
3. Elg, Campbell
4. Vcl, Boyd, twin fids
5. Vcl, Boyd; Trio: DeArman, Boyd, Willson

DAL-816. Texas Song of Pride (Marvin Montgomery)
1. Twin fids, Pitts, Brower
2. Vcl group, DeArman, Pitts, Boyd, Willson
3. Gtr, Campbell
4. Pno, Parker
5. Vcl group, quartet ending: Boyd, tenor; DeArman, lead; Pitts, baritone; Willson, b

June 15, 1939
DAL-827. Two More Years (And I'll Be Free)
1. Gtr, Campbell (playing two part harmony)
2. Vcl, Boyd
3. Gtr
4. Twin fids, Pitts, Brower
5. Vcl
6. Gtr
7. Vcl

DAL-828. Mama Won't Let Me (Campbell, Parker, Montgomery; I wrote the fid parts only)
1. Gtr (Campbell) & pno (Parker) intro
2. Gtr
3. Pno
4. Twin fids, Pitts, Brower
5. Gtr lead, pno harmony: Bridge, Pno lead, gtr harmony: gtr lead, pno harmony; Boyd, b.

DAL-829. All Because of Lovin' You
1. Gtr, Campbell
2. Vcl, DeArman
3. Twin fids, Pitts, Brower
4. Vcl
Notice: This is the worst performance of any song we had recorded so far—the Doughboys always played the same chords at the same time up until this song. I don't know how the mixed-up chords and bass got by Uncle Art and Pitts. Campbell and Pitts had the best ears in the band, not counting Parker.

DAL-830. Oh Baby Blues
1. Twin fids, Pitts, Brower
2. Vcl, Boyd
3. Gtr, Campbell, vcl out

DAL-831. Beer Drinkin' Mama (Marvin Montgomery)
1 Gtr, Campbell
2. Vcl, Boyd
3. Pno, Parker
4. Twin fids, Pitts, Brower
5. Bj, Montgomery
6. Vcl
7. Gtr (DeAman played b and Boyd rhy gtr)

DAL-832. Mama Gets What She Wants (Knocky Parker)
1. Pno, Parker
2. Vcl, Boyd
3. Gtr, Campbell
4. Vcl
5. Fid, Brower
6. Vcl (Yells, Parker; he felt so good about the way Boyd was singing his song he couldn't hold it in)
7. Gtr

DAL-833. My Gal's with My Pal Tonight (Marvin Montgomery)
1. Twin fids, Pitts, Brower
2. Vcl, Boyd
3. Twin fids
4. Vcl

DAL-834. I Had Someone Else Before I Had You
1. Twin fids, Pitts, Brower
2. Vcl, Boyd
3. Gtr, Campbell; pno, Parker
4. Vcl, Boyd, b

DAL-835. You Got What I Want (Marvin Montgomery)
1. Twin fids, Pitts, Brower
2. Vcl, Boyd
3. Gtr, Campbell
4. Pno, Parker, vcl out; Boyd, b

DAL-836. Jazzbo Joe (Marvin Montgomery)
1. Kazoo, Montgomery
2. Vcl, Boyd
3. Kazoo, twin fid background, Pitts, Brower
4. Gtr, Campbell
5. Fid solo, Brower
6. Pno, Parker
7. Gtr
8. Fid solo, Pitts
9. Kazoo fid background
10. Vcl with kazoo ending, Boyd, b

DAL-837. If I Had My Way
1. Gtr, Campbell
2. Vcl, Boyd
3. Pno, Parker; Twin fids, Pitts, Brower
4. Vcl out; Boyd, b
We recorded 25 songs in two days, eleven of which I wrote. In hindsight I think that if I'd been serious about my songwriting, instead of doing the off-beat stuff, I might have come up with something worth listening to.

Early September 1939, Fort Worth (At our broadcasting studio at the Burrus Flour Mill in Saginaw, Texas). Uncle Art Satherley sent us "I'll Keep on Loving You" and wanted it in a hurry—we cut it and "Little Rubber Dolly" and sent the master to New York. Musicians: fids, Pitts, Brower; b, DeArman; acoustic gtr, Boyd; bj, Montgomery; Elg, Campbell. Knocky Parker (pno) was not on this session. Engineer, our own radio engineer, Jerry (Snag) Stewart. Boss-Man, Parker Willson.

25317. I'll Keep on Loving You
1. Elg, Campbell
2. Vcl, DeArman
3. Twin fids, Pitts, Brower
4. Vcl out; Boyd, b

25318. Little Rubber Dolly
1. Fid, Brower
2. Vcl: DeArman, lead; Boyd, high, high tenor
3. Fid
4. Vcl
5. Fid; acoustic gtr fills played by Boyd. Campbell played acoustic rhythm.
Question: What did Pitts play? Answer: Pitts says he didn't play anything.

Late Oct. 1939, Fort Worth In our Saginaw Studio. Uncle Art wanted a quick "Truck Driver Blues." Same musicians plus Parker back on pno.

25525. Horsie Keep Your Tail Up
Horse, Boyd
1. Vcl: DeArman, lead; Boyd, tenor
2. Bj, Montgomery
3. fids, Pitts, Brower
4. Vcl
5. Gtr, Campbell; vcl: quartet ending, Boyd, tenor; DeArman, lead; Pitts, baritone; Willson, b voice

25526. Truck Driver's Blues
1. Gtr, Campbell
2. Vcl, Boyd
3. Fids, Pitts, Brower
4. Vcl out: Boyd, rhy; DeArman, b

Early December 1939, Fort Worth (Saginaw)
The two previous sessions worked out fairly well and so Parker Willson talked Uncle Art Satherley into letting us produce our own session, picking our own songs. Outside of "Green Valley Trot" we didn't pick very commercial songs. Same musicians.

25594. Green Valley Trot (Another mislabeled record. Joe "Bashful" Ferguson did not come down from Bob Wills's band until the first of January 1940 to

replace Boyd, who left to join Governor W. Lee O'Daniel and His Hillbilly Boys in Austin, Texas. Joe Frank Ferguson is the only musician to come from the Bob Wills band to the Doughboys. All the other musicians left the Doughboys to join Wills.)
1. Gtr, Campbell, full chord lead (no steel gtr)
2. Vcl: DeArman, lead; Boyd, tenor; Pitts, baritone
3. Fid, Brower
4. Vcl solo, Boyd
5. Gtr
6. Vcl, duet
7. Gtr, trio out

25595. Marinita (I think we did this song in order to get our picture on the music.)
1. Acoustic gtr intro, Boyd
2. Fid, Pitts, Brower
3. Vcl, Boyd
4. Acd, Parker; Pitts to rhythm pno
5. Three gtrs, tgtr, Montgomery; standard acoustic gtrs, Boyd, Campbell (Parker back on pno)
6. Vcl out

25596. Careless
1. Gtr, Campbell
2. Vcl, Boyd, fid and steel gtr fills
3. Pno, Parker; steel, Campbell; fids, Pitts, Brower
4. Vcl out. Parker Willson had been on Campbell to play some steel gtr. Campbell played it on this song although he really didn't want to and didn't especially like it when he heard it.

25597. Listen to the Mockingbird. Unissued.

April 24, 1940, Fort Worth (Our Saginaw Studio)
Untold Tales Til Now: Uncle Art Satherley didn't seem to like what we were doing on our own and so he, along with Don Law, came down to Saginaw to produce some sessions. At the same time he recorded several other groups, which probably included the Bob Wills band. The real reason, however, was due to the fact that all of the major record labels had just signed contracts with the American Federation of Musicians and could not record non-union musicians. At that period in time Local 72, AF of M did not seem to want C & W musicians in their union, although Kenneth Pitts, Knocky Parker and I were attending Texas Christian University at the time as part-time students studying every music class available and probably knew more about music history, etc. than a good percentage of the union members. (This is the feeling I had at the time.)

Brower, having traveled with Ted Fiorito's Orchestra, belonged to the L. A. Local. Joe (Bashful) Ferguson, who joined the Doughboys in January 1940, replacing Jim Boyd, came off the Bob Wills Band and was a member of the Tulsa Local. I had belonged to the AF of M local in Newton, Iowa, before I came to Texas, but was not a member at the time of this session. Uncle Art decided to let me play on the session anyhow, as there was not a union banjo player available. I don't know whether he listed me as playing on the session or not. I suppose that if the AF of M had found out that Uncle Art had done such a dastardly deed as to let a non-union banjo player play with union musicians on a recording session they would have taken him out and hung him by his thumbs. But until now, this fact has never been written down.

And so, for this session only, some of the regular Doughboys had to be replaced by union pickers. Leroy Millican, Local 72, replaced Campbell on electric guitar; Babe Wright, Local 72, faced up to the pno in Parker's place; Paul Waggoner, Local 72, picked the rhythm gtr; hence, the band consisted of Wright, pno; Brower, fid; Ferguson, b; Millican, Elg; Waggoner, rhy gtr and non-union Montgomery bj. Singing and arranging was not yet controlled by the union and so Pitts, DeArman, Willson and Campbell could get in on the singing. Also, Pitts wrote all the lead parts for the electric guitar to make the band sound as much like the Doughboys as possible. Although these records were given DAL numbers, they were recorded at our studio in Saginaw, Texas. Neither Pitts, Ferguson nor I could remember Millican playing on these sessions and so I located Millican, alive and retired in Dallas, and sent him a tape. He called back and said that he was playing the lead guitar on these sessions. Thanks, Zeke Campbell, for remembering about Millican.

DAL-1054. Goodbye Little Darling
1. Elg, Leroy Millican
2. Vcl: DeArman, lead; Ferguson, tenor; Pitts, baritone
3. Fid, Brower
4. Vcl
5. Fid, gtr duet, Brower, Millican
6. Vcl
7. Gtr
8. Vcl

DAL-1055. I Want a Feller (Marvin Montgomery)
1. Fid, Brower
2. Vcl, DeArman
3. Gtr, Millican
4. Vcl
5. Fid
6. Vcl
7. Fid

DAL-1056. Rainbow
1. Gtr, Millican
2. Fid, Brower
3. Fid
4. Gtr lead, fid harmony
5. Fid
6. Gtr and fid duet

DAL-1057. Alice Blue Gown
1. Fid, Cecil
2. Vcl, Ferguson
3. Gtr, Milliccan
4. Pno, Babe Wright
5. Vcl

Up to now the pno was not featured on a solo, due to the fact Willson and Uncle Art were afraid that people would realize that it was not Knocky Parker playing, but unto this day, none of the music historians, or anybody else, has ever questioned me on who the musicians were on this session. It seems Pitts did a good job arranging the music in the Doughboy fashion, regardless of the players. And we non-union musicians who swore on a stack of old broken Doughboy 78s to keep the secret from our radio fans, did, until now! I will, however, mention the fact that Bob Pinson noticed that Pitts was not playing fid on these sessions.

April 26, 1940. Same place, same musicians and singers.
DAL-1070. South (Uncle Art sent an old original record of this song down and Pitts wrote the parts out to sound like the Doughboys. It turned out to be one of our best juke-box sellers.) Notice: Some group cut twelve songs on April 25th—could have been Bob Wills.

DAL-1071. She's Too Young (To Play with the Boys) (Pitts, Campbell, Parker)
Vamp, voices: Pitts, DeArman, Willson, Ferguson
2. Fid, Brower
3. Vcl solo, DeArman, voices
4. Gtr, Millican
5. Vcl
6. Fid
7. Vcl
8. Pno, Wright
9. Vcl

DAL-1072. Mean, Mean Mama (From Meana) (Pitts, Campbell, Parker)
1. Gtr, Millican
2. Vcl, Ferguson
3. Fid, Brower
4. Vcl

DAL-1073. Cripple Creek (Pitts wrote lyrics to this old Breakdown. Pitts states that he thinks it was me. Come on, Ken, it's not that bad, go ahead and take credit for it.)
1. Fid, Brower; voice, Parker, Willson
2. Fid
3. Vcl solo, DeArman; quartet: Ferguson, Tenor; DeArman, Lead; Pitts, baritone; Willson, b
4. Fid
5. Vcl
6. Fid, yells, Willson, DeArman
7. Vcl

DAL-1074. Little Honky Tonk Headache (Marvin Montgomery)
1. Gtr, Millican
2. Vcl, Ferguson
3. Pno, Wright
4. Fid, Brower
5. Vcl

DAL-1075. Good Gracious Gracie (Marvin Montgomery)
1. Fid, Brower
2. Vcl, Ferguson
3. Gtr, Millican
4. Pno, Wright
5. Vcl

DAL-1076. If You'll Come Back (Marvin Montgomery)
1. Gtr, Millican
2. Vcl, DeArman
3. Fid, Brower
4. Gtr, vcl to end

DAL-1077. Snow Deer
1. Fid, Brower, playing double stops
2. Gtr, Millican in harmony with fid
3. Fid
4. Gtr and fid
5. Fid

The union musicians on these sessions were paid union scale. Ferguson, Brower and I put the money we got in the pot and it was divided equally between Pitts, Campbell, Parker, DeArman, Brower, Ferguson and yours truly.

February 27, 1941, Fort Worth in the old WBAP radio studios on top of the Blackstone Hotel. The Doughboys all belong to Local 72 AF of M now. For some reason or other Uncle Art gave these records Dallas numbers. Bob Wills and numerous other bands recorded here during this same series of sessions. I remember having a long talk with Tommy Duncan at the studio right after we finished our session. Producer: Art Satherley, Don Law. Musicians: J. B. Brinkley, rhy gtr and vcl, replacing DeArman who was accidentally burned to death. Frank Reneau, pno, replacing Ted Druer who replaced Knocky Parker when Knocky left to finish his college education. Plus Campbell, Pitts, Brower, Ferguson and Montgomery.

DAL-1184. Too. Late
1. Gtr, Campbell; steel gtr fills, Ted Daffan
2. Vcl duet, Brinkley, lead; Ferguson, harmony
3. fids, Brower, Pitts
4. Vcl, duet
Notice: Ted Daffan had just finished a session or was waiting to do a session, or was hoping Uncle Art would let him do a session. Daffan kept pestering Uncle Art to let him play on a Doughboy record, and so, with Parker Willson's approval, Daffan played on two songs with us on this session: "Too Late," and "Five Long Years." This is the only time Daffan ever played with the Doughboys.

DAL-1185. The Little Bar Fly (Marvin Montgomery)
1. Gtr, Campbell
2. Vcl, Brinkley
3. Fids, Brower, Pitts; pno, Reneau, fids
4. Vcl

DAL-1186. It's Your Worry Now (Marvin Montgomery)
I got the idea for this song while we were playing a personal appearance in Pine Bluff, Arkansas, when I overheard a young couple having an argument. As she walked away she heatedly said, "It's your worry, now." I've often wondered what he had to worry about.
1. Gtr, Campbell
2. Vcl, Brinkley
3. Fids, Brower, Pitts
4. Gtr
5. Vcl
6. Vcl

DAL-1187. Zip Zip Zipper (Marvin Montgomery)
1. Vamp, vcl group, Willson, Pitts, Ferguson, Brinkley
2. Vcl group
3. Gtr, Campbell
4. Pno, Reneau
5. Fid solo, Brower
6. Vcl chorus
7. Gtr and fids

DAL-1188. The Bartender's Daughter (Marvin Montgomery)
1. Gtr, Campbell
2. Vcl, Brinkley
3. Fids, Brower, Pitts
4. Vcl

DAL-1189. Don't Lie To An Innocent Maiden (Marvin Montgomery)
1. Gtr, Campbell
2. Vcl, Ferguson
3. Fids, Brower, Pitts
4. Vcl

DAL-1190. Little Honky Tonk Heartthrob (Marvin Montgomery). Unissued.

DAL-1191. Five Long Years (Brinkley)
1. Elg lead, Campbell; steel gtr fills, Ted Daffan
2. Vcl, Brinkley
3. fids, Brower, Pitts
4. Vcl

DAL-1192. Sweet Sally (Campbell, Pitts, Parker)
1. Gtr lead in, J. B. Brinkley, with fids, Brower, Pitts
2. Vcl, Brinkley
3. Gtr, Campbell
4. Pno, Reneau
5. Fid solo, Brower
6. Vcl
Notice: On this session we begin to lose our Doughboy rhythm style—due somewhat to the fact that on some of the songs the bj is almost out of the picture and we missed the 2/4 beat of Parker's pno. Reneau's pno (to me) seems over-balanced, I think because they ("they" being Parker Willson?) wanted to get the many, many, many b runs Reneau added (and there goes the rhythm.) J. B. Brinkley played good rhythm but again, most of it was lost due to the poor balance of the instruments.

DAL-1193. Slufoot on the Levee (Frank Reneau)
1. Pno vamp, Reneau
2. Gtr, Campbell with fids, Brower, Pitts
3. Gtr
4. Gtr and fids
5. Fid solo, Brower
6. Gtr and fids
7. Pno
8. Gtr and fids
9. same

DAL-1194. Honky Tonk Shuffle (Campbell)
1. Gtr, Campbell
2. fids, Brower, Pitts
3. Pno, Reneau
4. Gtr

March 3, 6, 14, Fort Worth.
These sessions were recorded at the old WBAP radio studios on top of the old Blackstone Hotel. In order to confirm this, I called Joe Frank Ferguson, and he remembers that when we finished one of our sessions, Bob Wills was waiting to record. Bob told Joe to go home and get his saxophone as they were going to record some big band numbers and needed Joe's sax to help out. (Big Beaver.) I also called Frank Reneau who now lives in Temple, Texas. Frank remembers doing all these sessions at WBAP, including the religious songs. He recalls that we had trouble with Campbell's electric amp, as it was picking up police calls. I remember that Uncle Art became somewhat upset due to the fact that it was messing up some of our cuts. No tape recording in those days and the acetates cost money. These were our last sessions before going off to fight WWII. Producer; Uncle Art Satherley, Don Law. Musicians: "Cecil" Brower (Coast Guard), fid; Kenneth "Abner" Pitts (Army inspector at American Manufacturing Company producing shells), fid, acd; Muryel "Zeke" Campbell, (Bookkeeper at vital food company), elg; Joe "Bashful" Ferguson (Coast Guard), b, vcl; "Frank" Reneau (Army - Italy), pno; "J. B." Brinkley (4F), rhy gtr, vcl; Marvin "Junior" Montgomery (Swing Shift Supervisor at Crown Machine & Tool producing six inch shells for the Navy), bj, tgtr, sometimes vcl; "Dolores Jo" Clancy, Little Light Crust Sweetheart, eleven or twelve years of age.

March 3, 1941.
Still using Dallas numbers, but recorded in Fort Worth. I think Uncle Art did this just to confuse future music historians, because some of them have sure been confused about where these sessions took place and who played on them.

DAL-1207. Be Honest with Me
1. Fids, Brower, Pitts
2. Vcl, Brinkley
3. Gtr, Campbell
4. Vcl
5. fids, gtr fills, vcl ending

DAL-1208. Bear Creek Hop (Marvin Montgomery, the old "Bear Creek Hop" breakdown; I wrote the words and the melodies that go with the words.)
1. Voice: Parker Willson; fid, Brower
2. Vcl, Brinkley
3. Quartet: Ferguson, tenor; Brinkley, lead; Pitts, baritone; Willson, b
4. Fid, Brower
5. Vcl
6. Quartet
7. Fid, Brower
8. Vcl
9. Quartet. All yells by Parker Willson (his version of Bob Wills).

DAl-1209. It's Funny What Love Will Make You Do. Unissued.

DAL-1210. Do You Ever Miss Me? Unissued.

DAL-1211. Won't You Wait Another Year (Marvin Montgomery. The tour of duty was two years in the Armed Forces, this poor guy had one year to go hoping not to get a "Dear John" letter.)
1. Gtr, Campbell
2. Vcl, Brinkley
3. Fids, Brower, Pitts
4. Vcl
5. Gtr
6. Vcl, two fids

DAL-1212. I Want a Waitress (Marvin Montgomery)
1. Vcl Group, Brinkley, Ferguson, Pitts, Willson, Montgomery
2. Vcl solo, Montgomery
3. Gtr, Campbell
4. Pno, Reneau
5. Vcl
6. Fid solo, Brower
7. Gtr
8. Vcl
9. Gtr & two fids. Due to the fact that I had to stand close to the mike to sing, I played the tgtr because the bj would have been too loud.

DAL-1213. Can't Ease My Evil Mind
1. Gtr, Campbell
2. Vcl, Brinkley
3. Fids, Brower, Pitts
4. Vcl
5. Pno, Reneau
6. Vcl. A very sloppy ending on this one

DAL-1214. After You Said You Were Leaving (Marvin Montgomery)
1. Gtr, Campbell
2. Vcl, Dolores Jo (Clancy) Little Light Crust Sweetheart
3. Pno, Reneau
4. Fids, Brower, Pitts
5. Vcl. Montgomery played tgtr

March 6, 1941.
DAL-1229. Big House Blues. Unissued.

DAL-1230. We Just Can't Get Along. Unissued.

DAL-1231. Have I Lost Your Love Forever (Little Darling)
1. Gtr, Campbell
2. Vcl, Ferguson
3. fids, Brower, Pitts
4. Vcl
5. Gtr
6. Fids
7. Vcl

DAL-1232. Why Did You Lie to Me?
1. Gtr, Campbell
2. Vcl, Brinkley
3. Gtr & twin fids, Brower, Pitts
4. Vcl

DAL-1233. I'll Never Say Goodbye (Marvin Montgomery). Unissued.

DAL-1234. Salvation Has Been Brought Down. Unissued.
Parker Willson talked Uncle Art into letting the quartet do some religious songs because during this time we were doing two programs a week (Tuesday and Thursday) of all religious songs. The quartet was made up of Joe "Bashful" Ferguson, tenor; J. B. Brinkley, lead; Kenneth "Abner" Pitts, baritone; and Parker Willson, bass. Frank Reneau played the pno. Campbell and I went home. These songs would never get on the juke boxes (our biggest market at that time),

hence Uncle Art was reluctant to release them. Besides, The Chuck Wagon Gang and the Stamps-Baxter Quartets had that market sewed up.

DAL-1235. I Shall See Him By and By. Unissued.

DAL-1236. I Know I'll See Mother Again. Unavailable.

DAL-1237. Beyond the Clouds. Unavailable.

March 16, 1941.
DAL-1323. This Life Is Hard to Understand

DAL-1324. In the Morning
Last song recorded by this group of Light Crust Doughboys

POST-WWII

September 1947, King Records, Session at Sellers Studio, Dallas, Texas
The Post-World War II Light Crust Doughboys. Mel Cox (Jack Perry), MC, vcl and fid; Wilson Perkins (Lefty), lead elg and steel gtr; Charles Godwin (Knocky), accordion; Hal Harris (Bashful), rhy gtr and vcl; Red Kidwell (Sleepy), b and vcl; Carroll Hubbard (Ezra), fid and vcl; Marvin Montgomery (Junior), tbj, rhy gtr and arranger; Sid Nathan (owner of King Records), producer.
K2563. The New Sow Song (words by Mel Cox)
Intro
1. Vcl verse, Cox; chorus, all sing
2. Acd, Godwin
3. Vcl
4. Elg, Perkins
5. Vcl
6. Twin fids: Cox, lead; Hubbard, Harmony
7. Bj, Montgomery; b, Kidwell; Rhythm gtr, Harris; vcl out, sound effects, Cox and Hubbard.

K2564. Pappy's Banjo Boogie (Mel Cox, words; Marvin Montgomery, music)
Intro, acd
1. Bj, Montgomery
2. Vcl, Cox
3. Bj
4. Vcl
5. Elg lead, Perkins; accordian, Godwin; fid, Hubbard
6. Vcl
7. Bj
8. Vcl, out

K2565. No Suh (Marvin Montgomery)
Fid intro, Hubbard
1. Vcl, Cox, all sing answers
2. Acd, Godwin
3. Vcl
4. Elg, Perkins
5. Vcl
6. Fid, Hubbard
7. Vcl
8. Fid and acd ending

K2566. Guitar Jump (Wilson Perkins)
Acd, Godwin; fid, Hubbard, intro
1. Steel gtr, Perkins
2. Acd, Godwin
3. Steel
4. Twin fids, Cox & Hubbard
5. Steel

K2567. Fisherman's Polka (Wilson Perkins)
1. Acd, Godwin; Twin fids, Cox, Hubbard
2. Twin fids
3. Elg, Perkins
4. Twin fids
5. Acd
6. Twin fids

K2568. It's a Dirty Shame (Marvin Montgomery)
Intro acd, Elg, twin fids
1. Vcl, Hal Harris; quartet BG, Hubbard, Kidwell, Cox, Godwin
2. Acd, gtr, twin fids
3. Vcl
4. Gtr
5. Vcl

K2569. Slow Down My Darling (Cox). Unissued.

K2570. Oh My Aching Back (Marvin Montgjomery)
Intro, acd, fid, Hubbard
1. Vcl (talking), Mel Cox; vcl chorus, Cox, Hubbard, Harris, Kidwell
2. Acd & fid, Hubbard
3. Vcl
4. Acd, elg, acd & fid, Hubbard
5. Vcl

K2571. Ezra's Waltz (Carroll Hubbard, music; Mel Cox, words)
1. Twin fids, Cox & Hubbard
2. Vcl, Cox; vcl chorus, Cox, Hubbard, Kidwell, Harris
3. Whistle, Cox
4. Vcl, vcl chorus
5. Twin fids, vcl out; steel gtr, Perkins; md, Montgomery

K2572. Oklahoma Waltz (Marvin Montgomery, music; Mel Cox, words)
1. Twin fids
2. Vcl, Kidwell
3. Twin fids
4. Vcl
5. Band, out; steel, Perkins; md, Montgomery
Notice: Starting with K2573 you will hear no more acd. The foregoing songs were recorded on Thursday night and on Friday Charley (Knocky) Godwin left town due to wife trouble. And so on Friday night we recorded with no acd. Godwin, an ex-Marine pilot, later died when he crashed his own plane.

K2573. I'm Gonna Be Gone, Gone, Gone (Mel Cox)
Intro fid, Hubbard
1. Talk & vcl, Cox
2. Steel, Perkins; bj, Montgomery; vcl, out

K2574. Just a World of Heartaches (Montgomery). Unissued.

K2575. Hook, Line and Sinker (Cox). Unissued.

K2576. Wedding Ring for Sale (Montgomery). Unissued.

K2577. I Cried and Cried and Cried (Montgomery)
1. Fid, Hubbard
2. Vcl, Cox with Hubbard
3. Elg, Perkins
4. Vcl
5. Fid, Hubbard
6. Vcl
7. Elg
8. Vcl

K2578. After We've Been in Love (Montgomery). Unissued.

Session, Sellers Studio.
Sid Nathan Producer. Sid sat in the control booth and talked with Mr. Sellers while I played the bj with Wilson (Lefty) Perkins playing rhy gtr and Red Kidwell picking the b.

K2579. Hear Dem Bells (arr. Montgomery)
(also released on Federal 10014, album)

K2580. Ring Ring De Banjo (arr. Montgomery)

K2581. Blue Bells Of Scotland/Sweet And Low (arr. Montgomery)

K2582. My Old Kentucky Home (arr. Montgomery)
(also released on Federal 10014, Album)
K2583. Raggin' on the Banjo (Marvin Montgomery)
Released on the back side of Cowboy Copas/Grandpa Jones record K2955 *The Feudin' Boogie*.
Last song recorded on this three-day recording session.

Session recorded at Seller's Studio, Dallas, in early part of 1948. Mel Cox signed a contract with Sid Nathan to record as The Flying X Ranchboys so that he could collect all the royalties from the record sales. As the Light Crust Doughboys, we shared the record royalties equally. This under the table act by Mel made some of the band members very unhappy. By the end of 1948 Mel was no longer with us. I took over as leader after Mel left. Hal Harris left before we did this session. Mel Cox, fid, leader; Carroll Hubbard, fid; Red Kidwell, b; Wilson Perkins, elg and steel; Marvin Montgomery, rhy gtr, arranger.

K2805. Tears in My Heart (Marvin Montgomery). Unissued.

K2806. Honolulu Lou (Music, Perkins; words, Cox)
Intro: Steel, Perkins
1. Vcl trio, Mel Cox, Carroll Hubbard, Red Kidwell
2. Steel
3. Vcl trio, out (rhy gtr, Montgomery; fids, Hubbard, Cox; b, Kidwell; steel, Perkins). Five members in band.

K2807. I Cried My Last Tear over You (Montgomery). Unissued.

K2808. Starlight Waltz (Mel Cox)
1. Twin fids, Cox, Hubbard
2. Vcl, Red Kidwell
3. Twin fids
4. Vcl, out; steel, Perkins; rhy gtr, Montgomery

K2809. Billy Goat Rag (Montgomery)
Intro, twin fids, goat, Carroll Hubbard
1. Twin fids
2. Elg turn around, Perkins
3. Vcl trio, Cox, lead; Kidwell, tenor; Hubbard, baritone and goat
4. Elg, Perkins
5. Hot fid, Hubbard
6. Elg
7. Vcl trio, out
K2810. I'm Moving You Right Out of My Heart (Cox). Unissued.

K2811. She's a Backwoods Woman (Cox). Unissued.

K2812. I'd Never Cry Again (Montgomery). Unissued.

This completes the list of commercial recordings made by the Light Crust Doughboys until 1979 when we recorded an album for Burrus Mills. Then in 1981 we recorded *50 Years of Texas Style Music* (Golden Anniversary) and in 1986 we recorded the album *150 Years of Texas Country Music* which Burrus Mills still sells by placing coupons in the Light Crust Flour packages.

From April 4, 1936, through March 14, 1941, the Doughboys recorded 163 cuts. We had two cuts on seven songs. We recorded 156 songs. Of these, twenty-eight titles were never released. We had 128 titles released.

I had thirty-four songs recorded of which four ("Tonight I Have a Date," "Old November Moon," "Little Honky Tonk Heartthrob," and "I'll Never Say Goodbye") were never issued. Most of the songs not issued were cowboy songs. Re: "The Big Corral," "Strawberry Roan," etc., and barbershop quartet type songs such as: "When You Wore a Tulip," "I Want a Girl (Just Like the Girl That Married Dear Old Dad)," etc. Uncle Art Satherley was looking for danceable, juke box type songs and we were giving him the stuff that we played on our daily radio programs. I think the reason Uncle Art took so many of my songs was because I was writing trash that we could never play on the air, but which the juke box operators liked, such as: "Pussy, Pussy, Pussy," "You Got What I Want," "Baby, Give Me Some of That," "She Gave Me the Bird," etc.

After WWII in 1945 all MCs of the Light Crust Doughboys were called Jack Perry after Jack Perry Burrus, founder of the Burrus Mil and Elevator Company. To name a few who were called Jack Perry: Mel Cox, Jimmy Jeffreys, Paul Blunt, Walter Hailey.

Quotes from Kenneth Pitts's letter to me after listening to the tapes of the Light Crust Doughboy recordings:

> My first general observation of this entire effort is that the band might have been better off under the leadership of someone other that me. I failed in many instances to exhibit any imagination and foresight musically—all I wanted was

to hear what I thought was good from a group with the ability that group had. My judgment, business-wise, and in the matter of dealing with other people, was very minus—I needed to be much more "political" than I was. On the other hand, I realize that it is easy to make great "hindsights" about anything.

My second general observation is that Mr. Satherley should have really taken us to task as to repertoire and style on the recordings. Possibly he was trying to let our natural inclinations lead us to some sound that would have been distinctive. As it was, the only distinctive sounds we had were Zeke (Campbell), you, Knocky (Parker) and the twin fiddle sound. But none of these four ever seemed to get together and really jell. However, I don't want these acid criticisms to be interpreted to mean the entire effort was a complete loss.

Back in those days, most everybody was in a sort of terror that he might have found himself suddenly without a job. I think it is to the credit of Bob Wills, Gross, and even "Snag" (Jerry Stewart, our radio engineer) that they at least drew some sort of line in their defense. It's hard to say which course might have been wise for us—probably the one we stuck to. Of course, Bob Wills's success is acknowledged. Gross, in case you didn't know, had some success after he went to Louisville (Kentucky) and organized his own band.

Excerpts from "Zeke" Campbell's letter to me after listening to the Doughboy recordiings.

Here are some things that might interest you. When I first joined the Doughboys in October 1935, they had seven men. I made the eighth. All the guys had either gone with O'Daniel or Bob Wills. Pitts and Gross were the only original ones left. Pitts and Gross on fiddles, Bruce (Roscoe) Pierce on guitar, Hubert Barham on bass, Doc Eastwood on banjo, Matt Welch on accordion, and a guy named Leonard Grider as vocalist. He didn't play any instrument. Ramon DeArman and Cecil Brower had gone to Columbus, Ohio, to make transcriptions for some cereal company. I don't remember whether Curly Perrin had gone with them or joined O'Daniel. You and Dick (Reinhart) and Bert (Dodson) joined the band exactly two weeks after I did. You three guys replaced five men.

I have been unable to find a picture of this group. Pierce states that they were Doughboys for such a short time no picture was made. Cecil Brower was not a Doughboy at that time. He left Milton Brown and the Musical Brownies to make the move to Ohio. He joined the Doughboys, replacing Buchanan, some time after returning from Ohio.

Thanks to Kenneth "Abner" Pitts (1934–1941), Muryel "Zeke" Campbell (1935–1941), Jim "Bashful" Boyd (1938–1940), Joe Frank "Bashful" Ferguson (1940–1942), Frank Reneau (1941–1942), and Leroy Millican (a Doughboy for a few hours during the month of April, 1940) for their assistance in compiling this Discography.

There are a few minor points that may not be exactly right, but this is as close as it's ever going to get.

Marvin "Junior" Montgomery (1935–1989), I've been Leader of the Doughboys since 1948. I lost "Junior" and became "Smokey" in September of 1948 when we went on WBAP TV, Channel 5, Fort Worth, Texas.

Appendix 2
Light Crust Doughboys Discography,
1969–present

We're the Light Crust Doughboys from Burrus Mills
Producer: Smokey Montgomery   **Date: 1969**
Light Crust Doughboys Theme: Jack Perry (Walter Hailey)
Double Eagle/Wildwood Flower
The Leaf of Love
Hear Dem Bells
Red River Valley/Yellow Rose of Texas/Beautiful Texas
Kelly Waltz/Good Night Waltz
A Fool such as I
Old Joe Clark
Beer Barrel Polka
A Petal from a Faded Rose
Tennessee Wagoner
My Best to You
I Really Don't Want to Know
San Antonio Rose
When It's Roundup Time in Heaven
Light Crust Doughboys Theme: Jack Perry

The Light Crust Doughboys Religious Memories
Producer: Smokey Montgomery   **Date: 1979**
Theme: Guide and Keep Us
Turn Your Radio On
Medley: (a) It Is No Secret (b) The Old Rugged Cross (c) Take My Hand
Precious Lord (d) Amazing Grace
Lord, Take All of Me
How Great Thou Art
I'll Fly Away
Just a Closer Walk with Thee
In the Garden
The Last Roundup
Medley: (a) Church in the Wildwood (b) the Lily of the Valley (c) When the
Roll is Called Up Yonder
Precious Memories
Theme: Guide and Keep Us

Golden Anniversary Album
Producer: Smokey Montgomery   **Date: 1981**
San Antonio Rose
Beautiful Texas
Sugar Moon
Red River Valley
Faded Love
Big Beaver
Hang Your Head in Shame
My Mary
Fraulein
Home in San Antone
Bandera Waltz
Lone Star Rag

150 Years of Texas Country Music
Producer: Smokey Montgomery   **Date: 1985**
Opening Radio Theme
The Yellow Rose of Texas
When The Bloom Is On the Sage (When It's Roundup Time in Texas)
Texas In My Soul
Beautiful Texas
Waiting For A Train
Old Joe Clark
You're From Texas
If You're Gonna Play In Texas (You Gotta Have A Fiddle In The Band)
Amarillo By Morning
Across The Alley From The Alamo
In The Mood
Does Fort Worth Ever Cross Your Mind
Sure 'Nuf Texas
Texas (When I Die)
Closing Radio Theme

Texas Swing (The Light Crust Doughboy Way)
Producers: Smokey Montgomery and Art Greenhaw   **Date: 1993**
San Antonio Rose
Blue Moon of Kentucky
Secret Love
Silver Bell
Your Cheating Heart
Just a Closer Walk with Thee
Smoke! Smoke! Smoke!
Maiden's Prayer
God Must be a Cowboy (at Heart)

Pine Top Boogie
Crying in the Chapel
Betcha My Heart
Cool Heart
Time Changes Everything
Sweet Dreams
No Vacancy
The World is Waiting for the Sunrise
When it's Round-up Time in Heaven
Happy Trails

Yesterday and Today
Producers: Smokey Montgomery and Art Greenhaw   **Date: 1994**
Opening Theme Song
You Are My Sunshine
Bonaparte's Retreat
Sugar Blues
Sixteen Tons
Twinkle, Twinkle Little Star
I'm So Lonesome I Could Cry
M-I-S-S-I-S-S-I-P-P-I
Lord, Take All of Me
South
I Really Don't Want to Know
Send the Light/Wildwood Flower
Yesterday
Spaghetti Rag
Hallelujah Yodel Lady
Old Rivers
Bells of St. Mary's
Toy Yodeler
Closing Theme

High Road on the Hilltop **(The Light Crust Doughboys and the Southern Methodist University Mustang Band)**
Producers: Smokey Montgomery and Art Greenhaw   **Date: 1997**
Introduction
Western Peruna & Light Crust Doughboys Theme
Doughboy Parade
The High Road
Smokey's Smoke
Texas Women
Johnny's Stomp
Bonaparte's Retreat
Spaghetti Rag

Pussy, Pussy, Pussy
M-I-S-S-I-S-S-I-P-P-I
You Are My Sunshine
Sugar Blues
Hangin' Round Deep Ellum
The World is Waiting for the Sunrise
Texas In My Soul
That's All Brother
Sit Down
Western Medley: Movie & TV Cowboy Themes
Varsity
Bill Melton & Light Crust Doughboy Closing Theme

Keep Lookin' Up: The Texas Swing Sessions **(James Blackwood & the Light Crust Doughboys)**
Producers: Smokey Montgomery and Art Greenhaw   **Date: 1997**
This Ole House
The Unclouded Day
Wayfaring Stranger
The Big Boss
Trouble in the Amen Corner
This World Is Not My Home
The Chair That Never Got Mended
I Am A Pilgrim
That's The Way It Used to Be
Riding the Range for Jesus
When All God's Children Go Marching In
Sheltered in the Arms of God
Six Days
Life's Railway to Heaven
Beautiful Texas
Lord, Take All of Me
Washed in the Blood Medley
Keep Lookin' Up

Folk and Blues of the American Southwest
Producers: Smokey Montgomery and Art Greenhaw   **Date: 1998**
Deep Ellum Blues
Cattle Serenade
Talkin' Too Much Taxes Blues
Chili and Beans Blues
Happy John's Waltz
Amarillo Where the Wind Blows Free
Once Ev'ry So Often (I Get the Blues)
Sending Me You

Hangin' 'Round Deep Ellum
The Entertainer
No Home, Motor Home, R.V. Blues
Hallelujah Yodel Lady
Brother Can You Spare a Dime
12th Street Rag
Red River Valley
Toy Yodeler
Last Night Waltz
Sittin' On Top of the World
The Bells of St. Mary's
Light Crust Doughboys Theme
Old Folks at Home

God Bless Amarillo (And All the Cowboys, Too)
Producers: Smokey Montgomery and Art Greenhaw   **Date: 1998**
Beautiful Texas
Sugar Moon
I'm So Lonesome I Could Cry
Sky Ball Paint
The Yellow Rose of Texas
Texas In My Soul
Smokey's Smoke
Texas Women
San Antonio Rose
Silver Stars
Red Wing Medley
Happy Trails
Send the Light/Wildwood Flower
Sugar Blues
Careless Hands
Spaghetti Rag
God Bless Amarillo Suite

They Gave the World a Smile: The Stamps Quartet Tribute Album **(The
James Blackwood Quartet and the Light Crust Doughboys)**
Producers: Smokey Montgomery and Art Greenhaw   **Date: 1998**
What a Savior
Give the World A Smile
I Want To Be More Like Jesus
Precious Memories
No Tears In Heaven
Where Could I Go (But to the Lord)
Turn Your Radio On
Farther Along

On the Jericho Road
Low Singin' Bass
Where We'll Never Grow Old
We'll Soon Be Done with Troubles and Trials
The Eastern Gate
I'll Fly Away
Where the Roses Never Fade
I'll Meet You in the Morning
When All God's Singers Get Home
Guide and Keep Us

James Blackwood & The Light Crust Doughboys:
The Ultimate All-Day Singing Songbook
(CD included with book, Mel Bay Publications, Inc., Pacific, Mo.)
Producers: Smokey Montgomery and Art Greenhaw   Year: 1999
Theme
Bless These Vows
The Eastern Gate
The Lone Prairie
Where We'll Never Grow Old
Send the Light
The Gift of Love
Medley: Are You Washed in the Blood/There is Power in the Blood
Let's Sing a Happy Song
Low Singin' Bass
Medley: The Church in the Wildwood/Lily of the Valley/When the Roll is
Called Up Yonder
The Unclouded Day
Sending Me You
In the Garden
Precious Memories
Just a Closer Walk
Farther Along
The Builder's Song
Red River Valley Memories
Give the World a Smile
He Leadeth Me

The Light Crust Doughboys Songbook: Pioneers of Western Swing
(CD included with book, Mel Bay Publications, Inc., Pacific, Mo.)
Producers: Smokey Montgomery and Art Greenhaw   Year: 1999
Doughboy Parade
Chile and Beans Blues
The Chair That Never Got Mended
Once Ev'ry So Often (I Get the Blues)

Texas Women
That's the Way It Used to Be
Hangin' 'Round Deep Ellum
Toy Yodeler
When All God's Children Go Marching In
Talkin' Too Much Taxes Blues
The Amarillo Suite
The High Road
No Home, Motor Home, R.V. Blues
Ticket for Speeding
Six Days
The Bells of St. Mary's
Lord, Take All of Me
That's All, Brother (Sit Down)
Keep Lookin' Up
Guide and Keep Us

Red River Valley Memories: The Texas Swing Sessions, Vol. 2
(The Light Crust Doughboys with James Blackwood)
Producers: Smokey Montgomery and Art Greenhaw   **Date: 1999**
The Bells of St. Mary's
Behold
A Mystery/Czardas
Red River Valley Memories
Scriptural Reading by James (four separate readings are included in the recording)
Render Unto Caesar Blues
When I Survey the Wondrous Cross
Scriptural Reading by James
The Gift of Love
Send the Light/Wildflower
Bless these Vows
In the Garden
Hear Dem Bells
Home on the Range
Tennessee Wagoner
When It's Round-Up time in Heaven
The Church in the Wildwood/The Lily of theValley/When the Roll is Called Up Yonder
Old Rivers
The Blood Will Never Lose Its Power
Spoken Introduction by Art,
Smiles and Laughter with James Blackwood and the Light Crust Doughboys

Adventure in Country Swing
(The Light Crust Doughboys with Nokie Edwards)
Producers: Smokey Montgomery and Art Greenhaw   **Date: 2000**
I'm Walkin'
Welcome to My World
Tumbling Tumbleweeds
I Love You Because
Beer Barrel Polka
Amarillo By Morning
Lonesome Town
Faded Love
Panhandle Rag
A Fool Such As I
Fraulein
Your Cheatin' Heart
Orange Blossom Special

Doughboy Rock
Producers: Smokey Montgomery and Art Greenhaw   **Date: 2000**
It's No Sin To Rock
Take Me Back To Tulsa
She Bops A Lot
Teenage Boogie
Milk Cow Blues
The B.S. Boogie
Jailhouse Rock
Miss Molly
That's All Right
Just Because
Hello Mary Lou
Pussy Pussy Pussy (The Pussycat Song)
Hey Good Lookin'

The Great Gospel Hit Parade **(The Light Crust Doughboys**
with James Blackwood, The Jordanaires and Tom Brumley)
Producers: Smokey Montgomery and Art Greenhaw   **Date: 2000**
I Believe
Lookin' Through a Stained Glass Darkly
It Is No Secret
Just a Closer Walk with Thee
The Gift of Love
He's Got the Whole World in His Hands
Peace in the Valley
Lord, Take All of Me
Keep Lookin' Up

Crying in the Chapel
Sending Me You
He

Steel Away **(The Light Crust Doughboys with**
James Blackwood and Tom Brumley)
Producers: Smokey Montgomery and Art Greenhaw   **Date: 2000**
The Keys To The Kingdom
How Great Thou Art
If I Can Help Somebody
The Lone Prairie
I Just Steal Away and Pray
Rank Strangers To Me
Gospel Music's Biggest Night
Amazing Grace
The Word
He's Got The Whole World In His Hands
In The Sweet By And By
The Old Rugged Cross
Lookin' Through A Stained Glass Darkly
If We Never Meet Again
Spoken Intro by Art
Danny Boy

A Surf 'n' Swing/Fret 'n' String Christmas **(The Light Crust Doughboys with**
Nokie Edwards)
Producers: Smokey Montgomery and Art Greenhaw   **Date: 2000**
Deck the Halls
Silver Bells
It Came Upon a Midnight Clear
The Gift of Love
Peace in the Valley
Swan Lake Christmas
O Holy Night
Silent Night
Christmas Carol Rock
O Little Town of Bethlehem
The Toy Yodeler
A Closer Walk
The Bells of St. Mary's
New Years' Rendezvous

References

"Announcing the Light Crust Doughboys are on the air with a new star!" Advertising poster. Collection of Art Greenhaw.

"Auto Injuries Take Life of Milton Brown." *Fort Worth Star-Telegram.* nd. Collection of Art Greenhaw.

Bacon, Tony, and Paul Day. *The Fender Book: A Complete History of Fender Electric Guitars.* San Francisco: Miller Freeman Books, 1998.

Baker, Jim. Interview with author, April 17, 2001.

Barber, Dan. R. "Doughboys Music Gives Rise to Hall of Fame Honor." *Dallas Morning News.* June 18, 2000.

Barber, Dan R. "Doughboys Put Jingle in their Swing on New CD." *Dallas Morning News.* November 29, 2000. 2-M.

Barnouw, Erik. *A Tower in Babel: A History of Broadcasting in the United States, Volume I — to 1933.* New York: Oxford University Press, 1966.

"Bashful's Baby." Light Crust Doughboys radio script, January 27, 1937. Collection of Art Greenhaw.

"Beat, The: Music of the 30s." Available at http://www.duck.org/30s.asp?SortBy=Artist&Page=2. Accessed February 18, 2002.

The Beatles Anthology. San Francisco: Chronicle Books, 2000.

Bensman, M.R. "The History of Broadcasting, 1920–1960." In *Radio Program Archive* [On-line]. Available at http://www.people.memphis.edu/~mbensman/HOMES30.DAT. Accessed March 22, 2001.

Biffle, Kent. "Pappy O'Daniel Won Hearts with Inaugural Festivities." *Dallas Morning News.* January 17, 1999.

Blackwood, James. Interview with author, April 5, 2001.

"Bob Wills and the Texas Playboys." Available at http://www.westernmusic.org/fame/BobWills.html. Accessed April 24, 2001.

"A Brief History of WBAP." Available at http://wbap.com/aboutwbap.asp. Accessed November 5, 1999.

Broadbent, Peter. *Charlie Christian: The Story of the Seminal Electric Guitarist.* Newcastle-upon-Tyne, UK: Ashley Mark Publishing Company, 1997.

Brown, Roy Lee. Interview with author, December 21, 2001.

Bruemmer, Bruce. Personal communication to author, March 9, 2001.

Brumley, Tom. Interview with author, February 26, 2001.

Bryant, Helen. "Hoping to Hoof it for Oprah." *Dallas Morning News.* January 24, 1998.

"Burrus Mill and Elevator Company vs. Jim Rob Wills, et al, no. 32483. In the 19th Court of McLennan County, Texas." Collection of Art Greenhaw.

"Burrus Mill and Elevator Company — Radio Stations Carrying Transcribed Light Crust Doughboys as of 11/7/46." Collection of Art Greenhaw.

Bus photo. Collection of Art Greenhaw.

Camp, Paul. Personal communication to author, April 26, 2001.

Campbell, William "Zeke." Oral history. University of North Texas Oral History Collection, No. 1138. Dallas. Interviewer, John Daniels, September 14, 1996.

Caro, Robert. *The Years of Lyndon Johnson: The Path to Power.* New York: Alfred A. Knopf, Inc., 1983.

Chandler, Chip. "Lone Star Ballet Opens Season with Curious Conceptual Display." *Amarillo Globe-News.* October 2, 2000.

Coffee Grinders photo. Collection of Art Greenhaw.

Coffey, Kevin. Personal communication to author, July 29, 2001.

—. Personal communication to author. November 25, 2001.

—. Personal communication to author. January 6, 2002.

—. Personal communication to author. February 20, 2002.

"The Complete Compositions of Duke Ellington." Available at http:// hsb.baylor.edu/html.vanauken/Duke.html. Accessed February 18, 2002.

Cook, R. "Musing on Movies: *O Brother, Where Art Thou?*" [On-line]. Available at http://www.headlinemuse.com/moviereviews.brother.htm. August 8, 2001.

Court documents, Case no. 32483, 19th Court of McLennan County, Texas. Collection of Art Greenhaw.

"Cowboys, The." Available at http://www.johnnywakely.com/cowboys.htm. Accessed April 27, 2001.

Cronkite, Walter. Interview with author, August 15, 2000.

Dawson, Ronnie. Interview with author, March 14, 2001.

Death certificate, Thomas E. Duncan. Collection of Art Greenhaw.

Dickerson, Sharon. Interview with author, May 2, 2001.

"Doughboys Make Change." *Fort Worth Star-Telegram.* June 6, 1937.

"Doughboys Return; Made Movie, Also Boosted Centennial." *Fort Worth Star-Telegram.* nd. Collection of Art Greenhaw.

"Doughboys to Miss First Broadcast." Unidentified newspaper article. Collection of Art Greenhaw.

Douglas, G.H. *The Early Days of Radio Broadcasting.* Jefferson, NC: McFarland and Company, 1987.

Douglas, C.L., and Francis Miller. *The Life Story of W. Lee O'Daniel*. Dallas: Regional Press, 1938.

"Dunn — biography." Collection of Art Greenhaw.

Dunn, Eddie. "In Memory of Will Rogers and Wiley Post." Light Crust Doughboys program, August 16, 1935. Collection of Art Greenhaw.

"Eddie Dunn's First Doughboy Program." Light Crust Doughboys script, May 22, 1935. Collection of Art Greenhaw.

Elliott, Jerry. Interview with author, March 8, 2001.

—. Interview with author, May 8, 2001.

Faig, Ronald. Personal communication to author, April 26, 2001.

"Famous Texans: Bob Wills." Available at http://www.famoustexans.com/bobwills.htm. Accessed April 25, 2001.

Fehrenbach, T.R. *Seven Keys to Texas*. El Paso: Texas Western Press, 1983.

Ferguson, Joe. Oral history. University of North Texas Oral History Collection, No. 1161. Dallas. Interviewer, John Daniels, November 9, 1996.

"Fiddler's Love of Music is Sixty Years Strong." *Fort Worth Star-Telegram.* July 5, 1998.

Floyd, Jacquielynn. "For a joyful noise, pick a banjo band." *Dallas Morning News.* July 13, 2000. 23-A.

Flying X Ranchboys promotional card. Collection of Art Greenhaw.

Fowler, Gene and Bill Crawford. *Border Radio*. Austin, Texas: Texas Monthly Press, 1987.

Garay, Ron. *Gordon McLendon: The Maverick of Radio*. New York: Greenwood Press, 1992.

Gilchriest, Gail. "All that Texas Jazz," *Ultra* 7 (June 1989): 90.

Gibble, K.L. *Mr. Songman: The Slim Whitman Story*. Elgin, IL: Brethren Press, 1982.

Ginell, Cary. *Milton Brown and the Founding of Western swing*. Urbana, Ill.: University of Illinois Press, 1994.

—. Personal communication to author, February 12, 2002.

"Gold Star Mothers to be Given Radio Salute on Armistice Day." Unidentified newspaper article. Collection of Art Greenhaw.

Gordon, Jack. "Banjo? 'Oh, NO.' But Yes, if Marvin Montgomery Plays It." *Fort Worth Press*. March 1, 1959.

Govenar, Alan B., and Jay F. Brakefield. *Deep Ellum and Central Track*. Denton, Texas: University of North Texas Press, 1998.

Gray, James. *Business without Boundaries: The Story of General Mills*. Minneapolis, Minn.: University of Minnesota Press, 1954.

Greenhaw, Art. Interview with author, March 26, 2001.

—. Personal communication with author, December 30, 2001.

—. Personal communication with author, February 19, 2002.

Guralnick, Peter. *Last Train to Memphis: The Rise of Elvis Presley.* Boston: Little, Brown & Company, 1994.

Guest, Melissa. "Doughboys, Other Greats Team up on *Steel Away." Dallas Morning News.* nd. Collection of Art Greenhaw.

Hailey, Walter. Interview with author, February 16, 2001.

Halsey, Nancy B. "Swing Guitarist William Campbell Dies." *Dallas Morning News.* March 9, 1997.

"Hank Thompson: Biography." In *Country.com.* Available at http://artist.country.com/cmt/art/search/art.bios.jhtml?ai_id=507613. Accessed Aug. 23, 2001.

Head, Sydney W., and Christopher Sterling. *Broadcasting in America.* Boston: Houghton Mifflin Company, 1991.

"Helen Forrest." Solid. http://www.parabrisas.com/d_forresth.html. Accessed May 5, 2001.

Hess, Neil. Interview with author, April 24, 2001.

"James Blackwood Sr. Celebrates 65 Years in Gospel Music." Available at http://www.jamesblackwood.comn/history.htm. Accessed April 6, 2001.

Johnson, Lori A. "Now Listen Everybody from Near and Far, If You Want to Know Who We Are, We're the Light Crust Doughboys from Burrus Mills." *Cargill News* 50 (August 1986): 11–22.

Jolesch, W. "Doughboys Make a Change." Unidentified magazine article. Collection of Art Greenhaw.

"Johnny Bond Publications." Available at http://www.johnnybond.com/bio2.htm. Accessed April 27, 2001.

Jones, Jim. "Modest Church Inspired an Elvis Hit." *Fort Worth Star-Telegram.* April 4, 1998.

Kelly, H.C. Interview with author, May 7, 2001.

—. Interview with author, May 9, 2001.

Kienzle, Rich. "Bob Wills and his Texas Playboys: Anthology, 1935–1973" (CD liner notes). Los Angeles: Rhino Records, 1991.

Kimzey, John Paul. Personal communication to author, March 8, 2002.

Kinney, Mrs. M. Frank. Letter to Parker Willson, July 7, 1942. Collection of Art Greenhaw.

Knapp, L.K. Personal communication to author, April 10, 2001.

KOYL radio recording. Collection of H.C. Kelly.

"Last Original Member of Wills' Band Dies." *Tulsa World*. February 22, 1984. C-11.

Lawson, John. "Willson Returns as Doughboys M.C." Unidentified newspaper article. Collection of Art Greenhaw.

"Leon Huff, Western Band Singer, Dies." Unidentified newspaper article. Collection of Art Greenhaw.

"Light Crust Doughboys appointed Texas Music Ambassadors." Texas Composers Forum. Collection of Art Greenhaw.

"Light Crust Doughboys: Picture Chart – 50 years of Texas Style Music." Collection of Art Greenhaw.

"Louis Armstrong and his Orchestra." Available at http://www.redhotjazz.com/lao.html; http://www.redhotjazz.com/Sebastian.html. Accessed February 18, 2002.

"Lugosi: Hollywood's Dracula." *Filmfax* 67 (July 1998): 36.

"Major Jazz Composers and Performers." Available at http://www.cftech.com/BrainBank/OTHERREFERENCE/THEARTS/MajJazComp.html. Accessed February 18, 2002.

Martini, Mike, Xavier University. Personal communication to author, February 19, 2002.

McKay, Seth Shepard. *W. Lee O'Daniel and Texas politics*. Lubbock, Texas: Texas Tech Press, 1944.

"Melody Lane: 'My Buddy.' " Available at http://www.melodylane.net/standards14.html. Accessed February 19, 2002.

Montgomery, Marvin. "Light Crust Doughboys Announcers in Chronological Order." Collection of Art Greenhaw.

—. "Light Crust Doughboy Recording Sessions," 1989. Collection of Janis Stout. Citations in the text are to this manuscript. A version of this list is reprinted in this book as Appendix I.

—. Oral history. University of North Texas Oral History Collection, No. 1152. Dallas. Interviewer, John Daniels, September 7, 1996.

—. Interview with author, January 3, 2001.

—. Interview with author, March 21, 2001.

—. Interview with author, May 3, 2001.

—. Interview with author, May 28, 2001.

Morrison, Susan. "Local Band Snags Grammy Nomination." *Mesquite, Texas, News*. January 15, 1998. 1-A.

Morthland, J. Interview with author, May 4, 2001.

Murillo, Lisa. "Rites held for Joe Ferguson III." *Dallas Morning News*. February 21, 2001.

Network program. Undated memorandum. Collection of Art Greenhaw.

"The New Light Crust Doughboys." Photo. Collection of Art Greenhaw.

"News release—Jack Perry and Light Crust Doughboys Help Celebrate Opening of Sally's Truck and Tractor Company," January 14, 1946. Collection of Art Greenhaw.

"'Pappy' O'Daniel." Texas State Library & Archives Commission. Available at http://castor.tsl.state.tx.us/treasures/characters/pappy/html. Accessed April 25, 2001.

Parker, Knocky. Interview with Cary Ginell, January 10, 1984.

"Parker, Knocky, oral history interview." Hogan Jazz Archive, Tulane University, New Orleans, Louisiana. Transcription of three reels. Interviewers: Ed Kahn and Paul R. Crawford, August 28, 1963.

Patoski, Joe Nick. Personal communication to author, May 9, 2001.

"Paul Whiteman and his Orchestra." Available at http://www.redhotjazz.com/pwo.html. Accessed February 18, 2002.

"Petrillo, James Caesar." Infoplease.com. Available at http://infoplease.looksmart.com/ce6/people/A0838631.html. Accessed February 23, 2001.

Pitts, Kenneth. Interview with Cary Ginell, May 27, 1986.

—. "Light Crust Doughboys." Unpublished manuscript. Collection of Janis Stout.

"Press release." *Wichita Falls Times-Record* review. Available at http://www.lightcrustdoughboys.com/news.releases\.asp?index=21, October 7, 2000. Accessed February 26, 2001.

"Press Release. A Grammy Nomination for the Light Crust Doughboys ... Again!" Light Crust Doughboys Official Web Site. Available at http://www.lightcrustdoughboys.com/news/grammy/htm. Accessed July 30, 2001.

"Primarily A Cappella: The Comedian Harmonists." Available at http://www.singers.com/jazz/vintage/comedianharmonist.html. Accessed February 18, 2002.

Putnam, Margaret. "Steps Back." *Dallas Morning News.* March 8, 1998.

"Radio Feature Transcribed Here." Unidentified newspaper article. Collection of Art Greenhaw.

Radio recordings, 1936, 1937, 1946, 1947, 1950. Collection of Kevin Coffey.

"Radio Timetable." *Dallas Morning News* May 31, 1954. Part 2, 7.

Rasmussen, Chris. "Risky Records (or, The 'Dirty Thirties'): Risqué Songs and Jukeboxes in the 1930s." Paper presented to the Popular Culture Association, Philadelphia, April 14, 2001.

Remick, Pat. "Light Crust Doughboys Still on the Road in the South." *Houston Chronicle.* January 5, 1983.

Rhoads, Jeff. "Lone Star Ballet to Perform with Forefathers of Western Swing." *Amarillo Globe-News.* February 8, 1998. 9-D.

"Ronnie Dawson: The Blonde Bomber." Available at http://www.ronniedawson.com. Accessed March 14, 2001.

Schreyer, Lowell. "Banjo Legend: Smokey Montgomery." *FIGA (Fretted Instruments Guild of America) Magazine* (May/June 1997). Available at http://www.texas-music.com/old/figa.htm. Accessed May 10, 2001.

Schroeder, Richard. *Texas Signs On.* College Station, Texas: Texas A&M Press, 1998.

Sheldon, Ruth. *Hubbin' It: The Life of Bob Wills.* Kingsport, Tenn.: Kingsport Press, Inc., 1938.

Simmons, Bill. Interview with author, March 16, 2001.

Smith, Joanne. "Seven Decades of Texas Swing: The Light Crust Doughboys." *Texas Highways,* 47 (January 2000): 12–19.

Smulyan, Susan. *Selling Radio: The Commercialization of American Broadcasting, 1920–1934.* Washington: Smithsonian Institution Press, 1994.

Southern Selectors newspaper photo. *Fort Worth Press.* 1938. Collection of Art Greenhaw.

Steen, Herman. *Flour Milling in America.* Westport, Conn.: Greenwood Press, 1963.

Stout, Janis. "The Light Crust Doughboys Were on the Air: A Memoir." *The Journal of Country Music,* 18 (1996): 5–9.

—. Personal communication to author, April 26, 2001.

Streetman, Jay. Interview with author, May 8, 2001.

"Ted Daffan: Hall of Fame." Available at http://www.nashvillesongwritersfoundation.com/fame/daffan.html. Accessed March 26, 2002.

Tarrant, David. "Smokey Montgomery: The Doughboys' Longtime Banjo Player is Far from Stale." *Dallas Morning News.* January 19, 1997.

Taylor, Lewis. "Rock Pioneer Still Riding the Curl." *Eugene, Oregon, Register-Guard.* December 23, 2000.

Thibodeaux, Julie. "Doughboys to Perform at Festival." *Fort Worth Star-Telegram, Neighborhoods Up Close.* October 8, 2000.

Thompson, Hank. Interview with author, March 8, 2001.

Townsend, Charles R. "About the Light Crust Doughboys." Available at http://www.rockabillyhall.com/Doughboys.html. Accessed July 21, 2000.

—. Display. Light Crust Doughboys Museum. Mesquite, Texas.

—. "The Light Crust Doughboys—Yesterday and Today." *Traveler* 33 (January 1998).

—. *San Antonio Rose.* Urbana, Ill.: University of Illinois Press, 1976.

—. "Thomas Elmer Duncan." The Handbook of Texas Online. Available at http://www.tsha.utexas.edu/handbook/online.articles/view/DD/fdu57.html. Accessed March 6, 2002.

—. "W. Lee O'Daniel and his Hillbilly Boys." *The Handbook of Texas Online.* Available at http://www.tsha.utexas.edu/handbook/online.articles/view/WW/xgwl.html. Accessed March 9, 2001.

"2 singles, 27 LPs certified by RIAA." *Billboard* 76 (January 4, 1964): 3.

Vacca, John. Letter to H.C. Kelly, April 18, 1958. Collection of H.C. Kelly.

Walden, John. Interview with author, March 29, 2001.

Watkins, Darren. "Greenhaw Record Grabs Grammy Nod." *Mesquite, Texas, News.* January 11, 2001. 1-A.

Weitz, Matt. "A Flood of Memories —The Levee Singers Regroup for a Good Cause." *Dallas Morning News.* January 18, 2001.

"'We'll Spend But $300' And WBAP Was Begun; Hoover Named Station." *Fort Worth Star-Telegram.* October 30, 1943. Special section, 3.

"WFAA, KGKO, WBAP Family Album 1941." Collection of Art Greenhaw.

"WFPK 2001 Greatest Songs of All Time." Available at http://www.wfpk.org/list1099_1000.htm. Accessed Feb. 18, 2002.

Whetmore, Edward Jay. *American Electric.* New York: McGraw-Hill, 1992.

White, Forest. *The Fender Story.* San Francisco: GPI Books, 1994.

White, Glenn. Personal communication to author, March 24, 2001.

"Willie 'The Lion' Smith." Available at http://www.redhotjazz.com/thelion.html. Accessed February 18, 2002.

Willson, Parker (son of Doughboys' announcer). Personal communication to author, May 7, 2001.

Young, Michael E. "Prime Real Estate – Legendary Longhorn Ballroom for Sale; Joint's Storied Past Thrown in for Free." *Dallas Morning News.* February 9, 2001.

Index